WARK ON

THE AUTOBIOGRAPHY OF JOHN WARK

WITH A FOREWORD BY KENNY DALGLISH

Know The Score Books Limited
118 Alcester Road
Studley
Warwickshire
B80 7NT
01527 454482
info@knowthescorebooks.com
www.knowthescorebooks.com

A CIP catalogue record is available for this book from the British Library
ISBN: 978-1-84818-511-1

Printed and bound in Great Britain
By TJ International, Cornwall

CONTENTS

Foreword by Kenny Dalglish	7
I Belong To Glasgow	11
On Trial	26
Work Hard Play Hard	38
To Cap It All	51
Bobby's Men	61
1981 And All That	68
Goodbye Robson, Hello Wark	80
Top Of The Kop	91
The Booze Brothers	106
Back Home	115
Renaissance Man	126
Scotland The Brave	138
Escape To Victory	151
I Am What I Am	158
Money Money Money	167
Career Statistics	171

ACKNOWLEDGEMENTS

MY THANKS GO to Mel Henderson, without whom this book would not have been possible.

Thanks as well to Neil Prentice and his staff at White Space Design for the wonderful double-header cover and Simon Lowe and all his staff at Know The Score Books, especially Richard Roper. Mark Lomas has been an invaluable help throughout the whole process of the production of the book.

Of course everyone who has helped me in any way throughout my career with all three of my clubs and the Scotland national team has to have a big thank you. There are so many so I won't attempt to name you all, but you know who you are and I couldn't have done any of it without you.

Finally all my love to Karen, Andrew and all my family, without whose support I would not have been able to write this book or have been as succesful throughout my career as I was able to be.

Lyrics to *I Am What I Am* reproduced by kind permission of Warner Chappell.

FOREWORD BY KENNY DALGLISH

THE REASON I accepted Warky's invitation to write the foreword to his autobiography is simple – it gives me an opportunity to tell you the truth about him and to embarrass him at the same time. I am going to go public and tell the world that Warky owes me money. I don't know the exact amount – to be honest I lost count a long time ago – but his royalties from this book should just about cover it. In our time together at Liverpool we used to have a modest wager on the outcome of the Old Firm games in Scotland. If his beloved Rangers won he would owe me a fiver, but if my former club Celtic did the business he would have to cough up a similar amount to me. Except that he didn't and nearly a quarter of a century later I'm still waiting for him to settle his account. Hopefully, this book will do well enough for him to square me up in the not too distant future.

When he rang me about writing the foreword I asked him what he expected of me. "Just say something nice about me," he responded, so I've racked my brains and can hopefully do him justice. He was more than a team-mate of mine with Liverpool and Scotland. He was also a room-mate on occasions and he doesn't know how lucky he was to have me looking after him. He might think he got a raw deal from me because I would insist he switched the television off, closed the curtains and took the telephone off the hook so that I would not be disturbed during my pre-match sleep, but when he roomed with Alan Hansen he had all that and more besides, including making the tea, cleaning his shoes and running his bath. A proper taskmaster, he was, and I wasn't surprised when Warky, having realised the grass is not always greener elsewhere, decided to come back to me.

Of course, I knew all about Warky long before he came to Anfield in 1984. I played against him on many occasions in his Ipswich days and he was also a colleague with Scotland. When he signed for Liverpool I knew he would have no trouble settling in. He's a good mixer. He loves a laugh, almost as much as he likes a drink, and he was one of the lads from day one. He was just what we needed on the field, too, because he had that precious, all-too-rare gift of being able to contribute goals from midfield. Not just one here and there, either. Warky got them by the barrowload, which was what prompted Joe Fagan to sign him. It was no surprise that he scored on his debut, for example, and if you check his overall record in almost four years on Merseyside it is clear he was an inspired signing.

Warky was very intelligent – I'm talking about on the pitch – and his impeccable timing should never be under-estimated. If he arrived too early or too late the goals wouldn't have flowed as regularly as they did. He got it spot-on virtually all the time. He would get into the box and if he didn't get on the end of a cross himself he would know when to hang back and pounce on the knock-downs from the strikers. Only a few midfield players in our game have had that priceless knack and he definitely added something to the Liverpool team when Joe brought him in.

Of course, he was an established player with Ipswich for a number of years before we benefited from his transfer to Liverpool. That Ipswich side was much admired and respected by us at Liverpool and by that I mean they were one of the teams we knew we had to beat if we were going to be successful. It had quality in every department but if there was something that set them apart it was Warky's phenomenal contribution in terms of goals from the middle of the park, and no more so than in the 1980-81 season when he scored an incredible 36 of them. Ipswich played 12 games in their successful UEFA Cup campaign and Warky scored 14 goals to equal a long-standing European record. For a midfield player – and that's the key – to score more goals than games played in a top competition like that was simply unheard of; in fact I wouldn't mind betting that his contribution was and still is unique at such a high level.

But while Warky's goalscoring statistics will forever impress, the record books say nothing about the other way in which he played his part in his teams' successes. He maybe didn't have as many touches of the ball as some of his colleagues, but he didn't half make them count. He was never one to shirk a challenge and he invariably came away with the ball when he launched into a tackle. Once he moved back to being a fantastic central defender during the latter stages of his career, he demonstrated his football brain in a completely different way, mopping up at the back. But he could still pose a major threat when he went up for set pieces because he was brave and relished an aerial battle, whether he was defending his own goal or attacking the other.

One of my abiding memories of Warky is him trying to nail Diego Maradona when Scotland played Argentina in a friendly at Hampden 30 years ago. Warky was sick and tired of Maradona running the show, but when he tried to halt him in full flight Maradona just shrugged off the tackle and carried on as if nothing had happened. None of the rest of us could get near him either and Maradona was so good that day that you'd have needed a gun to slow him down.

I believe a big part of Liverpool's success, not just in my time with the club but in the famous Bill Shankly era, was based on the off-the-field camaraderie among the players and Warky enjoyed that side of it as much as anyone. That was part of the reason that he fitted in so well. He could take the mickey but he could also laugh at himself, an admirable quality in anyone. Being Scottish he was keen on the social side of life as a footballer and never went thirsty. He liked a good swallow, as the saying goes north of the border, but come match day the statistics confirm that Warky invariably delivered. He was a good team player who knew his job and never gave less than his all.

When he won the Professional Footballers' Association Player of the Year award in 1981 I was not the least bit surprised because, as I said earlier, anyone capable of contributing 36 goals in one season from midfield is bound to be a leading contender. It was totally justified, a well deserved honour, and the PFA members deserve credit as well for recognising Warky ahead of the other nominees. Talking of nominees, Warky was always one of those in the running for Liverpool's very own Tube of the Week award, which worked on a points system based on things that players would say and do in front of their colleagues. For example, me, Alan Hansen, Warky and Steve Nicol were once travelling north by train from Birmingham to Scotland to report for international duty and one of Warky's little quirks was to keep touching his tie. Unknown to him, every time he did it Alan Hansen awarded him a point and by the time we arrived in Glasgow he was way ahead of the field.

When he first joined us at Liverpool we were within nine league games of the end of the season, but we nevertheless valued the part he played in helping us to complete a hat-trick of league crowns and that was why the club sought permission from The Football League to present him with a winner's medal. It was only right that he should share in our success because we were undoubtedly lifted by his arrival and his contribution over those nine games. The following season he was the club's top scorer with 27 goals and the year after that he was unfortunate to suffer two serious injuries that saw him miss a lot of football and cost him the opportunity to add to his medal collection.

I was manager of the club when Warky headed back to Ipswich in 1988 and I left it entirely up to him whether he moved on or not. I didn't see it as my job to prevent him doing what he wanted to do, so it was only fair that he should be informed of the fact that other clubs wanted to talk to him and that he made up his own mind about what he was going to do next. Had he said he wanted to remain a Liverpool player it would not have been a problem, but Warky preferred to move on and create another new chapter of his amazing career. You often get players returning to their former clubs, but in Warky's case he went back to

Ipswich twice and when you take into consideration his goals it is hard to imagine any other player in the club's entire history giving more for the cause.

Warky, I salute you. Great bloke, great player and I look forward to receiving your cheque in full and final settlement.

I BELONG TO GLASGOW

IN THE WORDS OF the song, I belong to Glasgow, a city with a huge heart that consistently welcomes me home with all the genuine warmth of a mother greeting her long-lost son. It still amazes me that virtually from the minute I arrive I am recognised and the greetings are exceedingly good-natured, even from those Celtic supporters only too aware of my long-standing affection for their arch-rivals Rangers. I know I am biased, but as far as I am concerned Glasgow is second to none and the same goes for the sense of humour displayed by its natives. I love the way I am still able to feel instantly at home in a city I left way back in 1973 to seek fame and fortune in faraway Ipswich, which could hardly be more different by comparison.

I had three spells with Ipswich Town and I love Suffolk, which has been my home for more than 35 years, but I have never needed much of an excuse to return to Glasgow. In my time as a player my return visits were far more frequent than they are today. For example, when I was a regular choice for Scotland I would congregate with my international colleagues in Glasgow and it provided me with an ideal opportunity to meet up with various family members. With both my parents dead, my older brother Alex settled in Australia and my younger brother Andy having relocated to Ipswich, which means I see him regularly, my visits north of the border invariably lead to me meeting up with my sister, Wilma, and her husband Peter, who have lived their entire lives in Glasgow.

I am reminded about the time when Wilma and I were 'in town' – that's Glasgow lingo for visiting the city centre – and we popped into a well-known pub called The Horseshoe, which enjoys legendary status thanks in part to boasting what the Guinness Book of Records recognises as the longest bar in Britain. On the day in question Wilma and I were minding our own business when an elderly customer, who had clearly been enjoying the hospitality on offer, stopped and stared in my direction. It was far from a new experience when he said: "I know you, don't I?" He continued to look me straight in the eye before adding: "You were a footballer – played for Scotland didn't you?" I smiled and nodded, at which point the punter added: "No, don't tell me, let me have a wee think." At that point he disappeared into a corner with his drink. Wilma and I laughed and, when we looked over, he had his head in his hands, clearly racking his brain to think who I was.

About half an hour later the chap returned and, with a huge grin on his face that suggested the penny had well and truly dropped, he announced somewhat triumphantly: "I've got it – you're Graeme Souness!" He shook my hand and was so pleased with himself for eventually 'identifying' me that I didn't have the heart to tell him the truth. That is the one and only time I have ever been mistaken for someone I played alongside for both Liverpool and Scotland, but these days I am regularly confused with one of my ex-Liverpool colleagues, goalkeeper Bruce Grobbelaar, oddly enough even when he is also in close proximity as we travel the world together as members of the Liverpool Legends side. Clearly, it must have something to do with the receding, or almost disappeared, hairline and the 'tache!

Of course, Glasgow is renowned the world over as basically a city of two halves, Rangers and Celtic. The message was rammed home from a very early age that Rangers were my club. That was the way it was and probably still is, and I am sure it is the same on the other side of the Glasgow divide with youngsters told in no uncertain terms that they must follow the family tradition and support Celtic. My father – and his father before him etc etc – were all Rangers supporters and I caught the bug before I was even attending school. On one occasion I actually threatened to leave home and head for Ibrox. I am told I was aged just five at the time and so upset that I was sobbing my eyes out. I was half-way down our road in Partick before my mother caught up with me. I was feeling aggrieved about something and instead of just having a 'greet' I also decided to run away, stating quite categorically that I was going to Ibrox. No one took me seriously until they realised I was actually missing. I was apparently headed for the local subway station and had my mother not been so quick off the mark I probably would have made it and the consequences of my action could well have been very serious. Instead, my relieved mother marched me home and drummed into me the error of my ways, although it did nothing to diminish my eagerness to attend a Rangers home game.

The pull of Ibrox remained and it was two uncles who eventually arranged my baptism as a fan. Hugh, my father's brother, and Duncan, my mother's brother, took me to my very first game there. My father was more of a Rangers follower than an actual match-by-match supporter. He attended some games but both Hugh and Duncan were among the most loyal fans and boasted virtually perfect attendance records around that time. It became a bit of a ritual for me, too, and I was always decked out in my favourite blue, white and red scarf. For home games we would travel across the River Clyde by ferry. There were always long queues and they crammed hundreds of fans on the Govan ferry, which operated on a shuttle basis between Water Row on the north side of the river to Ferry Road in Govan on the south. Far from enjoying a view of the water for the few minutes it took to cross, I was instead pressed up against other passengers' knees to the extent that I hardly even saw daylight. The Govan ferry actually closed in 1966, made redundant by the building of the Clyde Tunnel, the Kingston Bridge and the modernisation of the subway that was to become our favoured mode of transport in later years.

I'm not sure if kids these days experience the same thrill as I did when I attended my very first live game. The power of television, and the glut of games covered by a multitude of channels, means they are familiar with just about everything to do with all the Premier League clubs – the stadium, the players etc – and even those further down the professional structure. Young supporters are introduced to the game via what they see on the box, but in the 60s it was very much a case of having to find out for oneself. It is difficult to put into words how I felt on my debut as a fan at Ibrox. I was completely enveloped by the experience and the sheer scale of it. The excitement mounted from the moment I caught my first distant view of the red brick stadium, which was quite unlike anything I had ever clapped eyes on before, and it seemed to have a magnetic pull. Passing through the throng of fans zigzagging their way to various entrances, squeezing through the turnstile, climbing the massive staircase and then, at long last, catching sight of the pitch, which I regarded as a scene of outstanding beauty. If ever something was going to whet my appetite to become a footballer that was undoubtedly it. I just stood and gazed, taking it all in, open-mouthed, wide-eyed and completely enthralled.

Even the mention of it now tends to give me goose bumps because it was something to which I had looked forward so much and I would count the days until the next game. Once we disembarked from the ferry it would take us about ten minutes to walk to the ground and there were times when I would join hundreds of autograph hunters before the kick-off. We were usually in too much of a hurry to commence our journey home after the game to hang around until the players exited the stadium, but collecting signatures beforehand was far from easy either. The players couldn't have been expected to satisfy the demand or the kick-off would have had to be delayed, so they only obliged a fortunate few in the throng. My first target was John Greig, an inspirational captain I had the pleasure of meeting a few years back, and as I grew older Colin Stein, a strong, bustling centre-forward, and tricky left-winger Willie Johnston were big favourites of mine. I managed to acquire all three autographs but don't ask me where they are now.

Quite a few years later, in 1978, I actually played against Willie in an FA Cup semi-final at Highbury when I scored with a last-minute header to give Ipswich a 3-1 victory over his team, West Bromwich Albion. While I was fortunate enough to go to Wembley a few weeks later and help Ipswich defeat Arsenal 1-0 in the final, Willie went off to Argentina with the Scotland squad. The opening game against Peru proved to be his last for his country because he was found to have taken a banned stimulant and subsequently expelled from the tournament. He had come south in 1972 to join Albion and such was his impact at The Hawthorns that in 2004 he was named as one of their 16 greatest players of all time in a poll to coincide with the club's 125th anniversary celebrations. As far as I was concerned, the wee man could do no wrong.

The attendance figure published in the next day's newspapers bore little resemblance to the actual crowd packed into Ibrox and the same applied at all the grounds. It was common practice in those days for accompanied children to be admitted free as long as they squeezed in and the turnstile only clicked once. When we were in the ground and had climbed the steps to the top of the massive terracing, kids would then be passed over the heads of adult spectators until we reached the front, where we would spend the entire match. I was under strict orders to remain in place until after the final whistle and once the crowd had dispersed I would start climbing back up the terracing to be reunited with one or both of my uncles. The match at Ibrox was just one part of what I regarded as the perfect day out – calling in at the local 'chippy' for a fish supper, as we often did, was another highlight. No doubt about it, my uncles spoilt me – and for that I shall always be grateful.

In later years, when my parents allowed me to travel on my own, I was one of hundreds of kids looking to gain free entry to Ibrox. The trick was to find an adult willing to take you in. "Hey, mister, gonna gie us a lift over please," – note the word please, I am convinced it helped – was repeated every few seconds until you struck lucky and a man indicated he would do the necessary and hoist you over the turnstile. Once inside, you were free to take up your place on the terracing and I have to confess that on the first few occasions I went along unaccompanied I found the experience a bit scary, what with the constant swaying of the crowd. Needless to say, however, I never once owned up that I was frightened or my parents would have put their foot down and prevented me from going until I was much older.

I was not at Ibrox on January 2 1971, when a number of children were among the 66 fans who died when a stairway – the very one I had been up and down on countless previous occasions – gave way as spectators exited towards the end of the Old Firm game against Celtic. Another 200 supporters were injured and I will never forget how we faced an anxious wait of several hours before learning that Alex was safe. We knew he had gone to the game and that he would have been standing in the vicinity of where the tragedy occurred. There were no mobile phones at the time, or checking he was okay would have taken just a few seconds. We didn't even have a phone in the house and it wasn't until he eventually turned up at home at about 10pm that we stopped panicking that he may have been among the many victims. My brother-in-law, Wilma's husband Peter, was also at the game and left by the very same stairway that collapsed. He had gone for a drink with friends, totally oblivious to what happened just a few minutes later, and he was in the pub by the time news of the disaster started to filter through. He, too, was welcomed home with open arms when he returned that evening.

I also attended a number of away games with my uncles but they tended to be fixtures that did not involve too much travelling. Aberdeen, Dundee and Edinburgh were all on the banned list, and from what I recall my experience of away games stretched no further than those at St Mirren, Airdrie, Motherwell, Clyde and Partick Thistle. We travelled on a bus that left from the local pub, The Smugglers Inn in Dumbarton Road, and you can probably guess the state that some of the fans were in by the time the bus pulled away. It would never be allowed today but it was normal behaviour back then – fans would even take bottles and cans of alcoholic drinks into the stadium – and on the few occasions that the atmosphere turned ugly I was glad to have my uncles close by.

Rangers took up a huge part of my childhood and it remains the only regret of a long and successful career that I never achieved my ambition of playing for the club. Indeed, it is more than just a regret or a disappointment; it really, really bugs me that it never happened. If there was one thing I would change about my career that is it. Just one appearance would have been enough to plug that particular void. Daft as it might sound, even in my late 30s, by which time it was clear that my playing days were definitely numbered, I continued to dream about pulling on the famous blue jersey. Before I returned to my first club, Ipswich, from Liverpool in January 1988, there were rumours that Graeme Souness wanted to take me to Ibrox, but nothing materialised. Whether or not there was genuine interest, I have no idea, but one prominent Scottish club did speak to me around that time about returning north. It was none other than Celtic. Their manager at the time was Billy McNeill and I think he appreciated my predicament when I turned down his offer and, in all seriousness, explained: "My family would lynch me."

In fact that wasn't the only occasion Celtic showed interest in me. Aged 15 I was playing for Drumchapel Amateurs, a club that launched many a professional career, including those of Sir Alex Ferguson and Walter Smith, both of whom went on to enjoy their greatest successes in the game as managers. Ex-players Pat Crerand (Celtic and Manchester United), Andy Lochhead (Burnley), Eddie McCreadie (Chelsea), Bobby Hope (West Bromwich Albion), Tony Green (Newcastle), Tommy Craig (Newcastle), Andy Gray (Aston Villa), Kenny Dalglish (Celtic and Liverpool), John Robertson (Nottingham Forest), Asa Hartford (Manchester City and Everton), Francis Munro (Wolves), John O'Hare (Derby County and Nottingham Forest), Archie Gemmill (Derby County),

Frank McAvennie (West Ham), Jim Cruickshank (Hearts), Jim Forrest and Alex Willoughby (both Rangers) and Mo Johnston (Celtic, Everton and Rangers) are also Drumchapel old boys and I am immensely proud to feature alongside so many former Scotland internationals in the club's ever-expanding Hall of Fame. Ever since I was old enough to understand that it was possible to be paid for playing football, something that initially surprised me, it had been my aim to play for Rangers. They were my team and I was desperate to join them, but the only Scottish club to show any interest in me at that time was their fiercest rivals from across the city. It never came to anything so I didn't have to make a decision on whether to join Celtic, which is probably just as well!

I AM PROUD TO be a Glaswegian and, along with thousands of others over the years, I made my entry into the world at the city's Royal Maternity and Women's Hospital. The word Women's was dropped in 1960 and it was better known locally as the Rottenrow, named after the street in which it was located. Strangely, and no one close to me can explain why, I was the only member of my family who was not born at home. I am assured I was perfectly normal and there were no complications regarding the delivery, but for some reason my mother was taken into the hospital, which was situated to the east of the city centre, and she gave birth on August 4, 1957. I was child number three to Alex and Helen, who already had a daughter, Wilma, who was eight, and a son, Alex, aged seven. When my younger brother, Andrew, came along seven years later, apparently his arrival was many people's cue for a number of jokes about the seven-year itch, since that was the amount of time that separated each of the three boys.

As far as I am aware, there are two possible explanations for Rottenrow being so called. One, that it was formerly the site of a refuse and sewage dump, and the other that the name is derived from the Gaelic phrase rat-an-righ, which translates as Road of the Kings. Opinion between Scotland's historians appears to be divided, but I know which version I prefer. Either way, the hospital in which I was born has been demolished, except for some exterior walls that were retained to form part of a new development. The site was purchased by the University of Strathclyde, who converted it into a public park that opened in 2004 and the centrepiece of which is a magnificent Monument to Maternity sculpture by George Wyllie – a giant metal nappy pin. Full marks for enterprise must go to those responsible for coming up with the idea of using the ruins to make souvenir paperweights, each of which comprised one-inch stones featuring an imprint of a baby's face and the message Rottenrow 1834–2001 round the edge. I am told that thousands were snapped up, in the main by people who were born there, but I have to confess I wasn't one of them.

Since a taxi fare was beyond their reach, my parents boarded a bus to take the new arrival back to their modest 'single end' or 'room and kitchen' on the other side of Glasgow. Both terms were randomly used to describe the basic two-room accommodation that was rented from the city corporation. We were one of eight families, some of whom were even larger than our own, who lived in the four-storey tenement block, one of hundreds or perhaps even thousands dotted around the city. We shared a solitary outside toilet, the seat of which always seemed to be warm. The houses were known locally as 'middens', which is a far from complimentary term, but despite the lack of luxuries on offer it was rare to hear a complaint as people generally accepted, and were surprisingly happy with, their lot, a situation that I still believe prevails to this day.

The address was 14 Muirhead Street in Partick, a suburb on the north bank of the River Clyde right across the water from Govan, where Ibrox is located. Govan is also where Sir Alex Ferguson was raised and our paths have crossed many times over the years. One of Partick's claims to fame is that it was the home of comedian Billy Connolly when he was a child, while it was also previously home to the famous Partick Thistle FC. They were there for around 30 years until 1909, when the club relocated to the Maryhill area, to the north of the city centre, and this remains their home a century later. Staying with football, in 1872 Partick hosted the world's very first international football match, a goalless draw between Scotland and England, which was played on what is now the West of Scotland Cricket Club's ground in Hamilton Crescent. There were many more spectators at Hampden Park when I played in the very same fixture some 112 years later. In recent times Partick has started to shed its working class image and edged closer to becoming a part of the fashionable West End, where some of the city's trendy bars, cafés, restaurants and shops attract many visitors, and which boasts some of Glasgow's more desirable residential areas.

Many years ago my parents confessed to me that times were so hard when I came along that they were unable to afford a cot for me. They solved the problem by turning one of the drawers from a sideboard, which was one of the few items of furniture that they possessed, into a temporary bed. To be honest, my recollections of life in Partick are very scant, but Wilma remembers it well and has painted an accurate picture of a typical working class upbringing. Our house was on the ground floor and my aunt and uncle – Isobel, my mother's sister, and her husband, Andy Potts – lived immediately above us. Because they had a television, which was pretty rare at the time, my mother, with me a babe in arms, was a regular visitor, always climbing the stairs to arrive just in time to accept a cup of tea and sit down to watch the Scottish News. It was an evening ritual and once the programme was over, she would return with me to our own flat on the ground floor and finish preparing a meal in time for my father returning from work. He worked for his best pal, a boyhood friend called Alex McVey, who was Wilma's godfather and had his own furniture removal business. It was a case of simple pleasures in those days, one of the highlights of my parents' week apparently being a trip upstairs every Sunday evening to watch the popular variety show, Sunday Night at the London Palladium, and enjoy a few drinks.

My aunt and uncle had a son, Brian, who was just a couple of years older than me. We were inseparable, more like brothers than cousins, as we played together throughout our childhood and spent many a night at each other's homes. When he grew up Brian neither smoked nor drank and he enjoyed playing five-a-side football, so it was a terrible shock when I heard he had collapsed and died of a heart attack when he was only 41. A father of two, he was decorating his house when it happened. He was divorced but his life had seemed to take a major upturn as he had just met a new partner, who still visits Isobel on a regular basis, and they were looking ahead to many happy years together when tragedy intervened.

Unfortunately, there is a history of early deaths in the Wark family. My paternal grandmother died giving birth to twins, her eighth and ninth children. At the time my father was 14, the eldest child, and because he was ready to go to work he was taken in, although never officially adopted, by an aunt. His eight brothers and sisters were separated to go and live with other relatives and it wasn't until they were adults that they were reunited, most of them having spent years not even knowing the others existed. My grandfather presumably felt he was unable to cope with such a large family, so it astounded those closest to him when he later met a woman and moved in with her and her six children. I never knew my grandmother nor my grandfather on my mother's side, since both had died before I was born, and because my paternal grandfather was only a very rare visitor to our home I virtually missed out altogether in terms of having grandparents, although I never regarded it at the time as a loss because I had never known any differently.

I am certain that being parted from his eight brothers and sisters had a profound effect on my father, who never quite came to terms with why it had to be that way. It soured his relationship with his own father and, having lost his mother at such an early age, he also missed out on a great deal as a result of being parted from the other members of his family. His youngest brother, Hugh, who was one of the twins, spent some time researching the family tree and was able to provide the answer to one question that had puzzled other family members for several years. They were curious as to why I had been named John, because no one had any recollection of another family member of that name. It was a tradition to pass on the same Christian name, as in my father naming his first son Alex and he in turn doing exactly the same, but no one had any idea why I had been named John. It was not until after the death of my father, who had never volunteered anything by way of an explanation, that Hugh unearthed the answer. About a year and a half after my grandmother had her first child, who became my father, she gave birth to another boy. Tragically, he was just a year old when he died of bronchial pneumonia. Not only was he called John, but he was also born on August 4 – in 1930 – so I think it is safe to assume that I was named after him.

The fact that I was born on August 4, just as my father's younger brother had been many years earlier, is not the only example of coincidental dates in the family. My father passed away in his sleep on February 28, 1980, and not only had his mother also died on that date, it was the same date on which his twin brothers, Hugh and Neil, had been born. Also, my uncle James, my dad's brother, died on the same day that my son was born. Spooky or what?

Although my birth certificate records my Christian name as John, from the very beginning I was known as Johnny and to this day that is how every member of my family addresses me. I sign my autograph in that way, too, yet I can never recall being described as such on a team sheet or in a match report, although it suited the Ipswich supporters to constantly refer to me as Johnny, for the simple reason that it was more convenient for their 'He's here, he's there ...' chant that I'm delighted to say echoed round Portman Road on many an occasion. Also, thanks to the number of goals I scored from penalties, it became fairly common practice for newspaper sub-editors to dub me Johnny on the Spot.

But back to Partick and my early days. Having outgrown the drawer in the sideboard, I graduated to a proper-size bed that I had to share with Alex, seven years my senior. It was the bottom bunk and Wilma had the top one. The five of us were squeezed into just two rooms. My parents slept on a bed settee, which they made up every night in the only other room, which also had a recess kitchen area. Open-plan living, it would be called today, but it was anything but back then, with the 'living room' having to double as my parents' bedroom. From our only back window we could see the local police station, which had a court attached, and the women of the houses were regularly hanging out of their windows, checking out those who had been detained overnight, more often than not on drunk and disorderly charges, which was a ready-made starting point for the gossip of the day.

Thankfully, as far as I am aware, none of the Wark clan made an appearance in court, but that is not to say that my parents didn't enjoy a drink. Indeed, one of the 'highlights' of my week was when they returned from a night out in the company of some friends and our house became a party venue for a few hours. Maybe the noise – it was a regular occurrence for an argument or two to break out – meant we didn't get as much sleep as we should have done, but the guests' coats inevitably ended up spread over our bed and the extra warmth was a bonus, albeit a temporary one. I nearly split my sides when I heard a humorous story on this very subject told by Billy Connolly on one of his many television appearances because it could easily have been inspired by my very own childhood experiences.

Sadly, indeed tragically, the demon drink was responsible for my mother's death. She was 57 but because of the ravages of drink she appeared to be quite a few years older. Whereas my father was clearly unwell – he had undergone open-heart surgery in London a few years before the fatal heart attack that took him from us at the ridiculously early age of 51 – mum's demise was largely down to the fact that she was an alcoholic. It hurts me to say it, but it is the truth and there is no point in me trying to deny it. My father was no different to most working men in Glasgow in that he enjoyed an occasional trip to the local pub. When we lived in Scotstoun I recall him popping down to his local, The Smugglers Inn, and when I was old enough and back home for a visit we often went in together. Through my dad, I presented the pub with one of my Scotland shirts and I understand they display it proudly and prominently to this day. If they don't, I would love to know the reason why!

My mother's illness, for that is what it undoubtedly was, caused a lot of heartache within the family. It was not uncommon, for example, for Wilma to receive a call and the voice on the other end of the phone would say 'Come and collect your mum, she's not well'. It became a well-worn code for 'Your mother's under the influence'. Wilma knew what to expect when she got there, to a friend's house or maybe even the pub itself, and literally had to prop her up to get her home. Apart from my father, of course, Wilma took the brunt of the unpleasantness. She became increasingly frustrated and literally tried everything to make our mother see sense. She even attended a support group to gain advice on how to deal with having an alcoholic in the family, but to no avail. We would have done anything to make her better, but my mother stubbornly refused to help herself and eventually paid the ultimate price. She also suffered from depression and was prescribed antidepressants, but since she invariably washed them down with an alcoholic drink their effectiveness was reduced to nil and, as a result, her condition not only failed to improve but actually deteriorated.

I rarely saw my mum's darker days, mainly because I was resident in Suffolk or Merseyside, and for my own good, together with the fact that there was simply nothing that I could have done, I know Wilma spared me a lot of the gory details. My parents were probably similar to a lot of married couples at the time in that they would often appear to be at war with one another. Voices would be raised, usually a signal for the children to make ourselves scarce, but I must stress that there was never any sign of domestic violence. My father was actually quite a gentle soul, certainly not aggressive, but the launching pad for most of the arguments would be my mother's alcoholism. Wilma might intervene and Dad would say 'Leave it to me' and that invariably meant a war of words. But despite the fact that they were often at each other's throats – Wilma has often joked that they could have fought for Britain – the next morning would bring a total change of atmosphere and they could be seen going along the road arm-in-arm, like a young courting couple.

I find it devastatingly sad to state that my mother had neither a long, nor a particularly happy, life. When she was in her 30s, and not long after I had been born, she contracted spinal tuberculosis, which meant she was hospitalised for almost a year. She was a patient at Killearn Hospital, which made it far from easy for my father to visit on a regular basis. He had three children to look after – I was put into an all-day nursery while Alex and Wilma were at school – and a full-time job to hold down. It was a genuine problem. These days, the 15-mile journey by car would be no more than half an hour, but in the 50s, when most people were totally reliant on public transport, it was a very different matter altogether.

My mother certainly did not have an easy life. She worked as a part-time sales assistant at the local corner shop when we lived in Partick and after I started school she took a cleaning job at Glasgow Western Infirmary. Years later she was a cleaner at my former secondary school, Victoria Drive, which wasn't far from our home in Scotstoun. That meant starting at 6am until about 9am, when lessons got under way, and again from approximately 4pm, by which time the pupils were on their way home, for another couple of hours. Like many people, it was merely an existence, devoid of any genuine luxuries, and I cannot help thinking that this must have contributed to her lapse into alcoholism, by way of an escape from the frank realities of what must have been a tedious day-to-day life.

Mum's condition deteriorated fairly rapidly after my dad died. There was no beating the illness, which had her in its grip for years and saw her behaviour become increasingly irrational. One day, for example, she suddenly decided to pay me a visit. It was during my time as a Liverpool player and rather than phone first she simply jumped on a train from Glasgow. She was accompanied by the new man in her life, a fellow alcoholic, and what she didn't know was that my house was empty. I was away on club business abroad and because that meant an absence of several days, Toula, my wife at the time, had returned to Ipswich to visit her family.

Had either I or Toula been at home, of course, we would have invited her in and extended the usual hospitality. My mother knocked on the door of our home in West Derby and when it remained unanswered she convinced herself that I was there but refusing her entry. She had brought with her some old family pictures, which she proceeded to throw around our front garden, and this was behaviour totally alien to such a respectable area. Some of our neighbours rang Toula, who in turn tracked me down, and all I could think to do was phone Wilma, relay the information that had been passed on to me and ask if she had seen our mother. It was all news to Wilma, who immediately went round to our mother's house and discovered she had already returned from Liverpool. A bewildered Wilma asked if mum had, indeed, been down to my house and she replied: "Yes, but the bugger wouldn't let me in."

She did her very best as a mother but the one who suffered most from her illness was undoubtedly Andy, who was subjected to the side effects without at first realising what was actually wrong. There was even a period when he had to move out to live with Isobel and Andy, our aunt and uncle, until he was old enough to fend for himself. By now we had left behind the grey tenement building that was home in Partick – we had hardly reached the end of the road by the time the bulldozers were moving in to demolish it. Isobel and Andy had accompanied us to Scotstoun. While our new home was in a sandstone tenement block with all mod cons, they were the original tenants in a modern skyscraper just along the road. They lived about 12 floors up and for a time it was a real novelty to visit and take in the birds-eye view. Imagine the excitement of us kids seeing things from the air – and in my case especially the Ibrox floodlights!

Mum put a meal on the table every night and there was always a choice – take it or leave it. It was routine fare to the extent that we could virtually work out the day of the week from the meals placed in front of us. Mince and tatties – potatoes to non-Scottish readers – was a regular favourite, as were pies and sausages, served with beans and mash, and macaroni cheese. Wilma and I still laugh when we recall those days and how mum had the same knack as many housewives of that generation in somehow being able to make the macaroni cheese stretch far further than seemed possible once it emerged from the oven. The Sunday leftovers were recycled into a stew on the Monday and there was usually a pot of soup on the go, too, and again it would make several appearances on the week's menu. We very, very seldom had a dessert, only ever on a Sunday, and it usually comprised nothing more complicated than jelly and evaporated milk. Whereas nowadays there appear to be half a dozen takeaway establishments round every corner, fish and chips from the local 'chippy' was such a rare luxury that Christmas seemed to occur more regularly. Mum would feed the kids at around 4.30pm and then she would prepare a meal for herself and dad at around 6pm.

My father wasn't a big man and he was never the type to chuck his weight about. He wasn't averse to giving any of the children a clip – or skelp as we used to say – round the ear but he tended to get his point over by making it in a stern voice. We all knew the score, that there was no scope for argument or negotiation, and if we misbehaved he would confine us to barracks, or ground us, for days at a time. My mother often warned us 'Wait until your father gets home' if we were disobedient and that would result in an immediate improvement in our behaviour, since we knew only too well from previous experience that to continue misbehaving would result in far more serious consequences.

In our Scotstoun days most of the male population either worked at the Albion Motor Works or for Yarrow Shipbuilders. My dad worked for the former, where lorries and buses were built. Alex also served his apprenticeship there and when she left school Wilma, too, was employed by the same company. It was quite common at the time for other members of the family to join the payroll. The fact that they knew your father was considered to be the ultimate reference and in Wilma's case she started as an office junior before moving into the invoice department. Dad also worked at the Singer sewing machine factory in nearby Clydebank, where he was on the assembly line.

I am sure you will have worked out by now that we were like so many families at the time in that my parents struggled from one week to the next to make ends meet. I had only been out of Scotland once – to play in a Boys' Brigade football tournament held in Guernsey – before I ventured south of the border for trials at Ipswich and Manchester City, and it wasn't until I signed on as an apprentice at Portman Road, and the youth team were taking part in a tournament in Holland, that I had any need of a passport. Our annual summer holiday didn't extend to a fortnight, a week or even a few days. It comprised nothing more than a day trip to the seaside – Ayr was a big favourite – and always on the first Monday of the Glasgow Fair fortnight, traditionally the last two weeks in July, when all the city's major factories would shut down. Cue an invasion of places like Blackpool and Great Yarmouth by Scots holidaymakers, but the Wark family budget never extended that far.

As far as I can remember, the lack of cash only ever embarrassed me on one occasion. I was still at primary school and I awoke one morning to find it had snowed overnight. The shoes I wore to school – and also used for a playground kickabout with a tennis ball – were falling apart and I had been told I would have to wait a week or so, until my parents had been paid, before I could have a new pair. The short-term solution to the problem was that I wore my mother's ankle boots, made of a black suede-type fabric and with a zip right up the middle, which resulted in some mickey-taking from some of my classmates. Kids can be cruel and there was no fooling them, because they recognised them straight away since their own mothers had boots just like them.

Muirhead Street in Partick, which was just two streets away from the River Clyde, has long since been demolished to make way for the Clydeside Expressway, but we were still living there when I started at Church Street Primary School. After a year or so we were on the move, to the neighbouring area of Scotstoun. To us it was definitely a case of going up in the world. Our new home, again rented from the city corporation, was at 38 Larchfield Avenue and is still standing. It was a different world to the one we left behind in Partick but let me be clear that it bore no resemblance to the comparative affluence of areas to the north such as Milngavie, Bearsden and Bishopbriggs, where the more well-to-do types, who owned their own properties, lived.

The new house was situated on the first floor of a three-storey tenement but after Partick it seemed like luxury, especially as we had our own bathroom and the old tin bath became redundant. Wilma had a room to herself, while Alex and I shared the only other bedroom, at least until Andy came along. That left my parents to once again make do with having a bed settee – yes, the same one they had in Partick – as they converted the living room into their bedroom on a nightly basis. With Isobel and Andy also moving to the immediate area, I was able to maintain my close friendship with Brian. It seemed I had three, rather than two, brothers and we were just like one big happy family as we came and went between the two homes.

My earliest memory is of kicking a ball around in the street in Partick. It was before I started school so I imagine I would have been about four at the time. The details are sketchy but I recall lots of boys joining in, to the extent that rather than have 22 players in total taking part, on occasions it was more like 22 per team. It seemed there was nothing else for us to do but play football. I literally followed in my brother's footsteps and at first I had to settle for the role of spectator as he and his mates, up to seven or eight years older than I was, enjoyed a kickabout. In Scotstoun a former children's home was demolished and its acres of grounds became our home pitch. Many an enjoyable hour was spent at The Homie, as it was known. It was the focal point of the area for us kids and the tendency back then was for just about every single one of us to receive a new kit, boots or a football from Santa.

You never forget your first pair of proper football boots. Previously, I had several pairs of imitation boots, cheapies from Woolworth's with three white stripes to make the untrained eye think they were actually manufactured by adidas. But one year I awoke on Christmas morning to unwrap the real thing. Endorsed by the one and only George Best, they were called Stylo Matchmakers and seemed years ahead of their time. They were black and purple in colour and laced up one side, rather than in the middle, and I thought I was the bee's knees. On Christmas Day I was out in the street with the other kids, the Rangers strips far outnumbering those of Celtic and even fewer boys sporting the colours of Clyde, Partick Thistle, St Mirren and Clydebank. I am pleased to say that the nastiness that has clouded many an Old Firm fixture was nowhere to be seen.

Gradually, from about the age of six or seven, I began to integrate – rather than just make up the numbers – with the others, and safe in the knowledge that Alex was there to fight my corner if need be, I never held back. Our back yard in Scotstoun was also a ready-made 'pitch' and we used dustbins as goalposts. But the washing lines that criss-crossed it were a real nuisance. In fact, on one occasion I almost came to grief as I ran full pelt into a neck-high rope. There was genuine concern for my well-being as I was taken to hospital hardly able to draw breath. Fortunately, I was later allowed home and the damage amounted to nothing more serious than an embarrassing burn to my neck that was evident for some weeks.

Football seemed to occupy about 99 per cent of my time as a youngster. In the school holidays I would leave the house in the morning and I recall my mum telling me 'Come home for your tea' but it was not uncommon to return to the house before then for a mid-afternoon snack. The big favourite was a piece 'n' jam, which comprised two thick slices of plain bread to form a sandwich with jam in the middle, and we would wash it down with water. After tea I would be off again and often stayed out until 10pm, by which time it was getting dark. I was no different to thousands of other kids in Glasgow and across Scotland who spent the bulk of their time kicking a ball around. Occasionally, we might give football a miss and instead resort to our very own version of the world's foremost steeplechase, The Grand National. Our Aintree was a nearby street full of privately owned houses that were all surrounded by hedges offering increased privacy. We would start at the top of the street, scaling the hedgerows all the way down to the last house at the bottom. Looking back, it was a wonder none of us collected a serious injury because we never had a clue what was on the other side of each hedge. As it was, there were a few twisted ankles, plus assorted cuts and bruises, but thankfully no broken bones.

We also helped ourselves to apples from some of the gardens but that was about as far as I ventured towards the wrong side of the law. We had our gang, but nothing more sinister than a group of friends who would hang out together and spend almost every hour of daylight kicking a ball around. It was about as far removed from the city's dozens of notorious neighbourhood gangs, who were 'tooled up' and looking for trouble, as it is possible to imagine. I thank my lucky stars for my obsession with football because even with Alex and Wilma looking out for me I could easily have veered off the straight and narrow had I had been even slightly fascinated with the endemic gang culture of the time.

ON TRIAL

FROM A VERY EARLY age I wanted to become a footballer and follow in the footsteps of my older brother, Alex, who was a professional at St Mirren. It was Alex who whetted my appetite. He was my shining light, my role model, someone I looked up to from a very early age. He took me under his wing and generally kept an eye out for me, just exactly as big brothers are expected to do. At the slightest sign of trouble, for example if another kid picked on me, Alex was there to deal with it. He was also the one who made me see sense when a lot of my contemporaries saw it as 'big' to smoke and drink. "You can forget about being a footballer if you go down that road," he would tell me – and Wilma wasn't far behind with the very same advice. Thankfully I listened, although it was never a difficult decision. We would have dances at school and beforehand some of the lads would light up and open a can of beer or cider. It wasn't for me, but anyone branding me a goody two-shoes would be well wide of the mark. Believe me, I more than made up for missing out on schoolboy drinking when I got older and quite how I managed to consume so much, and still have as successful a career as I had, is completely beyond me. But more of that later.

Alex didn't play very often for St Mirren but his partner in the middle of the defence on a great many occasions, mainly in the reserves before he stepped up a level, was Gordon McQueen. To this day Alex maintains he was a better player. In fact, he is also adamant that he was better than me and simply won't hear otherwise. In 1973, the year I moved south to join Ipswich, Leeds United boss Don Revie paid £30,000 for big Gordon and five years later he cost Manchester United £495,000. He also won 30 Scotland caps, one more than I did. Despite all that, however, if you ask Alex – and this is when he is stone-cold sober, rather then when he's had a drink or two – he will still claim to have been a better player than either me or Gordon. I think one problem that held Alex back was his temperament and, in turn, his disciplinary record. There is a very thin line between uncompromising and unacceptable, and I'm afraid he crossed it a few times too many. He played in the junior ranks, one step down from the Scottish

League and a rich source of top talent, and in 1977 he played for one of the most famous sides, Kirkintilloch Rob Roy, in the Scottish Junior Cup Final at Hampden. He wore the number five shirt and it was the first time the game was televised live, which might have accounted for the below-average attendance of less than 12,000. Unfortunately, not only did Alex collect the game's first yellow card, but opponents Kilbirnie Ladeside also triumphed 3-1. Alex, who also played for Duntocher Hibs, insists he has no regrets that he didn't make it as a footballer and always winds up Andy and I that he's the most handsome of the Wark boys. He was made up when someone in Ipswich told him he looked like Sean Connery and I have to confess that there is more than a passing resemblance between him and the original, and for my money still the best, James Bond.

Alex originally moved to Australia over 25 years ago to play football and returned to Scotland when his contract expired. Although he was keen to go back to Australia, his wife Morag was less enthusiastic. She wanted to be closer to her parents, which is perfectly understandable, and took a bit of persuading. Even when they tried for a second time Morag found it difficult to settle and they again returned to Scotland. Sadly, her father died but the story eventually had a happy ending when Alex, Morag and her mother all emigrated. I have only been out there once to see them and that was in the late 80s so I am overdue a visit. Alex travelled over here in 1996, when I celebrated my testimonial at Ipswich, and he was back again the following year for my 40th birthday party. Their son, Alex junior, was only an infant when they moved out there and they also have a daughter, Allison, who is in her early 20s.

Alex and his family love the lifestyle Down Under and I cannot see them returning to the UK other than on a family visit. He went out there to work as a mechanical engineer – he served his apprenticeship at the Albion Motor Works near our home in Scotstoun – but was made redundant when he was 50. He changed direction completely to become a prison officer at a women's jail in Melbourne, working in the psychiatric unit. He was attacked by an inmate in 2008 but it didn't put him off continuing in the job. When he first told us of his new job there were lots of light-hearted references to the Aussie television programme, Prisoner Cell Block H. Also, during a telephone call, Wilma jokingly asked him if he was anything like nasty Jim Fenner, the wing governor in the ITV series Bad Girls, which she watched regularly. He replied that he was more like Mr Mackay, the senior officer played by Fulton Mackay in Ronnie Barker's hit comedy Porridge!

Another link between me and the pro game was provided by Joe Wark, a distant relative who is ten years my senior. My grandfather had a brother and Joe is from that side of the family. He was a very successful left-back, clocking up around 500 games for Motherwell and he also captained them for many years before retiring in 1984, at which point he joined the coaching staff. Joe represented the Scottish League against the English League at Hampden in

March 1976, with my Ipswich club captain Mick Mills in opposition, and after a testimonial game against West Bromwich Albion he was also granted a benefit match in January 1985. A select team comprising players from Rangers and Celtic took on 'Well, who have named one of the Fir Park guest lounges after him, and there was another tribute to come in 2007 when the Motherwell supporters voted him into the club's inaugural Hall of Fame alongside the likes of Ian St John and the late Davie Cooper.

Of course, wanting to be a footballer and actually fulfilling the dream are two very different things. A huge percentage of youngsters set their hearts on making the grade, only for the vast majority to fall by the wayside. In my own case, I think it first began to dawn on me that I might actually be good enough when I was still attending Scotstoun Primary School, where I understand they have a picture of me on display alongside other ex-pupils who fall into the 'local boy made good' category. I made it into the school team and was captain of the side when I picked up my very first trophy for being named player of the year. I still have it to this day – a small shield on a wooden background – and it stands side by side with a slightly more prestigious award I collected about 14 years later. That was when my fellow professionals throughout the entire Football League voted me their Player of the Year, the highest individual accolade going. It was handed over towards the end of the 1980-81 season that saw me score 36 goals, 14 of which went a long way towards winning the UEFA Cup for Ipswich.

Further confirmation that I was progressing came after I had moved to Victoria Drive Secondary School, or VD as it was 'affectionately' known, and I was selected for the Glasgow Schools team. If I remember correctly it also contained a lad called George McCluskey, who went on to have a very successful career, playing more than 200 games for Celtic before going on to Leeds, Hibs, Hamilton, Kilmarnock and Clyde. At that point I began to take seriously the idea that my future could be in football. Nowadays, I imagine most, if not all, the parents would be in attendance to share their sons' proud moment, but it was different back then. Leaving work for a few hours was more difficult than it is now, while so few people had their own cars that locating the venue was another problem altogether. My headmaster, Mr Brown, who also picked the school team, drove me to the trials and then to the game itself. I knew how proud he was of having one of his pupils in such elite company because he told me so on more than one occasion. The school also made a fuss of me at an assembly and because I was never going to excel academically it made me feel ten feet tall to know that I was actually good at something.

Actually, to say that I was never going to excel academically is a bit of an understatement. I definitely wasn't the brightest and there is no point in me trying to deny it. My strengths lay in other areas and I was determined to make the most of them. I was only interested in one thing, football, and it helped to perfect my skills that I kicked a tennis ball around the playground with friends at breaks and lunchtime. Long before my time, when parents could not afford to purchase full-sized balls for their kids, the stars of the future had no alternative but to use a smaller, cheaper ball as they played in the streets, kicked it against the walls and controlled it, before repeating the exercise hundreds of times. They became known as tanner ba' players, on the basis that the rubber ball cost a mere sixpence, and once they were able to play with a proper ball they discovered they could perform all manner of tricks with it. It was a bit like that with me and the more I practiced the better I became in terms of being able to make the ball do what I wanted it to do, and that improved my confidence, which is undoubtedly one of the most important factors for any professional sportsman.

Discipline is also vital to becoming a footballer. There were a number of boys who were blessed with more natural ability than I was, but where they perhaps discovered other ways of occupying their spare time, and were distracted, I had tunnel vision in that I devoted virtually every hour to football and neither my dedication nor my determination wavered. I have both the Lifeboys and the Boys' Brigade to thank in part for that, and once again it was a case of following the path set out by my older brother. Our parents taught us right from wrong, and were not slow to reprimand us if they felt it was warranted, but being a member of an organisation like the BB also benefited me a great deal. Mind you, if I'm honest I was first attracted to joining when I heard they ran a football team. I was perhaps less keen on the church parades but I was quickly made aware that I could not do one without the other. I also learned about discipline, taking a pride in one's appearance and attention to detail, while also developing my social skills. Some locals were quick to take the mickey when I was in full uniform and I'd love to know how their lives have panned out.

Over the years I have discovered that I have a fair bit in common with Sir Alex Ferguson, to the extent that our families are known to one another and have mixed at weddings and other events. Sir Alex was born and raised in Govan, on the other side of the River Clyde to where I was brought up. Not only do we share a strong affection for Rangers, he also belonged to the BB and from reading his autobiography I know he also appreciated its part in his development as a person. He was also privileged to play some of his earliest organised football with Drumchapel Amateurs, one of Scotland's top nursery sides, and I remember my time there with great fondness. My older brother also played for them and, once again, it was a simple case of following in his footsteps. I was very proud to play for them – I regarded it as quite a feather in my cap to be deemed good enough – and I was even prepared to forgive them the fact that they played in green and white hoops. Drumchapel was only a small area to the west of Scotstoun towards Clydebank until the 1950s when they constructed a sprawling council estate to accommodate more than 30,000 people. It was part of the city's overspill policy but they neglected to add any amenities and Billy Connolly wasn't wrong when he described it as "a desert wi' windaes." They were an exceptional club thanks to the tireless efforts of Douglas Smith, who unquestionably ran the show. He was a millionaire who owned a shipyard and he instilled a lot of good habits in the boys, including sportsmanship and not swearing. Punctuality was another thing he encouraged and to this day I am never late for an appointment. I might arrive early, but I will never keep anyone waiting.

Having been welcomed into the under-14 squad, managed by Eddie McDonald, I could not believe the big-time treatment that we received. Douglas Smith was a top man and he invested a lot of his personal wealth in the club. On Saturdays, I would play in the morning for my school team, and then I would join the rest of my Drumchapel team-mates for a pre-match meal in one of Glasgow's best-known restaurants, Reid's, located in the city centre close to Central Station. This was unheard of in local football and, quite naturally, we felt superior to our opponents, something we consistently demonstrated en route to winning the league title. Another of my managers was David Moyes, father of the current Everton manager of the same name. I have never actually met David since he made his name as a footballer and then manager, but I remember him as a reddish-haired youngster, probably aged about seven. He accompanied his father to our games and was a near-permanent fixture alongside him on the touchline. That image comes alive in my mind every time I see him on television, barking out instructions to the players at Everton, where he has done such a marvellous job that he is often mentioned, and rightly so in my view, as a possible candidate to succeed Sir Alex, should he ever actually retire, at Manchester United.

It was on the strength of my performances for The Drum, as we were known, that I came to the attention of one of Glasgow's big two clubs. As I have already indicated, my ambition was to play for Rangers, but when an invitation to training did eventually transpire it came from their arch-rivals, Celtic. Although my loyalties lay elsewhere, I was not about to turn down such an opportunity and so I made my way there, via one bus to the city centre and another eastwards to Parkhead, every Tuesday evening. This lasted for a couple of months, despite the fact that I committed something of an own goal on my very first night. We were instructed we had to turn up in collar and tie, and I remember my father making sure I toed the line. There was just one problem, I slipped on a royal blue tie, but despite that faux pas they still invited me back. I was among a group of about 30 boys and the sessions took place in what was a rather large area behind one goal. The distance between the terraces and the goals was a feature of Celtic Park, which was oval-shaped in those days, but it disappeared when the stadium was developed into what is now one of Europe's leading grounds and fans behind the goal are a great deal closer to the action.

Eventually, having waited in vain for a knock on the door from a Rangers scout, Celtic invited me to sign schoolboy forms. It was well known in Scotland at the time that of the youngsters signed as schoolboys by the Old Firm clubs, only a handful tended to progress to the professional ranks. I have to admit, though, that had I received the same offer from Rangers I would have instantly agreed and taken my chance. However, I was able to stall on Celtic's offer because by that time I had attracted interest from several English clubs whose scouts were in regular attendance at Drumchapel games. Quite often, our manager would inform us beforehand which clubs were represented. That may have made some boys nervous, but in my case I was inspired to give of my very best, so eager was I to impress. The scouts stood out from the crowd and could have been spotted a mile away. But there was no way of knowing who represented which clubs until, if you were one of the lucky ones, they approached you afterwards. The first club to declare an interest were Bristol City, who invited me to take part in a trial game they had arranged in Ayr. By the time that game was looming, however, I had also been approached by both Manchester City and Ipswich Town, both of whom, in the early 1970s, I considered to be far more attractive propositions.

At this point in my life my education was suffering. Not through any fault of my teachers, I have to confess. Few, if any, of the pupils lived closer to the school than I did. I would leave the house and walk no more than 50 yards down the road, turn left and there it was. But in common, it has to be said, with a large number of the pupils, I was not the least bit dedicated to my studies. The fact that it seemed I was headed for a future in football – at least that was how I saw it, even if it was still very early days – provided me with an easy excuse to virtually desert them altogether. It wasn't that I was totally opposed to school and rebelled, but I was never academically inclined and remaining as a pupil, hopefully passing sufficient O-levels and then Highers, the Scottish equivalent of A-levels, then attending university, simply wasn't an option. As far as I was concerned, the quicker I could leave school the better. I used to enjoy the science subjects, and in particular the many chemical experiments we conducted in the laboratory, and although I never excelled at mathematics I always felt I had a good head for figures and was above average in my group. I certainly wasn't an unruly or disruptive pupil and have no recollection of my parents being summoned to the headmaster's office, but I have to confess that there were a few occasions when I felt the full force of the corporal punishment in general use at the time. It was meted out by a leather belt about half an inch thick and which was so solid it could stand up in the teacher's clenched fist, a bit like a cobra when it is hypnotised by a snake charmer.

My crime, invariably, was to get involved in playground dust-ups, of which there were quite a few. I am no longer in touch with old school friends but I remember two guys, Sammy Miller and David Peacock. They were with me at primary school and we all stepped up to Victoria Drive at the same time. We would 'hang about' together a fair bit. Sammy was quite a bit taller than me and because he could look after himself we tended to avoid trouble most, although certainly not all, of the time. For instance, I was caught in the act one day when I was carving the initials of one of the girl pupils on a desk. I had a crush on her and that was regarded as a 'cool' way in which to demonstrate my undying love. I remember using a compass from my geometry set to write CAD, which I believe stood for Carol-Ann Davey, but from what I can recall my feelings were never reciprocated. She wasn't the first object of my affection. That was Virginia Dorey – I think that's how she spelt her surname – who was generally acknowledged as the most attractive girl at Scotstoun. Consequently, I was not her only admirer. She lived in what I regarded as a 'posh' house – privately owned, large, detached, with its own garden – and I recall going round there one day after school with several other lads, at which point she made us form a queue and then proceeded, in turn, to kiss every single one of us.

While the belt should have been an ample deterrent, I was one of many pupils on the receiving end several times before the message sunk in. I was required to stand there, with one hand on top of the other, while the teacher brought down the belt with as much force as he could summon. A lack of accuracy meant that it often came into contact with the wrist, rather than the palm of the hand, which made it all the more painful. After three blows the hands were reversed, whereupon the teacher would repeat the routine. It simply wasn't on to let your classmates see you suffer, but anyone given the belt was automatically allowed to pay a visit to the toilets and once there I don't mind admitting that I shed a few tears as I soothed my 'burning' hands under the cold water tap.

The bottom line, as far as my schooling is concerned, is that I left at 15 without a single qualification. I found it got in the way of other things I wanted to do more. For example, I had ventured into the fairly lucrative area of part-time employment, which I regarded as a far more attractive proposition to sitting behind a desk for most of the day. My morning paper round, during which I devoured the back page football news in between the 200 or so deliveries I had to make in one long street, did not interfere with school. But it was a different story when I later took on a milk delivery job that required me to be up and ready to start work at 6am. The early start meant I would regularly fall asleep in class and then, having extended my working hours to 12 noon, there were days when I never even bothered to attend school. I was working virtually full-time and having my own independent income was very welcome. However, as I cast my mind back almost 40 years, I can see it was a very short-sighted strategy, since it would undoubtedly have limited my options had I failed to make it as a footballer. I prefer, of course, to say that it underlined my determination to fulfil my dream. But for football I have absolutely no idea where I would have turned. I am left with the inevitable conclusion that I would have taken a factory job and maybe played football, as my brother Alex did, at junior level for an extra few quid each week.

My life dramatically changed direction when I agreed to visit both Manchester City and Ipswich Town for trials. Their scouts visited my home to make the necessary arrangements and I was pleased to hear that one of my Drumchapel team-mates, Alan Godfrey, was also wanted by City. To be honest, I started to think in terms of the pair of us joining up at Maine Road. It seemed to me the perfect way to combat the problem of homesickness and I convinced myself that there could be nothing better than to be launching a new, exciting chapter of my life in the company of someone I knew well. We duly travelled together to Manchester in the school holidays on two separate occasions, but while City confirmed their desire to sign Alan on apprentice forms they were reluctant to commit themselves as far as I was concerned. Twice, I also made the long journey to Ipswich and not only was I made extremely welcome but I also gained the impression right from the off that they were keen to take me on. Sure enough, Bobby Robson spoke to me and formally invited me to sign as an apprentice, only for me to delay because I was still waiting on a final yes or no from City. I remember Bobby looking none too pleased with my response and asking 'Are you sure you are doing the right thing?'

Back in Glasgow, I feared I had blown it. What if Manchester City decided not to offer me anything and if Ipswich were so offended by my initial reluctance to accept their offer straight away that they withdrew it? I was in a bit of a sweat when I went to my Aunt Isobel's house to use her phone. A call to Maine Road, where they remained non-committal, made up my mind for me. Taking a rather deep breath, I then called Ipswich and asked to speak to Mr Robson. When he came on the line I asked, rather nervously, if he still wanted to sign me. He said he most certainly did and rather bluntly – he didn't mince his words – told me to get myself on the next train south, which I did the very next day. I had a couple of farewell parties, one at my house and the other on the platform at Glasgow's Central Station, where my family and friends waved me off. I settled down for the long journey with tears in my eyes and a nagging doubt in my mind because I had no way of knowing how things were going to work out. As the miles went by I had plenty of time to sit and wonder, inwardly voicing my concern as to whether or not I was doing the right thing.

Being greeted with open arms at the other end by Mr Robson, who made me feel he had signed a real gem of a player, was just the welcome I needed. To be honest, he made it seem as if I was a club record signing rather than a schoolboy hopeful. Sure, he probably said precisely the same things every time a new youngster checked in at Portman Road, but I have to say it worked as far as I was concerned and right there and then I decided I would do my very best to meet his expectations. The club's Scottish scout, George Findlay, was also delighted that I was joining Ipswich and it goes without saying that I owe him a debt of gratitude. George, who still lives in Kilmarnock, had already taken George Burley to

Portman Road and later snatched Alan Brazil from under Celtic's noses. It was no mean feat, bearing in mind the competition he faced from clubs on both sides of the border, to unearth three youngsters who not only went on to play for their country, but were all members of the Scotland squad for the 1982 World Cup finals in Spain.

I was booked into a hotel within walking distance of the ground and the following day I strolled into Portman Road to start work in the form of pre-season training, which actually took place at HMS Ganges, a Royal Navy training establishment out on the Suffolk coast at Shotley. Typically, I was a bit apprehensive, but I quicky settled into the routine and by the time the season got under way I had moved out of the hotel and into digs in the town. I was still feeling homesick and the only contact I had with my family was a weekly telephone call from Wilma, who would visit her local launderette in Glasgow every Friday evening to use their phone. The club found me a Scottish landlady in Norwich Road and no doubt thought they were doing me a huge favour, but she was too intense for my liking. She wanted to mother me but it actually felt like she was smothering me and her cooking didn't really agree with me. When she rang the police one Saturday night and reported me for being out too late at night it was to prove the last straw.

I remember being called into the manager's office on the Monday morning and immediately thinking 'I must be in trouble' although I had no idea why that should be the case. Mr Robson sat me down and with a stern look on his face said he had heard from my landlady that I had returned home the previous Saturday night at 10.30pm. I couldn't deny it and explained I had only been to the cinema. I said that by the time the film finished and I had walked home it was indeed 10.30. At that point the manager smiled and it was clear he was having a laugh at my expense. He simply said 'I think we need to find you some new digs.' I don't know if it was me, or whether I was just unlucky, but I had about six different digs in a few months. One was a house on the outskirts of the town, where I shared a room with David Geddis, and one night we were lying awake chatting when we heard a strange noise. It wasn't very loud and we couldn't fathom what it was – well, not until David let out a roar from his bed as he managed to grab a mouse that was scurrying across his chest. We were out of there pretty quickly.

The funny thing about David and I was that we spent a lot of our time arguing. We were like an old married couple, bickering away over this and that. Although we shared digs and played in the same youth team we weren't really that close. We used to kick lumps out of each other when we had short-sided games in the gym because it would be Scotland against England, which meant we were always in opposition to each other. There were several Scottish lads at the club – George Burley, David McKellar, Murdo Finlayson, Jimmy McNichol, Tommy O'Neill, Alec Jamieson, Kenny Taylor and Robert Hamilton – and we tended to stick together. We would visit the cinema a couple of times a week because the club received free passes, which was a nice perk when we had so little money in our pockets. It was not uncommon for the apprentices to borrow cash from the senior players, or on the odd occasion for the first team players to wave them away when they attempted to repay it. I managed to slip two £1 notes into an envelope and send it home to my mother every week. I wanted to do my bit and felt good about it.

I had never been in a pub before I came to Ipswich and in my first season I started to accompany some of the other youth team players to the Falcon in the town centre. It was the 'in' place to go on a Thursday evening but we were not supposed to be out beyond a Wednesday and youth coach Charlie Woods often tried to catch us out. Had he been six feet plus he might well have done. He would reach the entrance to the crowded pub and crane his neck to see if any of his players were breaking the club rules. That was our signal to hit the deck and because the place was packed solid Charlie never ventured much beyond the front door. Had he taken the trouble to work his way across the bar he could not have failed to spot as many as a dozen of us crouching down on the floor.

My early appearances in the youth team were at left-back and although it was not my best position I managed to equip myself reasonably well. One day I found myself up against a lightning-quick, full-of-tricks winger when we played Orient and it was none other than Laurie Cunningham, who went on to play for West Bromwich Albion and then became the first British player to sign for Real Madrid. He was also one of England's first black internationals and in 1989, when he was tragically killed in a road accident in Spain, he was still only 33 years old. I had played most of my football in Scotland as a centre-half and the club knew that, but it was perfectly normal for them to try kids in different positions to see where they had most to offer.

The South East Counties League proved a launching pad for many a successful career. The standard was extremely high and we were the best team by some distance, which is supported by the fact that we won the title by a considerable margin. The other 15 clubs represented were Arsenal, Chelsea, Tottenham, West Ham, Fulham, QPR, Charlton, Crystal Palace, Millwall, Orient, Portsmouth, Southend, Reading, Gillingham and Watford. I often felt we were at a disadvantage because of our location. The A12 took us right through the middle of Chelmsford, where there always seemed to be a traffic jam, and with the M25 still to come the journey time was a lot longer than it is today. Daylight was often trying to break through when we climbed on to the team bus at Portman Road to head south for games that would kick off at 10.30am. If the first team were at home we sometimes made it back for the start of the game, but more often than not we would only return in time to take in the second half. Our home games were played on the Portman Road practice pitch and used to attract a couple of hundred spectators, sometimes more.

We couldn't get enough football. Sunday was supposed to be a day off but I was one of a group that had a weekly routine I wouldn't have changed for anything. A group of us would rendezvous at the house where Eric Gates, David McKellar and Kenny Taylor had digs and their landlady, Mrs Garrod, would cook a magnificent roast dinner for us all. As word got round the numbers increased, but dinner wasn't the only thing on the Sunday menu. The Murray Road recreation ground was close by and we also looked forward to our weekly football match with some local lads. It would have been about eight-a-side and I still see some of the lads around town from time to time. Sadly, Mrs Garrod has passed away, but I often see her son, Graham, when I pop into one of my regular haunts, the Newton Road Conservative Club in Ipswich.

My dream back then was to make the first team, win major honours, play for my country and earn plenty of money. I was no different to all the other young players, although I can guarantee none of them wanted it more than I did. I will admit there were times when the homesickness kicked in and I wondered if I should pack it in and head back to Glasgow. If it hadn't been for the fact that I felt I was making progress I might well have quit. Bobby Robson's influence was another important factor. Of all the many top football people I encountered during my career, he had the biggest single influence on me. He took a close interest from day one and was always there for me. If I had a problem, whether it was football-related or a personal matter, he listened and he always had a sensible answer. He made me the player I was and I will always be grateful to him. Throughout my career, long after we parted company when he left Ipswich to become England manager in 1982, I sought his advice on a variety of subjects.

I suppose you could say I made fairly rapid progress after I joined Ipswich. I was a regular choice in the youth team and after those opening games at left-back I went on to spend more and more time in the middle of the defence, which I regarded at the time as my best position. I even managed to play in the reserves, celebrating my debut at right-back against Chelsea at a near-deserted Stamford Bridge in January 1974 by scoring the only goal, a shot five minutes from the end that deflected off one of their defenders. The thing I most remember is that Peter Bonetti was in goal for them and it was hard to believe that I'd stuck one past the same guy who was playing in goal for England in a World Cup quarter-final against West Germany less then four years earlier, which I could remember watching on television. Other familiar names in the Chelsea side that day were John Dempsey, Marvin Hinton, Peter Osgood, Kenny Swain and Ray Wilkins. I couldn't have asked for more. I gradually overcame the homesickness, too, and that was a huge help. Mr Robson appreciated the problem – he had left the family home near Newcastle to start out in London with Fulham – and he allowed me to nip home to Scotland at fairly regular intervals during that first season. Then, refreshed by a decent summer break back home in Glasgow, I returned to start my second year and once again Shotley was our base for pre-season training.

The routine was that the younger players would be chauffeured out there by the senior stars and when the cavalcade took off from Portman Road I found myself in Kevin Beattie's car alongside Glen Westley and Dale Roberts, who were not much older than me. We were about half-way there, along the windy coastal route, when we were involved in an accident that might have killed all four of us. Kevin – or Beat as he is universally known – could not control the car as he took a bend and it left the road, somersaulted three times and landed upside down. The wheels were still spinning when the manager's car came along moments later and with no visible sign of life he naturally feared the worst. Miraculously, although the car was a crumpled wreck and written off to the extent that only one wheel and the battery could be salvaged, none of us was injured. We managed to crawl out of the shattered back window, much to Mr Robson's relief, but we were all shaking and suffering from shock.

He realised straight away that we were in no shape to train and arranged for us to be ferried back into Ipswich. The car, an Opel Manta, was Beat's pride and joy but as he only had third party, rather than fully comprehensive, insurance cover, he was unable to claim and lost £1,400. That was a fair amount of money at the time – for example, my weekly wage back then was just £7.43 after deductions, although the club paid for my digs. Beat invited us back to his house, where we replayed the incident over and over. None of us had suffered as much as a scratch and we could not believe our good fortune. I remember Beat, despite his considerable financial loss, lightening the mood by joking 'Anything for a day off training, eh, lads!' Unfortunately, the crash affected me so much that it was a further ten years, by which time I was a Liverpool player, before I could even think about learning to drive.

WORK HARD PLAY HARD

LATE IN 2008, as I was flicking through a football magazine, a particular article caught my eye. It was about the Leeds United team crowned champions in the 1973-74 season and referred to them as 'the best team in the country, the most talked about team in the country and the most fashionable team in the country'. No sooner had they won the title than their manager, Don Revie, left to become England boss. His successor was Brian Clough, only for that to be one of the shortest partnerships in football history. Clough, who had won the League Championship for Derby County and would go on to even greater success with Nottingham Forest, was gone within 44 days and it was to former England captain Jimmy Armfield that they next turned. To Armfield's eternal credit he did more than just steady the ship. However, because the earlier upheaval had inevitably affected league results, they had very little hope of retaining their title. Instead, it was on the FA Cup and the European Cup, where they were eventually beaten 2-0 by Bayern Munich in the Paris final, that they were most firmly focused. That they did not get to Wembley for what would have been the third time in four seasons – they beat Arsenal in the 1972 final and were surprisingly beaten by Sunderland, of the Second Division, the following year – was down to Ipswich. And yours truly, much to my surprise and delight, played a part in their quarter-final KO.

It couldn't happen today because of the Football Association's ruling that ties have to be decided by the first replay, but the marathon clash with Leeds extended to four games and a total of seven hours of football before the two sides could be separated. A goalless draw at Portman Road that attracted what is still the club's record attendance of 38,010 was followed just three days later by a 1-1 stalemate at Elland Road in front of a 50,000-plus crowd. Ipswich led through David Johnson's 17th minute header and had further chances to score before Duncan McKenzie equalised in injury time to take the tie to a replay. There was no further scoring and manager Bobby Robson declared afterwards that he had never been so disappointed in all his time in football. His team was just 20 seconds away from winning through but instead the action switched to a neutral venue – Filbert Street,

Leicester – for a second replay a fortnight later. Once again, there was nothing between the two sides and following a 0-0 draw it was announced that they would reconvene at the same ground just 48 hours later for the fourth instalment.

As a youth team player with a few reserve games behind me, I followed developments from afar. I had seen the first tie but after that I depended on television highlights and press reports to keep me posted. In fact, while Ipswich and Leeds were locked together at Filbert Street on the Tuesday evening I was otherwise engaged. I was actually playing in the first leg of an FA Youth Cup semi-final at Huddersfield. We won 1-0 thanks to a goal from Keith Bertschin and the celebration party got under way as soon as we returned to our hotel. None of the hard stuff, obviously, because we were too young to drink, even if our chairman, John Cobbold, who had accompanied us, wanted to order a dozen bottles of champagne. Our youth coach, Charlie Woods, was on the prowl just to make sure none of the bubbly passed our lips. It was fairly late when Charlie informed me that he had spoken on the phone to Bobby Robson and said that I would be required for the first team game against Leeds at Leicester two days later. Kevin Beattie, he explained, was struggling after picking up a hamstring injury that same night, John Peddelty was still sidelined after fracturing his skull three months earlier and Dale Roberts had also picked up a knock in the youth game at Huddersfield that meant he was also out of contention. I was so far down the pecking order – fifth choice to be precise – that I was playing in midfield for the youth team and even after the initial shock of being diverted to Leicester I virtually convinced myself that I was only going along for the ride. I felt certain Kevin would respond to treatment and play, so my excitement at being promoted to the senior squad was tempered somewhat.

I was dropped off at Leicester on the Wednesday and knew that I would be missing a trip to West Germany for an international youth tournament over the Easter period that Ipswich went on to win without me. I learned that Kevin was a long way from being a certain non-starter for the next day's game, which did nothing to alter my feeling that I was merely there as a precautionary measure. However, on the Thursday morning Bobby Robson pulled me to one side during a training session and explained that Kevin was not going to make it after all and I would definitely be playing alongside Allan Hunter at the heart of the defence that night. From what I can recall of that precise moment I was completely stunned and, initially at least, I couldn't come to terms with it. I think the manager could tell from my reaction that I was struggling and immediately sought to reassure me. 'Look,' he said, 'I'm throwing you in for one reason and one reason only – you can do the job we require of you and if I didn't believe that you could cope there is absolutely no way that I would even think of doing it.'

On the day of the match, following a loosening-up session, there was a light-hearted moment at our hotel before we assembled for our pre-match meal. The telephone rang in my room and I found myself chatting to someone who said he was a newspaper reporter and would like to interview me. Ten minutes later I had given him my life story and even told him what I'd had for lunch. Only when we were sat in the restaurant at about 5pm did I realise the truth, that rather than giving my first big interview I was merely the latest victim of ace hoaxer Eric Gates. It was news to me but his party piece was to pretend to be a journalist and he was never rumbled as he stacked up a long list of young victims. I was Mr Gullible and I don't mind admitting it, so the senior players had a laugh at my expense. They pushed their luck a bit too far, however, when they suggested I should order steak and chips, which I probably would have done had Mr Robson not realised what was happening and put me right. It was par for the course for a new lad making his debut and while I was on the receiving end on that occasion, I have to confess that I was to exact revenge on countless unfortunate victims in the years to come.

As far as the outside world was concerned, Beat would be in his usual place for the third replay against Leeds. I knew differently, of course, but Ipswich were anxious to keep the starting line-up under wraps for as long as possible, so much so that when Leeds manager Jimmy Armfield popped his head into our dressing room about an hour before kick-off I was asked to hide. I was already kitted out with the number six shirt and if I'd been spotted it would have given the game away. Mr Robson and Jimmy were, and still are, the best of pals, a friendship that started in their playing days when they were colleagues in the England side, but there was no way he was going to let this particular cat out of the bag until he had to submit his team sheet. The rest of the players were doing their best to calm my nerves and took it in turn to offer words of advice, but to be honest all I wanted was to get out there and get on with it.

During the warm-up I looked around and saw so many familiar faces on the Leeds side, including some of my heroes, people like Billy Bremner, brothers Frank and Eddie Gray, and Joe Jordan, most of whom were established Scottish internationals I had been happy to cheer on numerous occasions at Hampden Park. Who could blame me for being a tad star-struck? There was very little time to settle down because the pace was pretty hectic right from the start, far quicker than anything I had previously experienced. The one thing that helped me to adjust was that I made a good early tackle on Allan Clarke and from that moment on I enjoyed myself in a game full of incident.

We took a fifth minute lead through Trevor Whymark but Clarke equalised before half-time and although Bryan Hamilton put us ahead in the 50th minute Leeds came back again through Johnny Giles in the 73rd minute. In the end the game was decided by a goal fit to grace the final itself as Clive Woods cut in from the left and hit a curling, right-foot drive that beat goalkeeper David Stewart and crept just inside the far post. We still had 11 minutes plus stoppage time to keep

Leeds out before Ipswich were eventually through to the FA Cup semi-finals for the first time in their history. Billy Bremner was quick to congratulate me after Jack Taylor, who I remembered from seeing the World Cup Final of 1974 on television, blew the final whistle. He shook my hand and said 'Well done, son' and most of the other Leeds players, while clearly devastated to have lost, were also sporting in defeat.

The one exception was Allan Clarke, who gave me as tough an introduction to the big-time as it was possible to imagine. I didn't mind the fact that he was clearly determined to make life difficult for me, nor was I fazed with his gamesmanship, the use of the elbow and several fouls committed on the blind side of the ref. What really wound me up was that he spat in my face a few times. It was his bad luck that Allan Hunter, who had promised beforehand that he would look after me, caught him in the act. Big Al wasn't amused and told him in no uncertain terms, 'Do that again and I'll break your f***ing leg'. Clarke wisely took the advice on board and there was no repeat. When asked years later to identify my least favourite opponent I always nominated Clarke, whose older brother Frank was a successful Bobby Robson signing for Ipswich from QPR in 1970.

Clarke's strike partner, Joe Jordan, gave me a very different welcome. He had a reputation as an uncompromising centre-forward, a bit of a battering ram, who never gave less than 100 per cent. No more than ten minutes into the game I challenged him in the air and he gave me what I can only describe as a head-butt. It was no accident. He just ignored the ball. Between them, Clarke and Jordan did their best to rough me up and intimidate me and I was pleased that they didn't succeed, although that word in Clarke's ear from Big Al certainly helped. When I eventually joined Joe in the Scotland squad I recalled my debut as a bit of an icebreaker. 'Do you remember head-butting me?' I asked him with a smile on my face. Joe, as lovely a man off the field as he was feared on it, just shrugged and replied 'That's me, that's how it is' and the conversation was brought to an abrupt end. Clearly, it had been a normal day at the office as far as he was concerned.

As we came off the pitch at Filbert Street I saw Bobby Robson was waiting to shake my hand. In fact, he came several yards on to the pitch to do it and was clearly thrilled for me. He later told the press I had 'performed heroics' and that was nice to read. I agreed to do an interview for ITV Sport – Gary Newbon was the man with the microphone – and being new to that side of things I have no qualms about admitting that my performance was nowhere near as good as it had been in the game. It was not possible for my parents to attend the game but once we were back at the hotel I made sure I found a phone to give them a call. Actually, I had to ring their neighbours along the road as so few people had phones in their own homes at the time. The following day's Daily Record reported the occasion, the first of many cuttings that my mother stuck in a series of scrapbooks charting my career.

I looked upon the win over Leeds as a one-off and having helped the club reach the semi-finals I felt I would be taking a back seat for the rest of the season. I couldn't have been more wrong. Beat was again absent less than 48 hours later for our home league game against Leicester, as were another three of the Filbert Street side – George Burley, Brian Talbot and David Johnson – so our 2-1 win was all the more welcome. I was up against one of the most talented centre-forwards I have ever seen in Frank Worthington and although he scored no one could change the fact that I was again on the winning side. In the space of just two days I had helped Ipswich into the semi-finals of the FA Cup and to three hugely important league points as we chased the title, but that was by no means the end of my first team experience that season.

Hard to believe, perhaps, but within the space of another 48 hours we were in action again, this time in the Easter Monday fixture at Chelsea. The Stamford Bridge side were nothing like the force they are today – in fact they were relegated a few weeks later – but in the circumstances a 0-0 draw was a satisfactory outcome. Incredibly, we had another game the very next day, a home clash with Birmingham, but with Messrs Hunter and Beattie both fit I was left out of the side as we won 3-2 and kept alive our Championship challenge. Incidentally, today's Premiership managers who feel the need to rotate players when commitments demand might be interested to know that the game against Birmingham was Ipswich's tenth in the space of just 24 days, starting with the first FA Cup clash against Leeds. That sort of workload is unheard of today but Bobby Robson managed to get by using just 19 different players in his starting line-ups and only four – Mick Mills, Allan Hunter, Bryan Hamilton and Trevor Whymark – played in all ten. With such a demanding programme, and bearing in mind the lack of depth to the senior squad, it was clear to see how a complete rookie like yours truly had been able to feature as often as I did.

But I still wasn't finished. When Ipswich drew the semi-final against West Ham United 0-0 at Villa Park, with around 23,000 fans from Suffolk in attendance, they were not only without David Johnson when he failed a late fitness test, but Beat was crocked early on and limped his way through the remainder of the game up front as Trevor Whymark went back into defence to replace him. Our other centre-half, Allan Hunter, was also injured to the extent that he had to go off and with both George Burley and Bryan Hamilton picking up knocks it was a relief to keep the scoreline blank and earn a replay four days later. Stamford Bridge was the venue and with Big Al ruled out I was drafted in alongside Beat at the back for what Bobby Robson called the most important game in the club's history. Our 2-1 defeat will be remembered for the controversial display of referee Clive Thomas and his decision not to allow what we considered to be two perfectly good goals, in particular when Bryan Hamilton found the net, although I have to also admit that a defensive header of mine was less than perfect and allowed Alan Taylor the opportunity to score one of his two that knocked us out.

The semi-final replay was not my last first team experience that season but it left a lasting impression. The extreme high of my senior debut, winning through to conclude the marathon tie against Leeds, was followed by the desperate low of going out to West Ham as Wembley beckoned. No one will ever be able to convince me that we did not deserve to reach the final, where we would have faced Fulham, who were just above the half-way point in the Second Division at the time. We would have beaten them, of that I am certain, but instead of leaving Stamford Bridge for a celebratory journey home to Suffolk we were a thoroughly dispirited bunch. It was quite an experience for me at such an early stage of my career to see so many seasoned pros emotionally distraught and many a tear was shed. Very few words were spoken but for the older players it must have been absolute torture to have their hopes dashed. As they reflected silently on whether the chance of appearing in an FA Cup Final had passed them by, I have to confess that at 17 I couldn't decide whether my one and only chance had gone or whether another opportunity would present itself. Thankfully, for all of us, our prayers were answered three years later.

There remained the significant matter of trying to win the League Championship. We were sitting fourth at the time of our FA Cup exit and because we could only muster two wins from our final four games – just two points per win in those days – we came up short. Ironically, we lost 2-1 to Leeds at Elland Road to virtually end all hope but there was no disgrace in finishing third on the same points as runners-up Liverpool and just two adrift of Brian Clough's Derby. I say 'we' but in truth I was removed from the first team picture after playing in the 2-1 home win over QPR, our fourth from last league fixture, and instead finished what I had started with the youth team. It was my goal that beat Orient 1-0 in the first round of the FA Youth Cup and we simply kept going all the way until we actually got our hands on the trophy. Having seen off Huddersfield at the semi-final stage we then set ourselves up for the second leg of the final at Portman Road by beating West Ham 3-1 at Upton Park. A crowd of 16,000-plus created a fantastic atmosphere at Portman Road and goals by Tommy O'Neill and Keith Bertschin earned a 2-0 win and a comfortable 5-1 aggregate success. The Hammers had Alvin Martin, Alan Curbishley, Geoff Pike, Paul Brush and Terry Hurlock in their side. With the South East Counties League title also in the bag – we only lost three of our 30 games – it was something to celebrate.

The official dinner to mark the club's second FA Youth Cup success in three seasons was a glittering affair. With John Cobbold at the helm there was always a sense of style about how the club did things. It certainly wasn't a case of taking our success for granted after a handsome first-leg win in East London because the club stated its intention to host a celebration before that game had even taken place. Invitations were sent out to all the boys' parents around the UK to state that the club would pay all expenses – travelling, accommodation, everything – so it was hardly a shock that there was a full house at the Copdock Hotel. In my own parents' case it was their first time in Ipswich and I can still see the looks on their faces after Mr John made one of the shortest speeches on record. In his own inimitable style he congratulated the players and then virtually ordered the parents to retire immediately. His actual words were, 'I want you to get to bed straight away, f*** like rabbits and make us another FA Youth Cup-winning team for about 18 years from now'. Those who had never met him before, including my mother and father, didn't know how to react at first but the rest of us just doubled up in laughter. That was typical of Mr John, although it is clear from the way things panned out that few, if any, parents took his request seriously. Either that or they were taking the necessary precautions.

By the end of the 1974-75 season, my second at the club, I had played more games, 24, for the reserves than for the youth team and bearing in mind I had also made five first team appearances, including two in the FA Cup, I was very satisfied with my progress. But it was during a trip home that summer that I saw the other side of the coin and counted my lucky stars for my own good fortune. I caught a bus into the city centre and couldn't believe it when the bus conductor approached me to take my fare. It was none other than Alan Godfrey, my former team-mate at Drumchapel Amateurs, who had accompanied me for trials to Manchester City. Not only had he been taken on as an apprentice at Maine Road, but the club had handed him a professional contract after one year. He explained that he had broken his leg and the injury had led to him returning to Glasgow and staying there. His experience had been in stark contrast to my own and I felt for him. We arranged to meet up the very next night and I could say or do nothing to ease the blow. It was a real shame because Alan was a far more gifted footballer than me, with similarities to Tottenham and England star Glenn Hoddle in the way he played the game.

I had signed as a £30-a-week professional on my 17th birthday in August 1974. I also received a £100 signing-on fee and that was sent back, in its entirety, to my parents. I signed a two-year deal and despite the fact that I had graduated to the first team ahead of schedule, so to speak, no wage rise was forthcoming in the summer of 1975. Still on the subject of money, Bobby Robson was always encouraging the players to invest the maximum permitted into a pension scheme. It was sound advice for which I was later very grateful, but in those days I had very little to invest. Clearly, as my earnings improved, I was able to allocate more to my pension but there was no way I could compete with fellow countryman George Burley, whose enthusiasm to stockpile cash actually led to him being informed he had contravened the rules by adding more than he was permitted to do.

Despite the fact that I had clocked up a few first team appearances I never in any way felt I had established myself as one of them. Indeed, far from it, and for a time I was so ill at ease with my new status that I would even knock on the first team dressing room before entering. That was me obeying the 'rules' as relayed to me by Allan Hunter. On more than one occasion he shouted 'I'm not decent, you'll have to wait outside' and of course I did. In those days the youngsters did all sorts of menial tasks, like cleaning the senior players' boots, sweeping out the dressing rooms, scrubbing the floors, cleaning the baths, showers and toilets, and making sure the entire complex, which incorporated the laundry room, treatment room, weight room and boot room, was spick and span. There would be an inspection by Charlie Woods before he would give the OK to leave. On a Friday you could be there until 5pm preparing the place for the next day's game, either first team or reserves. Thankfully, I had only one season of it because once you turned pro you said goodbye to all that.

I started the 1975-76 season in the first team, deputising for Allan Hunter, but it was a game to forget for anyone connected with Ipswich. We lost 3-0 at home to Newcastle United and it was the first time in 16 years that we had been beaten on the opening day of the season. It wasn't all down to me, of course, but it certainly wasn't one of my better games. Big Al was able to take over the number five shirt for the 0-0 draw at Tottenham four days later, when I was an unused substitute, and thereafter I faded from the first team picture. I am the first to admit that I still had a lot to learn and I had no complaints with anyone as I returned to playing for the reserves on a regular basis. I was fortunate in having a football brain that enabled me to anticipate what was going to happen and because of the maturity I showed on the pitch Bobby Robson used to say I was five years ahead of my time. Even so, I was quite happy to have a break from first team duties and was always confident that another opportunity would come along.

It was not until late January 1976 that I was again required to plug a gap in the first team. Once again I covered for Allan Hunter as we lost 1-0 in an FA Cup fourth round replay at Wolves. Soon after that I played in a 1-0 league win at Burnley when I partnered Big Al and Beat, who scored the only goal from his first penalty for the club, was at left-back because Mick Mills switched to midfield to replace the injured Brian Talbot. A fortnight later, when I played in our 3-1 defeat at QPR, I had John Peddelty alongside me because on this occasion Big Al was again an absentee. We looked to be heading for at least a point when I conceded a 68th minute own goal – pretty spectacularly it has to be said since my fierce volley gave goalkeeper Paul Cooper no chance – as I tried to clear a cross from the England captain, Gerry Francis. Mick Lambert equalised with nine minutes left but goals by David Webb and Dave Thomas in the last four minutes put the game well beyond us.

Come the end of the 1975-76 campaign I had added a further four first team appearances – three in the league and one in the FA Cup – and that brought my total to nine. Having been at Ipswich for three years since leaving school, I considered my progress to be satisfactory, rather than spectacular. I had no complaints and certainly no axe to grind with anyone, for the simple reason that I knew I wasn't good enough to be a first team regular. To be honest I was quite surprised by how well I had done when given the opportunity and it was almost a relief when I took a step back. I knew I had a lot of developing to do, both physically and with regard to learning the game, and while a taste of first team football had given me an appetite for more, I knew I had time on my side. I collected the club's Young Player of the Year award at the end of a season in which I spent most of my time playing for the youth team and the reserves. It was the decision of youth coach Charlie Woods and the manager, Bobby Robson, that I should win the individual accolade. Mr Robson wrote in the match-day programme: "I think John would have been chosen by any of the players for this award. His play, whether in defence or midfield, has been of a consistently high standard and we expect him to make the grade and become a first team player for years to come." Happily, he was absolutely spot-on!

I was appointed captain of the Scotland youth team, which I regarded as a tremendous honour. I had attended the trials the previous year, before I was called up for my senior debut against Leeds, but they told me I was too young and sent me back. In February 1976, along with my Ipswich team-mates Robert Hamilton and Alec Jamieson, I was in the Scotland team to meet Partick Thistle's youth side at Firhill. I was captain that night and I returned north of the border for a game against Ayr United before my place was confirmed in the squad to play in France, in the popular Cannes tournament that also involved Brazil, Italy and Finland. We actually won the competition and it was a bonus that we were invited to parade the trophy before the following month's Scotland v England senior international at Hampden in front of an 85,000 capacity crowd. As we crawled round the track in an open-top vehicle, I will admit that I gazed round and wondered if I would ever be back for the same game in a few years' time, but this time to play in it.

It was in the 1976-77 season that my career took off in a big way and not just because I started our first six games of the season, four in the League and two in the League Cup as we were eliminated by Brighton. Allan Hunter was walking his dog the night before our opening game against Tottenham at Portman Road and somehow managed to injure himself. I deputised against Spurs and at the age of just 22 Kevin Beattie was actually the oldest member of our back four, which also included George Burley and John Peddelty. It looked like ending all square until goals by Keith Bertschin and Mick Lambert earned us a 3-1 win. Allan had still not recovered by the time we went to Everton just three days later for a 1-1 draw and although he was back for the home clash with QPR I stayed in the side to partner him at the heart of the defence in our 2-2 draw.

The following week I scored my first senior goal for Ipswich, a shot from outside the box, but the fact that we were beaten 5-2 at Aston Villa took a lot of the shine off the occasion. I shouldered a lot of the blame – and rightly so – as Andy Gray, long before he landed that cushy number with Sky Sports, netted a hat-trick and I was supposed to be marking him. Andy was an outstanding striker and as brave as a lion, as I witnessed at very close quarters. One of his goals was a diving header at the near post and, I kid you not, the ball could not have been much more than a foot off the ground. I intended to make a straightforward clearance on the volley and I could not believe how he got there ahead of me and in such an unconventional way. At the time there was only one player in the English game fearless enough to have scored such a goal and that was Andy, who was a dab hand at making late runs that unsettled opponents. He gave me as torrid a time that day as any striker throughout my entire career. Ian Wright was a real handful, too, but in fairness that was during the latter stages of my career when my legs were constantly reminding me that they wouldn't last for ever.

I was dropped after the game at Villa Park and left out of the side for the next four league games and the manager also made a number of other changes so that a new-look side began to emerge. Eric Gates came into midfield but had the misfortune to be injured three games later and that paved the way for me to make my very first appearance in midfield, a position I had occupied for only a short time in the reserves. The game was at West Ham and the manager told me beforehand that I was to mark Trevor Brooking, who was an England regular at the time. We won 2-0 thanks to two goals from Clive Woods and I remember coming close to scoring with a shot that flew narrowly over. I felt I equipped myself well and the manager seemed to agree as he gave me a pat on the back afterwards. The fact that I retained my place in midfield for a further 23 games speaks for itself.

The arrival of Paul Mariner from Plymouth in October 1976 was extremely significant for the club. David Johnson had departed for Liverpool in the summer and my former youth team colleague, Keith Bertschin, took over the number nine shirt. Mariner, or PM as he was known, was an instant success, his debut in a win at Manchester United being followed one week later by his first outing at Portman Road in a game that people still talk about to this day. It was one that I, too, will never forget. We really turned it on to trounce West Bromwich Albion 7-0, with Trevor Whymark scoring four times and the others coming from Paul, Beat and myself. I was delighted to get my first goal from midfield, even if I had not struck the ball as hard as I had intended and goalkeeper John Osborne, I felt, was a little bit slow to react. If anyone had suggested then that I would go on to become the third highest goalscorer in the history of the club I simply wouldn't have believed it.

We went on a 15-game undefeated league run, winning 12 and drawing three to bank 27 points from a possible 30, and going into 1977 we were second behind league leaders Liverpool with just two points fewer than them but three games in hand. On a personal note, I took over penalty duties from Beat after he missed against Aston Villa. The way I remember it, Bobby Robson asked for a volunteer and my hand shot up. I had never missed one for the youths or the reserves so I was confident. There wasn't exactly a long queue so the manager said the job was mine. The very next day I scored from the spot against Norwich to give us a 12th minute lead and we went on to crush the Canaries 5-0, much to the delight of most spectators in a near-35,000 crowd. I put my kick to goalkeeper Kevin Keelan's left because I noticed that he was playing with a heavily strapped left thigh and I felt he may struggle on that side. Another factor was that I had seen him on television and I made a mental note that he tended to dive to his right more often than not when facing a penalty, which is exactly what he did. My penalty goal was overshadowed, and rightly so, by Trevor Whymark's hat-trick. It was the first of four penalties I took that season and I finished with a 100 per cent record. One of them came in our away game against Liverpool and silencing the Kop was a great feeling, although we were already trailing 2-0 by the time I beat Ray Clemence with just four minutes left to play. I scored in the 4-2 win at Birmingham that took us into pole position in the First Division with just 17 games played and 11 games later, after my 89th minute goal at Newcastle earned us a 1-1 draw, we were still in a strong position. We may have been second behind Liverpool, but while they had one point more we had two games in hand.

In the end it was our indifferent form when it mattered most, with the finishing post in sight, which cost us the big prize. We managed just one win from our last six games, eventually finishing third behind champions Liverpool and runners-up Manchester City, both of whom we managed to defeat at Portman Road. As always seemed to be the case during my first spell at Portman Road, injuries took their toll and in my own case I required a manipulative operation to clear up a foot problem that not only kept me out of Ipswich games but also the Scotland Under-21 side, which I was later to captain. Talking of captains, I was bowled over when I picked up a newspaper one day to find my club skipper Mick Mills saying nice things about me. He said: "The day manager Bobby Robson switched 19-year-old John Wark from defence to midfield was the day Ipswich launched their assault on the top of the First Division. John moved forward to become our anchor man in midfield and we have not looked back. He is an unspectacular player but the skill is there. John has the maturity of a seasoned professional and I find it difficult to pinpoint any flaws in his game. I'm delighted to give the lad the credit he deserves."

But I quickly learned about the down side of football when I was dismissed for the first time in my career at Derby along with their forward, Charlie George.

It was the penultimate game of the league campaign and the home side needed a point to be sure of avoiding relegation, which they managed courtesy of a 0-0 draw in the Baseball Ground mud. George was a big-name player – he won the League Championship and FA Cup double with Arsenal in 1971 when his spectacular extra-time goal beat Liverpool at Wembley – and I was still relatively unknown. I remember that I was having a decent game in midfield. I was especially pleased that I was getting a few tackles in and generally giving as good as I got. It was after one of my challenges, to which he took great exception, that he sprang to his feet, put his face close to mine and head-butted me. Instinctively, I flicked out with my right leg and caught him on the shin but it wasn't a full-blooded kick.

In all seriousness, had I known the referee was going to send us both off I would have kicked him a lot harder. We were walking off and George was muttering something in my direction when Allan Hunter shouted to him, 'Leave him alone or I'll sort you out in the players' lounge'. It was more than two years since my first team debut but Big Al was still looking out for me. Afterwards, I made sure I accompanied him to the players' lounge, just in case George was lurking round a corner.

George went right down in my estimation for his reaction to my firm, but undoubtedly fair, challenge. He was by no means one of the game's tough guys, although there were a few around at the time. Joe Jordan, as I found to my cost within a few minutes of my debut, could dish it out. Much later in my career I found myself up against a burly striker called Billy Whitehurst, who had come up the hard way. He worked as a bricklayer and played non-league football before signing for Hull City and five years later, in 1985, he earned a move to Newcastle. He was back at Hull when I encountered him in the 1988-89 season and I had returned from Liverpool for a second spell at Ipswich. Whitehurst's game was to try to unsettle his opponents with a spot of old-fashioned bullying, although there was no doubting his bravery as he hurled himself into situations most players would have avoided. His reputation had gone before him but when I heard him shout something about sorting out Linighan I realised he had targeted my defensive partner, David Linighan, one of the game's genuine hard men in whom he more than met his match.

John Fashanu and Vinnie Jones were a right pair. The Wimbledon duo liked to throw their weight about and often operated as a double act. They had a well rehearsed routine that I saw at close quarters one day. Basically, they were awarded a corner and as the ball was crossed into the area Fashanu made out he had been fouled and fell to the ground. This attracted the referee's attention and as he was occupied elsewhere Jones elbowed my team-mate, Jason Dozzell, in the face and broke his nose. They both had their fair share of controversy as players and my take on their antics was that they were covering up their deficiencies as players, although no one can take away the fact that four months after I left Anfield to return to Portman Road they defeated Liverpool at Wembley to record one of the biggest FA Cup Final upsets of all time.

The Manchester United and Northern Ireland forward, Norman Whiteside, could look after himself. In my time at Liverpool we had a player, Steve McMahon, who thought he was hard, but I could tell he was scared of Whiteside, who at 16 had an awesome physique. Another Liverpool player, Graeme Souness, was nobody's favourite opponent, but I fared well against him and never had any trouble. Maybe it was because we are both Scottish, but there seemed to be a mutual respect between us. Still at Liverpool, perhaps the hardest of the hard men was Tommy Smith. In one of Paul Mariner's first trips to Anfield with Ipswich he caught Tommy when he was a fraction late with his challenge. 'You shouldn't have done that,' I warned him, but PM was unconcerned and shrugged off the incident. But I was not surprised a few minutes later when our goalkeeper, Paul Cooper, sent a long clearance down the middle and Smith picked his moment for retribution. PM jumped to meet the ball with his head and Smith came in from behind in what appeared to be a genuine challenge. As PM headed the ball Smith headed PM's head and he slumped to the ground. He was stretchered off suffering from concussion.

But to give PM his due that incident didn't see him withdraw into his shell. Indeed, far from it. As a centre-forward who refused to shirk any challenge, he had to be able to look after himself and as he dished it out so he took it and then went back for more. Both he and Terry Butcher had a pre-match routine that I often saw strike fear into opponents. In 1981, when we won the UEFA Cup, they were extremely vocal and glowered at players from the other side in the tunnel. They were at it in France, when we handed out a football lesson by defeating St Etienne 4-1, and they staged a repeat performance in the next round, the semi-final, against Cologne. My goal was all that separated the sides at Portman Road and in the build-up to the return game we kept hearing how Cologne felt they had done the hard bit in restricting us to a slender, one-goal advantage and were ready to turn us over. Come the night of the game, when the two teams were lined up in the tunnel, which was more made of wire mesh and resembled a cage at the zoo, Butch and PM were in full voice. Not just that, they were like a couple of mad men. PM spotted one of their defenders and pointed at him as he roared 'You're going to get it'. As I looked across at the Germans, a number of whom were visibly unsettled, I grew in confidence and I'm sure that went for the rest of the Ipswich side. Just over 90 minutes later we were celebrating the fact that we were in the final and, appropriately enough, it was big Butch who headed the only goal. Daft as it may seem now, Butch was close to packing football in when coach Bobby Ferguson 'bullied' him to show more aggression. Unquestionably one of Bobby's biggest successes, that.

TO CAP IT ALL

IN THE SUMMER OF 1977, as pre-season training with Ipswich gathered pace and the new campaign was just around the corner, I went from feeling on top of the world to desperately low as I was seriously injured for the very first time in my career. The reason for my euphoria was that Scotland manager Ally MacLeod named me in his senior squad for the very first time. With the World Cup finals in Argentina less than a year away it was a significant step in my career and I would be lying if I said the thought of representing my country at the very highest level did not, fleetingly, cross my mind. I was with the Ipswich squad in Holland for a series of pre-season games when Bobby Robson delivered the good news – on my 20th birthday – that I had been selected for the friendly against East Germany to be played in Berlin in September. But within a few days, in the final game of our Dutch tour against FC Twente, I knew my international debut was going to have to wait. It was a real pity because although Scotland lost 1-0 in that game it would have given me an opportunity to play alongside one of my boyhood heroes, Willie Johnston. Instead, it was almost two years later that I finally made my senior debut and by that time Willie's international career had come to an end following his controversial exit from the tournament in South America.

I suffered the injury in fairly innocuous circumstances. I went up to head the ball and my momentum carried me over the opposition player who challenged me. I landed on my left leg and that very instant I felt my hamstring go. It was a 'ping' feeling and it felt as if I had been hit by a sniper's bullet. I was helped off and had no idea how serious it would turn out to be, but I wasn't the least bit surprised to learn that it was a bad tear. It wasn't long before the bruising started to appear and that was pretty frightening on its own. To go with the pain, the top of my leg all the way down to the knee was black and purple in colour. To this day I have never witnessed anything remotely like it. Had I seen someone else in that state I would have assumed they had been given a good kicking. We had travelled to Holland by boat and during the return journey there was no way I could get any sleep in a cramped bunk. For a couple of weeks it was the same at home as I found it virtually impossible to get comfortable in bed. We were also without skipper Mick Mills for the start of the season after he had been forced to undergo a cartilage operation, but the lads started with two wins and two draws without conceding a goal in our first four league games and things looked promising.

Every club wants to get injured players back as quickly as possible and Ipswich were no exception. Physiotherapist Brian Simpson encouraged me to start jogging before I felt comfortable and after a while I sensed it was going to be a long job. I had been named captain of the Scotland team for the European Under-21 Youth Championship but I was absent from the first qualifier against Switzerland and the fact that it was to be played at Ibrox made it doubly disappointing. One week earlier I was able to participate in a practice game for the reserves against the youths and I appeared to come through with no ill-effects. That made me think in terms of maybe making a proper comeback for the reserves a fortnight or so later and then being ready for the first team a week or so after that. I had no idea it would take me until January 1978 to make my first team return and even then it was said to be earlier than expected. It was for the FA Cup third round tie at Cardiff that launched us on a run all the way to the final at Wembley four months later, but even though I survived the entire 90 minutes at Ninian Park I knew I was only about 60 per cent fit. I could have done with another week or two but we had a lot of injuries at the time, which forced me to come back before I considered myself fully fit. To be honest the hamstring affected me a fair bit over the next few months and even in the FA Cup Final I could feel it wasn't perfect, although it didn't prevent me from doing what I was asked to do on the day. It's debatable whether the hamstring was ever 100 per cent again because I adopted a sort of lop-sided running style during the remainder of my playing career to compensate and try to avoid a repeat. Even years later I was regarded as a bit of a freak because of the protruding muscle and I remember how David Bingham, the Ipswich physiotherapist in the late 80s and 90s, would bring people into the treatment room just to show them my leg. David never could understand how I was able to extend my career as long as I did, so just think how many games I might have managed to clock up if my hamstring injury had never occurred.

But back to the 1977-78 season and while I kept plugging away to make sure my hamstring was right, the first team were having a mixed time of it. They were in a mid-table league position, whereas in previous seasons we had been genuine title challengers. There was nothing to suggest that a relegation struggle was on the cards, although that scenario became more and more likely as the season progressed. Ipswich also exited the UEFA Cup in cruel fashion. Leading 3-0 from the first leg clash with Barcelona, they were 2-0 down in the Nou Camp return but within two minutes of qualifying for the last eight. As they tried to hang on the Spaniards were awarded a penalty, which they converted, and after no further scoring in extra time it was Barcelona who went through via the penalty shoot-out. I would have loved to have played against Barcelona, who were captained by Johan Cruyff and also included his Dutch colleague Johan Neeskens in their ranks, but as luck would have it we drew them in the European Cup Winners' Cup the following season, although the outcome was the same and we went out. My return for the FA Cup-tie at Cardiff was well timed because the following week, when we played Manchester United at home in what was my first league game of the season, my father and sister were there to see me. They had planned their trip some weeks earlier so I was pleased to be back playing, even though we lost 2-1 to the Reds.

I scored my first goal of the season as we went down 5-3 to Chelsea at Stamford Bridge and I was on the bench for the following week's FA Cup fourth round tie at home to Hartlepool. The manager experimented with a formation that included two wingers, Mick Lambert and Clive Woods, and I only appeared for the last three minutes as I replaced George Burley. I was back in the starting line-up seven days later at Leeds, where a 1-0 defeat was our fifth on the trot in the league, but from a fitness point of view I was able to play in every game right through to the end of the season in what could not have been a more exciting climax. The records show that we could only win three of our last 15 league games but fortunately it was enough to ensure we survived and I think our supporters forgave us because of our FA Cup success, even if the win over Arsenal at Wembley provided my colleagues with an opportunity to take the mickey, something they still do to this day as they remind me it took me about 18 minutes to actually touch the ball.

Wembley was the only good thing about the 1977-78 season. Had it not been for the FA Cup win it would have been a total non-event – and any of the players will tell you the same. A lot of the lads were in and out with injury and we never at any stage looked like mounting a challenge for the league title, as we had done in each of the previous three seasons. Indeed, it was the exact opposite, the nagging fear of whether we would be dragged into a relegation scrap never far from our minds. I was lucky that I got myself fit just in time to get involved in the Cup run. Poor old Trevor Whymark was stretchered off during our Boxing Day defeat at Norwich with a suspected broken leg, although it turned out to be damaged knee ligaments, and while he was listed in the Wembley programme his place went to David Geddis. It was cruel luck for him but football is like that and I thank my lucky stars that I was able to achieve what I did. Margaret Thatcher was Leader of the Opposition back then and attended the game, as did James Callaghan, the Prime Minister. When asked who she would nominate as Man of the Match she said her vote would go to 'Number 10, Trevor Whymark'.

I suppose it was a typical FA Cup campaign in that we defeated Cardiff and Hartlepool to earn a fifth round trip to Bristol Rovers, where we suffered an almighty scare and were fortunate to scrape a 2-2 draw. The match should never have gone ahead. As we reached the city and checked into our hotel it was snowing and we virtually convinced ourselves the next day's game would be postponed. To our shock, Bobby Robson returned to the hotel following an early pitch inspection to tell us the game was going ahead. He was none too pleased having seen the state of the pitch and described it as a skating rink, which was exactly right. We scored first through Robin Turner but were trailing 2-1 and seemingly on our way out when Roger Osborne bundled the ball into their net four minutes from time. The goal was actually credited to Robin as Roger was too modest to admit he got the last touch and I don't see the record books being rewritten more than 30 years on. Luck was on our side that day because Rovers scored a perfectly good goal and would have been 3-1 in front had it not been ruled out for offside. We won the replay 3-0 and that booked us a quarter-final trip to Millwall, where the hooligan element among the home crowd invaded the pitch. As we defended a corner, a bottle flew past me and smashed on the turf. Both sets of players were removed to the dressing rooms for an unscheduled break lasting almost 20 minutes. Some of our fans were injured, but at least they saw us canter to a 6-1 victory in which Paul Mariner took the scoring honours with a hat-trick and I weighed in with a volley for the first of my 12 FA Cup goals for Ipswich.

We faced West Bromwich Albion in the semi-final at Highbury and outside Ipswich there were very few people who gave us a prayer against Ron Atkinson's team. The Baggies may have been better placed in the First Division but we were nevertheless confident that we could beat them and it turned out to be one of the most remarkable days of my career. We scored two early goals through Brian Talbot and Mick Mills and even after Brian had to withdraw, following a clash of heads with Albion skipper John Wile as he dived to head us in front, we remained firmly in control. Until, that is, about 15 minutes from the end when Allan Hunter handled the ball to concede a penalty. When Big Al stuck his hand up and touched the ball as it came over I don't think any of us could believe what we were seeing. Some of the players had a go – Mick Mils gave him a real ear-bashing – but me and a few others never said a word. In all honesty we were scared of the big man so we stayed silent. Tony Brown scored from the spot and all of a sudden it's about more than just seeing out the game. Albion hardly celebrated the goal because the only thing in their minds was to get on with the game and try to score another. We were in a bit of a fix at that point because we didn't want to go chasing a third goal in case we left space at the back for them to exploit. But nor did we want to sit back and try to hang on to what we had. That wasn't our way and we knew it might be asking for trouble to retreat into a defensive shell.

In the end everything was fine but it seemed an age until I headed our third goal, which was officially timed at 89 minutes. It came from a Clive Woods corner and of all the goals I scored for Ipswich that was probably the one that gave me most pleasure. I can think of many better ones, but none that I greeted with more exhilaration. It was the extreme importance of it and you could tell what it meant to the rest of the lads, too, as they piled on top of me. It was just like a rugby scrum with me right at the bottom. The sheer relief is something I can't describe. It was a killer for Albion because they knew the clock was against them, but for us it was a case of 'Wembley here we come'. We had a couple of minutes to play and then it was absolute bedlam as we started the celebrations. I was pleased for our supporters, all 26,000 of them, because we had given them something they had never had before, a place in the FA Cup Final. I cast my mind back three years to the tears that flowed after the semi-final replay defeat to West Ham at Stamford Bridge and I was chuffed to bits for everyone who had suffered then and wondered if another chance would come along. Back in the dressing room we got stuck into the champagne and we were drinking it in the bath. The manager threw open the doors to the press and the photographers had a field day. Just a very special moment, the realisation that you are going to Wembley to play in what back then, if not now, was the one all pros wanted to appear in.

In those days the build-up to Wembley started straight away. We did what every final team did and formed a players' pool. Why shouldn't we cash in on what could be a one-off occasion? We did commercial deals, like making a record, and it was great fun. We were complete rookies in terms of playing in an FA Cup Final, not that clued up, but we had been around long enough to know that the biggest earner of all would be selling tickets to the touts. Other teams had done it so why shouldn't we? Nowadays it is illegal, but in those days it was regarded as a perk to dispose of tickets in this way. Stan Flashman wasn't called King of the Touts for nothing. He had been doing it the longest and would boast that he could lay his hands on tickets for any occasion – at a price. Major sporting events, a Frank Sinatra concert at the Albert Hall, even a Royal Garden Party at Buckingham Palace. Fat Stan, as he was known, was never beaten. Some of the Ipswich players dealt with him but there were other touts, too, and my tickets went to a guy I knew only as Ginger. He was known to some of the senior players and I simply agreed to throw my tickets into the pot along with theirs, trusting them to look after my interests. We were allocated 100 tickets each and since I needed about 30 for family and friends that meant 70 or so going to the tout. Multiply that by the number of players dealing with the same guy and we're talking a lot of tickets – and a huge amount of cash.

We agreed a price – I think it was four, or maybe five times the face value – and the tout would clearly add on his mark-up before disposing of them. Clive Woods was nominated to deliver the tickets to the tout and a rendezvous was arranged for the exchange to take place. I never knew this at the time, but I have since learned that Woodsy was so apprehensive about the meeting that he took a gun with him in the car. Apparently, he knew someone in Norwich and borrowed the gun for the day. Yes, it was loaded and no, thankfully, he had no need for it. The transaction complete, we arranged to get together at a local hotel and distribute the cash. I had never seen so much money in my life. Paul Cooper was a part of the syndicate and made no bones about it – his share was going to be spent on a two-room extension to his house in Capel St Mary. It was just a few weeks before I was to be married so I had a hundred and one things on which to spend my own windfall. Others lavished theirs on more expensive holidays than they might normally have booked and I seem to recall a few new cars putting in an appearance when we reported for pre-season training a couple of months later.

But we were concerned about more than lining our pockets. We had other important business to take care of, namely winning enough league games to make sure we didn't get relegated. Of course, we wanted to go to Wembley and win, but it would have counted for very little if we were going to be playing in the Second Division the following season. There was genuine danger of that happening if we had taken our eye off the ball. As it was, we only managed one win and two draws from our final eight league games, but crucially it was enough. We suffered a 6-1 defeat at Aston Villa in our penultimate league game, just seven days before Wembley, and that was one to remember for all the wrong reasons. It was the manager's team selection that provoked an angry reaction from the players or, to be more precise, the senior players. At 20 I had very little to say for myself and I've a feeling that if I had piped up it wouldn't have made things any different.

Bobby Robson decided to give Colin Viljoen a chance to prove his fitness at Villa Park with a view to being included in the starting line-up at Wembley. That was his prerogative as manager but it went against the grain with most of the players for the simple reason that Colin had hardly played that season because of injury. As soon as the manager named the starting line-up there was a huddle of senior players muttering away and questioning his thinking. Roger Osborne was white with shock at being left out and just sat there, staring into space. At that precise moment, he was to admit later, he thought it was all over in terms of playing at Wembley. The players were clearly very unhappy and some of them just went through the motions – there is no other way that I can describe it. Half of them didn't try so it wasn't surprising that we got thumped by Villa. The daft thing is that we got off lightly. Villa might have scored 10 or more, that's how bad we were on the day, if it hadn't been for Paul Overton, who was making his debut in goal. He was only 17 and he was brilliant, but that was his first and last game for the club, and I felt desperately sorry for him. I can honestly say I was doing my best and putting in the effort but I looked around me and it was obvious that some of the players couldn't have cared less how many goals we let in. The papers had a field day, which was hardly surprising when you stop to think how many FA Cup Final teams receive a 6-1 walloping in their last game before Wembley. They called it player power and that's exactly what it was. You couldn't call it anything else, since the senior lads challenged the manager's decision and he changed his mind.

You could say it worked. After all, we did win the FA Cup, but I am glad to say that was the one and only time I ever saw that happen. I just sat in the Villa Park dressing room and the row was going on around me. I must admit that I felt sorry for Colin Viljoen. It couldn't have been much fun for him, since he clearly wasn't wanted in the side by the majority of the players. He was treated like an outcast and never played for the club again. He took it badly and I felt for him but had the manager stuck to his guns and picked him at Wembley I'm not sure how we would have fared. The upheaval might have cost us, because to accommodate Colin it would have meant that both me and Brian Talbot would have been required to change our roles in the middle of the park. Bringing him in against Villa wasn't just a simple one-in-one-out switch. With the positional changes, too, it was all a bit much with the FA Cup Final just a week away. It meant things were up in the air and the senior players who complained couldn't really see the point. I played out on the right of midfield at Villa Park and that wasn't really my scene. I knew we would be better with Roger out there and me in the middle, and I think my record proves it. Over the years, my one recurring thought has been 'What if it had been a must-win game at Villa?'

By the time we departed for our pre-Wembley base, Sopwell House Hotel at St Albans, on the Wednesday of FA Cup Final week it was clear that Colin Viljoen would not be playing as he was conspicuous by his absence from the team coach. But with both our central defenders, Allan Hunter and Kevin Beattie, nowhere near 100 per cent fit, our starting line-up was still a long way from being confirmed. We stopped off in Colchester to pick up our Wembley outfits of light blue jackets and charcoal trousers, and the mood on board was such that we could have been a bunch of mates heading off for a stag weekend rather than a team just three days from the biggest game of our lives. I can't imagine there has ever been a more confident side in the history of the famous tournament. We were in a relaxed frame of mind all the way through. Big Al and Beat were declared fit on the morning of the game and most of us had a bet on the outcome. We saw the odds of 5-2 against us winning and thought 'We'll have some of that'. Mick Lambert, who probably knew more about gambling than the rest of us put together, gathered up the cash and placed the bet. The bookies were writing us off, perhaps, but we just knew we were going to win it. Easy money, we thought.

We were in for a shock when we got to Wembley because the referee was making it known the game was in doubt. The heavens had opened that morning and there had been a lot of rain in the previous few days, so much so that a planned training session at the stadium a couple of days earlier had been of no great value to us. Although the rain had stopped, the ground staff were working hard to pump water off the pitch and it was to everyone's relief that the referee quickly confirmed that all was well. But while the rain had ceased, the surface was very spongy, and with the hot sun beating down on us it wasn't long before the tiredness kicked in. I never suffered on any other occasion as much as I did that day. I'm not sure about the playing surface at the new Wembley but the one in 1978 felt bigger than any other. It was doubly tiring because of the conditions underfoot, combined with the effects of the sun, and there wasn't one player who didn't feel it.

I mentioned earlier how the players love to poke fun at me for the fact that I took 18 minutes to come into contact with the ball. Every time we get together – we have had 10, 20 and 30-year reunions – they remind me. I can't deny it is true. My first kick came when I ran about 60 yards to stop the ball going out for a corner and the fact that the game was 18 minutes old at the time hardly seems possible. But this is my explanation. Just as Roger Osborne was told to mark Liam Brady, I was told to stick close to Arsenal's other midfield playmaker, Alan Hudson. They were both talented players who would soon start to influence the game if we allowed them time on the ball. I took the instructions literally and stuck to Hudson like glue. When he went deep and picked the ball up from Willie Young or David O'Leary, the Gunners' central defenders, I was there. He played little passes here and there but not once did he get the other side of me. In other words, he wasn't hurting us and shadowing him the way I did made perfect sense. I was making a nuisance of myself but I wasn't actually getting a kick. When the lads start taking the mickey I have the perfect answer to shut them up. As far as I am concerned there are only a few things that people remember about the FA Cup Final – first and foremost Roger's goal, PM hitting the bar early on, an unbelievable save by Pat Jennings from George Burley's header and, wait for it, my two shots that both cannoned off the same post. It tends to shut them up when I remind them about that.

If you are dominating a game and it is still 0-0 with little more than 10 minutes left for play you tend to get a bit concerned that you have not been able to make your superiority count. At the back of your mind you are thinking 'What if they score?' That was Ipswich in the 1978 FA Cup Final. We were all over Arsenal and just couldn't put the ball in the net. Our tactics worked a treat, with David Geddis coming into the side in an unaccustomed role on the right after Bobby Ferguson spied on Arsenal and spotted that left-back Sammy Nelson was the launching pad for most of their attacks after he took possession of the ball from Pat Jennings. David was brilliant on the day and it was no surprise that when we did eventually score he played a major part in it. His low cross was only half cleared by Willie Young and who should be there to drive low past Jennings with his left foot but

Roger – the same Roger who thought his world had collapsed seven days earlier at Villa Park. If ever there was a fitting match winner it was him. Overcome with emotion and exhaustion, he had to go off and Mick Lambert came off the bench to play on the right of midfield for the first time in his career.

There wasn't really one anxious moment when we feared Arsenal might get back into the game. We killed time as much as we could, just as any team would have done in that situation, and when I see replays of the game I have to laugh as Paul Cooper throws the ball out and Kevin Beattie just rolls it back to him on a number of occasions. I often wonder if the rule change that prevents the keeper picking up the ball from a back-pass was influenced by our tactics towards the end of that game. As always, the final whistle seemed to take for ever, but once it sounded we went straight into party mode. We climbed the steps to receive the trophy and our medals from HRH Princess Alexandra and then posed for a few pictures before commencing our lap of honour. It was as we were running down the track on the other side of the pitch that I spotted my sister, Wilma, and some other family members. There were about 24 of them and they had hired a coach to travel south, leaving Glasgow on the Thursday. Wembley had perimeter fences so when I spotted them I made a beeline for them and chatted through the wire mesh. As I got close I couldn't believe my eyes. No joking, their faces were just about tripping them. I was over the moon but they all looked bloody miserable. 'What's up?' I asked and they explained that they had all placed bets at odds of 20-1 that Ipswich would win and I would score the first goal. That seemed a bit generous to me after I had scored in both our quarter-final and semi-final victories.

There I was, with my FA Cup winner's medal in my hand, and all that lot could say was 'Why didn't you score?' I couldn't believe the reception they gave me but the story had a happy ending, even if it was more than a year later. I was just three games into my international career and playing for Scotland against England at Wembley. Among a batch of telegrams I received at the stadium was one from the family. The message was short and simple. It read 'This time hit the net' and I'm glad to say I did, so not only did the gamblers among them recover their losses but they also made a handsome profit thanks to my tap-in to open the scoring. Even if England did come back and score three times, at least some of the Wark clan were able to drown their sorrows free of charge. Back in 1978, some of my family made a detour via Ipswich on their way back to Glasgow and we all got together and had a session. That whole weekend – the game, the club banquet at the Royal Garden Hotel in Kensington, the journey back to Ipswich on the Sunday, the open-top bus ride through the town centre, the civic reception and the family reunion – is something I will never forget.

Towards the end of the 1977-78 season Scotland manager Ally MacLeod included me in a 40-strong squad from which he was going to name his final 22 for the World Cup finals in Argentina. There were eight midfield players in total and I was one of the outsiders because I was still waiting for my first cap. But Toula and I thought it wise to delay our wedding until after the event, just in case I made it into the travelling party. It was not exactly a major surprise when I didn't make the cut – I was still only 20 and uncapped – but while I was still disappointed I at least had the consolation of missing all the flak that came the players' way. Ally whipped the nation into a frenzy to the point where some people really believed that he and the players would bring the World Cup home, but instead they lost to Peru and were held to a draw by Iran before almost, unbelievably, snatching a place in the next stage by beating eventual runners-up Holland 3-1. Archie Gemmill scored a fabulous goal against the Dutch but I suspect that few of the Scots players will look back on their involvement in the 1978 finals with any pride.

BOBBY'S MEN

WE SPENT A GREAT deal of time in the company of the FA Cup in 1978, dragging it all over Suffolk to one event after another. To see people's faces light up when it was brought out of its old wooden cabinet was special. As a community club, rather than one of the big-city outfits, our supporters were able to share in our success. The trophy was on show throughout the year at a series of events. It was an historic achievement and 31 years on it has never been repeated. Indeed, who is to say it will ever happen again? To be one of the players responsible fills me with pride and the fact that I, together with Allan Hunter, Mick Mills, Roger Osborne and Mick Lambert, am still resident in Suffolk means we are constantly reminded of its continued importance. People say 'I was there' and there can't be many who do not have a picture of themselves with the famous trophy. Photo opportunities were plentiful and for most people the Wembley experience provided them with one of the greatest days of their lives. It meant no more to anyone than directors John and Patrick Cobbold, whose father had been instrumental in bringing professional football to the town. Apparently, he had quite a job to convince people in 1936 that they should ditch the amateur club and I guarantee no one then would have envisaged Ipswich Town winning the League Championship, as they did under Alf Ramsey in 1962, and then, 16 years later, the FA Cup. What we didn't realise at the time was that we had further glory to come, this time in the UEFA Cup, and Bobby Robson took a significant step towards securing that success with what I still regard as one of the best transfer deals of all time, convincing a wonderfully talented Dutch midfielder to cross the North Sea and join us at Portman Road.

Arnold Johannus Hyacinthus Muhren – you can probably imagine the rest of the players' reaction after he revealed his full name in a match-day magazine article – was undoubtedly one of the best players ever to represent Ipswich. He found his way here after Bobby Robson was speaking to Hans Kraay, an ex-Feyenoord defender, during a pre-season tournament in Bruges. Kraay was with AZ Alkmaar, who were also taking part, and when he was chatting to Bobby the conversation turned to the inflated prices in the British transfer market. Kraay suggested there would be greater value in signing players from Holland and straight away he recommended Arnold to him. Bobby relayed the story a few weeks later because Ipswich were paired with AZ in the first round of the European Cup Winners' Cup. It turned out to be a tremendous coup to sign Arnold, with Bobby offering the view that the £150,000 fee represented an outstanding bargain. He even argued that he would have had to pay twice as much in England for a player of comparable quality. Arnold was certainly not completely sold on the idea of moving to England and took a lot of persuading. Bobby was good at that, though. There wasn't the same movement of players then as there is now, but around the same time Tottenham unveiled their Argentinian imports, Osvaldo Ardiles and Ricardo Villa, and naturally the media focused on them ahead of Arnold, who was nowhere near as high profile. The manager pulled out all the stops to persuade Arnold to join us and even hired a small plane that flew the Muhren family around the area. When it passed over the practice pitch at Portman Road we gave them a wave. The location actually appealed to Arnold and his wife, Geerie, because it was easy to load the car, drive the short journey to Harwich and be on the ferry to the Hook of Holland, from where they didn't have long to travel to their home town of Volendam, not too far from Amsterdam. Had he not changed his mind about joining Ipswich – he was initially dead set against the idea – I wonder how we might have fared. Not nearly as well is the inevitable answer.

Arnold had pedigree, having started out with Ajax and playing alongside the likes of Cruyff, Neeskens and Krol. He had also been capped twice by Holland and further international honours were to come his way as a result of his convincing displays for Ipswich. Mind you, he must have wondered if he had done the right thing when he made his debut in our first home game of the season. He did not sign in time for the opening game of the campaign, when we lost 2-1 at West Bromwich Albion, and three days later we suffered another defeat, this time more comprehensive, as Liverpool turned us over 3-0 in front of our own fans. Poor Arnold spent most of the 90 minutes looking to the sky, watching the ball being transferred from back to front, a style totally alien to him. He had very few touches but we told him things would improve because Liverpool were far and away the best side in the country that season and proved it by winning the League Championship for the third time in four years. In actual fact, however, it was clear that Ipswich would have to change their style of play to accommodate a player like Arnold. When I first started to establish myself in midfield we were quite direct, the ball being played from the back to our front two of David Johnson, later Paul Mariner, and Trevor Whymark. I would pick up a lot of knock-downs from these guys and I would find myself with a few shooting opportunities in each game. Going back to Wembley in 1978, that was what I would call a typical display by me. I was in a position to have a go with two near-identical shots that both came back off the same post – in fact virtually the exact same spot on the post.

Once Arnold arrived on the scene the team that won the FA Cup a few months earlier started to evolve into an entirely different side. Some players stayed the same but the system altered, not overnight of course but over a period of months. A major change in personnel saw Brian Talbot transferred to Arsenal, a move that had been on the cards since before we beat them in the FA Cup Final, and Ipswich again went Dutch to replace him. I don't think the manager could believe his ears when Arnold suggested Frans Thijssen should come on board. He and Frans were team-mates at FC Twente and Arnold was adamant that the English game would be right up Frans' street. 'Is he that good?' Bobby asked and when Arnold replied 'Yes, he is better than me' I think the manager was already half-way to the travel agents to book his ticket to Holland. It was a great bit of business because Ipswich received £450,000 for Brian, spent a total of £350,000 on Arnold and Frans, and stuck a hundred grand in the bank. Brian was a big success at Highbury so everyone was happy.

We were actually in the bottom half of the First Division when Frans came on the scene. He guested for us in the Trevor Whymark Testimonial game against Norwich, a deal was quickly agreed and he made his debut in a 1-0 win at Derby on February 28, 1979. We were 12th in the table after our triumph at the Baseball Ground and of our remaining 15 games we only lost one, and eventually finished sixth to once again book a place in Europe the following season. It wasn't all down to Frans but he more than played his part and, like his fellow countryman, the crowd took an instant shine to him and were particularly grateful when his first goal in English football secured a vital win over Norwich at Carrow Road. Only yours truly and skipper Mick Mills were ever-present that season but it was also a campaign in which a new central defensive partnership was born, Russell Osman and Terry Butcher appearing on many more occasions than Allan Hunter. Another change saw my fellow countryman Alan Brazil emerge as a serious challenger for a regular place in the team and the same could be said of Eric Gates, who was to perform a key role as we continued to improve as a unit. Gatesy's cause was championed by coach Bobby Ferguson and rightly so. Bobby knew what Eric could do from their time together with the reserves and he dovetailed perfectly into the withdrawn role that Bobby had in mind for him. He revelled in the space, firing a lot of spectacular goals and also winning a lot of penalties, for which I will always be grateful. Gatesy's frustration at not breaking into the first team a couple of years earlier than he did actually saw him return north and go potato-picking. The press loved the fact that he had essentially gone on strike but he was eventually sweet-talked into returning by Bobby Robson, who also loved him to bits. From thinking he had no future at Ipswich he played his way into the England team, although it was difficult for him to transfer his talent to the international stage because the manager at the time, Ron Greenwood, didn't send his team out to play the Ipswich way. Opposition teams couldn't cope with Gatesy. They often pushed one of their two central defenders out to try to pick him up, only to come unstuck because it left them short at the back and we inevitably cashed in, the 6-0 home win over Manchester United being a case in point when Martin Buchan found it impossible to pin Eric down and he created havoc.

On a personal note, I scored nine goals in 54 games during the 1978-79 season, a modest return compared to what I was to achieve over the next few seasons, but we were going through a transitional period after the arrival of the Dutchmen. It took us time to adjust to Arnold's presence but we picked up in the second half of the season, losing just twice in 23 league games after Christmas. We were back at Wembley for the season's annual curtain-raiser, the Charity Shield meeting between the league champions and the FA Cup winners, but perhaps the less said about that the better. I was required to fill in at the back in a side depleted because of injuries. It could hardly have been in starker contrast to the FA Cup Final three months earlier as Nottingham Forest thumped us 5-0. We reached the quarter-final of the European Cup Winners' Cup but after beating Barcelona 2-1 at home we were beaten 1-0 in front of a 100,000 crowd at the Nou Camp a fortnight later and went out on the away goals rule. The fact that the Spaniards went on to win the trophy was of no consolation whatsoever. We were the FA Cup holders, of course, and we reached the last eight, only surrendering our grip on the trophy to a Kenny Dalglish goal which earned Liverpool the narrowest of wins in a pulsating tie at Portman Road. We pushed them all the way in that game and only Kenny's class ultimately separated the sides. Another disappointment was missing my first penalty. After ten successful conversions I got it wrong in our final home game against Tottenham when Milija Aleksic saved my kick, but at least we managed to record a 2-1 win. Milija had been at Ipswich on loan from Plymouth and actually played in a friendly win at Celtic two seasons earlier before he moved on to Luton and he had plenty to say for himself afterwards. I tried not to dwell on the miss, reasoning that I was always going to miss at some point.

It was no surprise to anyone when Arnold Muhren was presented with the supporters' Player of the Year award for 1978-79, such had been his influence on the team in his first season, and with Frans Thijssen also making a tremendous contribution in his 16-game run, there was no doubting the two Dutchmen's growing influence on the team. Much better was still to come, of course, but at this early stage of their English careers I felt I was benefiting more than anyone else at Portman Road since I was growing into a role that saw them operate either side of me in midfield. One of Ipswich's biggest victories, if you like, around this time was to retain the services of manager Bobby Robson. He celebrated the tenth anniversary of his appointment and at one stage it seemed he could have his pick

(Left) That's me when I was only a few months old.

I was about 12 and attending Victoria Drive Secondary School when this picture was taken.

Hampden Park, May 1976. I captained the Scottish youth team to victory in an international tournament in Cannes that also involved Brazil, Italy and Finland and we paraded the trophy before the 2-1 win over England in front of 85,000 fans.

The two captains with the officials before the game between Scotland and Brazil in Cannes.

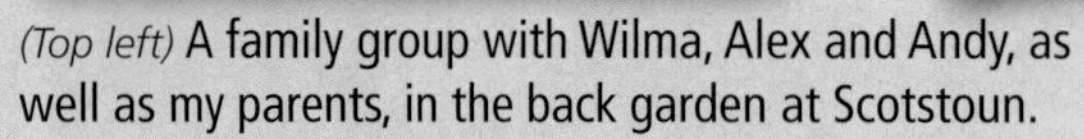

(Top left) A family group with Wilma, Alex and Andy, as well as my parents, in the back garden at Scotstoun.

(Top right) This picture of me with my parents was taken in Ipswich at the banquet held to celebrate our win over West Ham in the FA Youth Cup Final on April 30 1975.

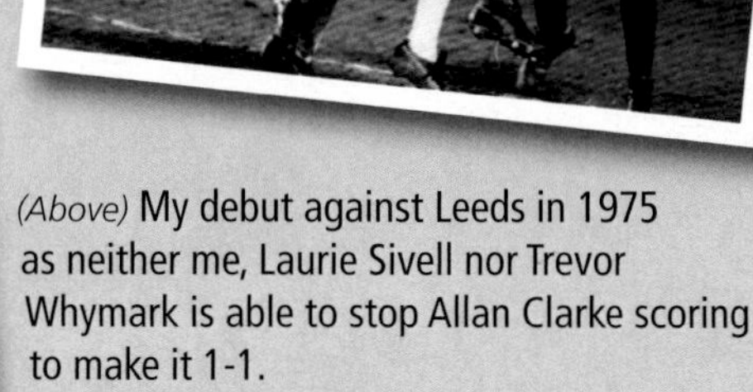

(Above) My debut against Leeds in 1975 as neither me, Laurie Sivell nor Trevor Whymark is able to stop Allan Clarke scoring to make it 1-1.

(Left) No prizes for guessing who has just scored an own goal in Ipswich's 3-1 defeat by QPR at Loftus Road in February 1976.

(Right) August 1976 and my first appearance in an Ipswich first team squad picture. That's me on the left of the back row alongside, left to right, Paul Cooper, John Peddelty, Laurie Sivell and Pat Sharkey. Middle row, David Johnson, Eric Gates, Terry Austin, Colin Viljoen, Keith Bertschin, Allan Hunter, Kevin Beattie and Trevor Whymark. Front row, Cyril Lea (coach), Brian Talbot, Clive Woods, Mick Mills, Roger Osborne, George Burley, Mick Lambert and Bobby Robson (manager).

Training at Portman Road alongside, from left, Paul Mariner, Allan Hunter, Roger Osborne, Trevor Whymark and Brian Talbot. Big Al never used to move that much in training – he must have been going for a fag.

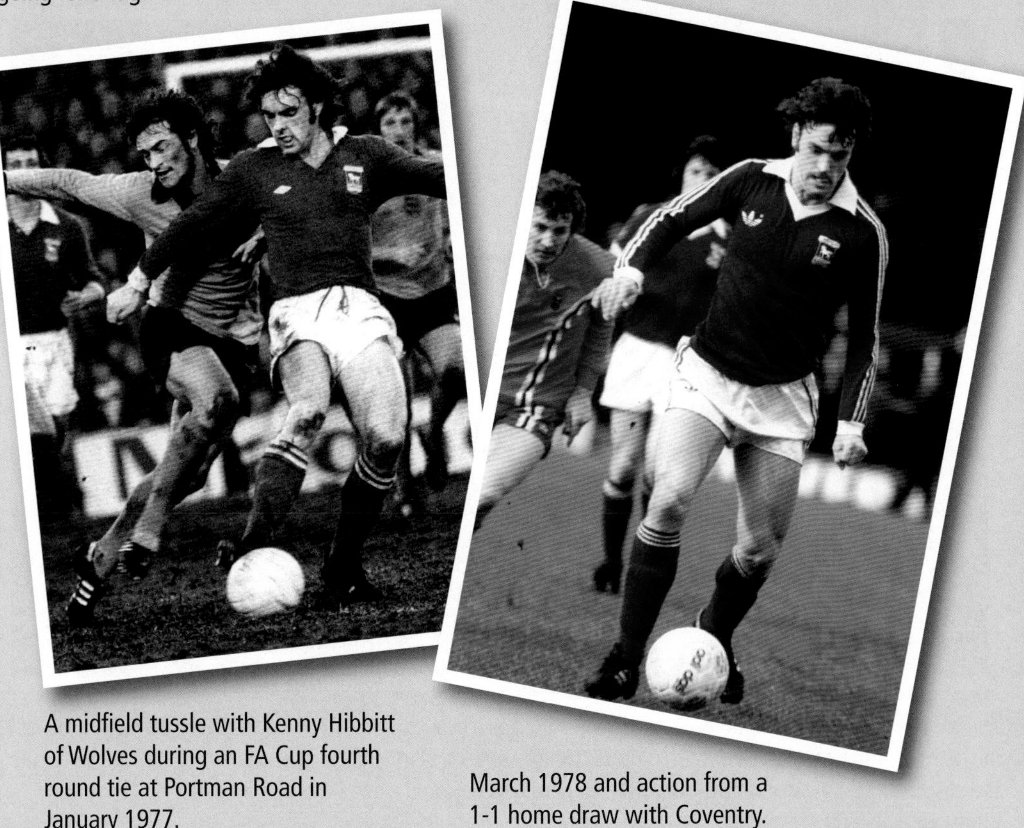

A midfield tussle with Kenny Hibbitt of Wolves during an FA Cup fourth round tie at Portman Road in January 1977.

March 1978 and action from a 1-1 home draw with Coventry.

A volley against Millwall in the FA Cup quarter-final at The Den in March 1978 – our fourth goal in a 6-1 win.

I am celebrating the first of my two goals for Ipswich in the 2-0 defeat of Coventry at Portman Road in September 1980, the same day Bobby Robson stirred up the home supporters by calling some of them 'zombies'.

The moment when we all knew Ipswich were going to Wembley in 1978. I have headed our third goal in the 3-1 defeat of West Bromwich Albion in the semi-final at Highbury and there is so little time on the clock that they can do nothing about it. Paul Mariner and Clive Woods join in the celebrations along with 23,000 supporters.

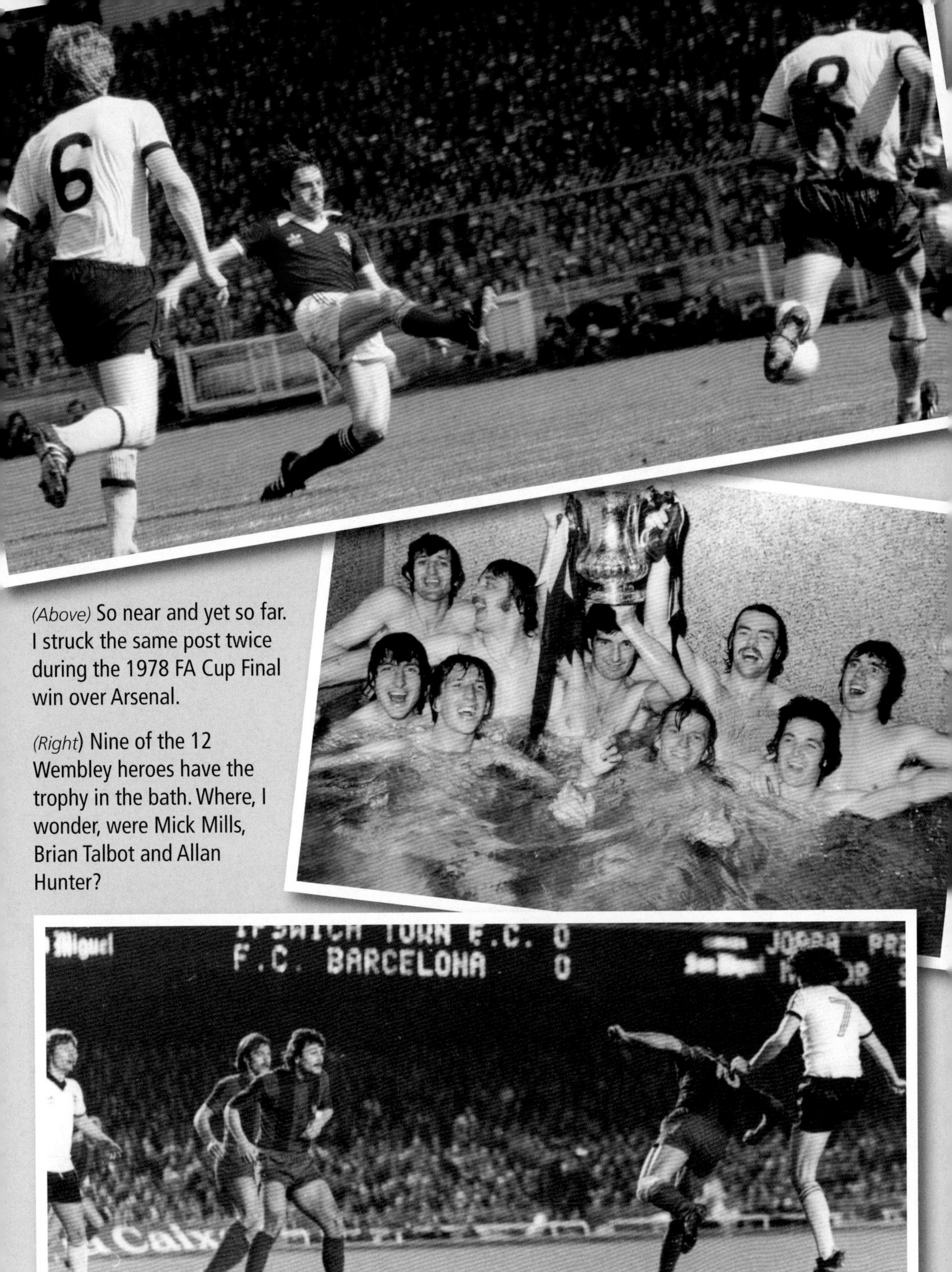

(Above) So near and yet so far. I struck the same post twice during the 1978 FA Cup Final win over Arsenal.

(Right) Nine of the 12 Wembley heroes have the trophy in the bath. Where, I wonder, were Mick Mills, Brian Talbot and Allan Hunter?

The early stages of Ipswich's European Cup Winners' Cup third round, second leg, game against Barcelona in the Nou Camp in March 1979. The scoreboard changed when their defender Migueli scored from a corner and we went out on the away goals rule.

It may look as if I have sent Diego Maradona sprawling during Scotland's 3-1 friendly defeat by Argentina at Hampden in June 1979, but he somehow managed to ride the tackle and continue on his way.

Another picture from the same game as Kenny Dalglish joins in our pursuit of Maradona.

The front cover of Ipswich's programme for the Boxing Day 1980 clash with Norwich features George Burley and I with Billy Connolly, who was in Ipswich and invited us into his dressing room after the show.

Baby Blues! Alan Brazil, me, Terry Butcher and Paul Mariner all became dads for the first time within a few months of each other. Alan is actually my son Andrew's godfather.

(Below) Me and Alan Brazil before Scotland's 3-0 defeat by Spain in Valencia in February 1982.

Here I am surrounded by family and friends outside Ibrox Stadium in Glasgow after I scored both Ipswich's goals in a 2-1 win over Rangers in August 1981.

Showing a young fan in Scotland a few souvenirs, including an international shirt and caps, along with my PFA Player of the Year trophy.

Bobby Robson tries to find words of encouragement as me and Frans Thijssen get ready for extra time in our FA Cup semi-final defeat by Manchester City at Villa Park in 1981.

of any job at home or in Europe. Among the clubs who tried to lure him away were Sunderland, Athletic Bilbao and Barcelona, who had clearly been impressed by the way he so nearly masterminded wins over them in successive seasons. In the end, while he must have been tempted, he remained loyal to Ipswich, with chairman Patrick Cobbold making it clear that he would only leave with the board's blessing if it was to manage England. In a sense it was payback time for the Ipswich directors as they had stayed loyal to their manager during the early, leaner years. Other clubs would not have been anywhere near as patient and, no doubt, when Bobby stopped to consider any offers that came his way he would have recognised that as being the case.

It would be fair to say that we anticipated making a better start to the 1979-80 season than was actually the case. After 12 games we were rock-bottom of the First Division with only seven points from 12 games while leaders Nottingham Forest, who defeated us 1-0 at Portman Road on the opening day of the campaign, boasted 17. We lost five league games on the trot, although a 2-1 defeat at Manchester United, who were on the same points tally as Forest, emphasised the narrow margin between sides at opposite ends of the table. As we prepared to face Manchester City at home we had added a further seven points from six games to move to third bottom and a tremendous 4-0 win – with Eric Gates claiming a brilliant hat-trick – was the launching pad for a magnificent 23-game unbeaten run in the league. Only on the very last day of the season, in the reverse fixture at Maine Road, did we suffer our next defeat. It was an amazing turnaround as we finished third, just seven points behind champions Liverpool and five adrift of runners-up Manchester United, to clinch European qualification for the sixth time in seven seasons. Not bad for a team that had managed just six wins from the first 18 league games. At that stage I had only managed to score five goals in all competitions so to finish the season with 15 from a total of 50 appearances, one of which was my first as a substitute, was satisfactory, to say the least.

One of our most remarkable results was to thrash Manchester United 6-0 at Portman Road, but I cannot claim any of the credit as I was absent from the team on that occasion. I had been ever-present in the side until then but I was in no fit state to play after the death of my father. I had been in Scotland that week and actually accompanied my dad to his local for a drink just hours before he died. Dad was in top form. My older brother, Alex, was also with us and it was just like old times as we reminisced. I had arranged to stay at my parents' home and I was awoken in the night by my mother's screams. Dad had simply passed away in his sleep. I ran into the bedroom and checked for a pulse but it was clear we had lost him. I consoled my mother, who was beside herself with grief, and my younger brother, Andy, who was asleep in his room when he heard the commotion. It wasn't long before other family members arrived at the house to provide support. It was a terrible shock to all of us and I decided to phone Bobby Robson to explain the situation. He was very understanding and sympathetic, and he agreed that I should have compassionate leave. My father's death hit me hard – he was only 51, the same age as me as I write these words – and I was angry that he had been taken from us. There was so much for him to live for – I still had a lot to achieve in my career and he never got to see his grandson, my son Andrew. Pleased as I was to hear about our 6-0 win over Manchester United, it did nothing to alter my mood. I made my way back to Suffolk a few days later and when the manager asked if I was feeling well enough to play in the FA Cup quarter-final at Everton I foolishly said I was.

Within a few minutes of the game at Goodison I knew I had made a mistake in deciding to play. The game bypassed me completely and by half-time, when the manager sat me down and queried whether I was in the right state of mind to continue, we were trailing 1-0. Everton were not a top side by any stretch of the imagination. We had thumped them 4-0 in a league game at Goodison the previous month and the fact that they finished the season fourth from bottom, narrowly avoiding relegation, said it all. Kevin Beattie replaced me but Brian Kidd scored to make our task more difficult still. Beat leapt higher than any other player could have done – there are pictures that clearly show he was above the crossbar as he made contact with the ball – to head our goal in the closing stages. The manager was criticised for changing the side that had annihilated Manchester United just seven days earlier and he stubbornly defended his decision. Knowing the part I had unintentionally played in our downfall, I was grateful to him for that. After another chat between the two of us I was left out for the 1-1 draw at Middlesbrough three days later, which Bobby said was 'in everyone's best interests' and I was only too happy to go along with that.

The Manchester United game was one of four on the trot that produced a remarkable total of nine penalties – and seven of them were missed. Frans Thijssen and Kevin Beattie twice, if you count the fact that he failed each time with a twice-taken penalty, could not beat United keeper Gary Bailey, then I took centre stage for all the wrong reasons in our 1-0 home win over Leeds. After John Lukic saved my first effort the referee ordered a retake and this time I smashed the ball against the bar. Next up it was Derby at Portman Road and the main reason we earned a point courtesy of a 1-1 draw was that goalkeeper Paul Cooper saved two penalties by Rams' pair Barry Powell and Gerry Daly. Finally, we defeated Norwich 4-2 and I scored my first Ipswich hat-trick that included two penalties. Coop had an amazing record when it came to facing spot-kicks, also saving from Terry McDermott and Micky Thomas at Liverpool and Manchester United respectively that season and his impressive record was that he kept out seven from 10 that he faced between August 1978 and May 1980. He was always very modest about his achievements, pointing out that all the pressure was on the guy taking the penalty. Spot-on, I reckon!

I did once quit as Ipswich's penalty taker but I soon got my old job back. It was in September 1979 that I missed one as Scotland drew 1-1 with Peru at Hampden. That was a friendly and it would have been worse had it been a vital qualifying game, but I still decided it would be best to step down. We badly wanted to beat Peru because they had beaten us in the World Cup finals in Argentina, but we couldn't beat the Glasgow weather. It was a miserable night of wind and rain, and the ball twice rolled off the spot before I was able to take the kick. It definitely wasn't one of my best and when I watched the highlights later on television I could see I had made it quite easy for their keeper to save it. I had also missed for the Scotland youth and under-21 sides, so I made up my mind not to risk a repeat and quit. My confidence was affected to the extent that I also asked to be relieved of my duties with Ipswich. The plan was that I would step down and we would play it by ear, but when Paul Mariner took over and fired his first penalty over the bar in our home win against Southampton he virtually pleaded with me to come out of my brief retirement. Within a few days we were awarded a penalty at Coventry and much to my relief I scored, although it was merely a consolation goal as we went down 4-1. I settled into the role again and kept it until I departed for Liverpool four and a half years later, by which time I had taken a further 31 penalties, failing to score from four of them. My complete spot-kick record in my first spell with Ipswich saw me score from 38 of the 43 penalties I took.

Just as Arnold Muhren being voted the fans' Player of the Year in 1979 was entirely predictable, so was the fact that fellow countryman Frans Thijssen succeeded him a year later. There was a double Dutch celebration, in fact, because in the summer of 1980 Arnold's two-year contract was due to expire and the club were desperate to retain his services. For a while it seemed he would be moving on, as he was perfectly entitled to do, but after a lot of negotiating between Arnold and Bobby Robson a sensible compromise was reached. The outcome was that Arnold signed a further two-year deal on the proviso that he would be entitled to a free transfer when it ended, allowing him to move wherever he wanted and, since there would be no transfer fee, he would also pocket a sizeable signing-on fee. Arnold's impact in two seasons with Ipswich was such that when he went public with his decision to stay, him and the manager were whisked off to the BBC studios in Southampton on the day of our match at The Dell to appear live on the lunchtime preview show, Football Focus. It seemed fitting that Arnold should score the only goal of the game to keep us on course for Europe. Arnold also explained his decision was not all about finances. "Next season," he said, "could be very exciting for Ipswich." Just how exciting, we wouldn't have dared dream.

1981 AND ALL THAT

WHILE EVERYONE AT IPSWICH started the 1980-81 season in confident mood – that had been the norm for a number of years – none of us were to know that we were launching into the most momentous season in the history of the club, one that would stretch across Europe, run to an amazing 66 games and see us chasing an unprecedented hat-trick of major honours – the League Championship, the FA Cup and the UEFA Cup. Maybe it was just as well that we were eliminated from the League Cup at the fifth round stage, or quarter-finals, although by then we were thinking in terms of winning that competition as well. We were the last team in the Football League to be beaten that season, and not until our 15th fixture at Brighton, but the fact that we did not have the depth of squad to battle on so many different fronts was to prove our downfall, although to land the one major honour we did was a marvellous achievement for a club of our size. Furthermore, for yours truly and my Dutch team-mate Frans Thijssen it was to prove the season of our lives as we won the highest individual prizes the English game has to offer. In my own case, I also won a special European accolade as Young Player of the Year and as I reflect on it now the memories come flooding back.

If I ended the season on a high note, the same could be said of the way I started, as I scored the only goal of our opening-day league game at Leicester. We were without injured pair Arnold Muhren and Alan Brazil at Filbert Street, and after Paul Mariner struck a post it seemed we would have to settle for a goalless draw. But two minutes from the end Eric Gates found me with a cross and I headed past Mark Wallington. It was goal number one – you always like to get off the mark as quickly as possible – of 36 I scored that season as I revelled in my role between Frans and Arnold in the middle of the park. I was still regarded as a defensive midfielder, but I perfected the art of breaking up attacks at one end of the pitch and then, after passing to one of the Dutch lads or a full-back, I would motor to the other end and add my weight to the attack, invariably getting on the end of crosses or knock-downs from the strikers. Defensively speaking, I suppose I was similar to Javier Mascherano of Liverpool and Argentina, although the former Tottenham Hotspur manager, David Pleat, wrote the following on behalf of a national newspaper early in 2007 when he was asked to cast his eye over Reading midfielder Steve Sidwell, who subsequently moved to Chelsea and is now with Aston Villa: "He is quiet, unassuming but ruthlessly efficient. Sidwell reminds me of John Wark, the former Liverpool and Ipswich Town midfielder. His ability to transfer the ball with energy, allied to a football brain, took him into goalscoring positions on several occasions and his runs between strikers were perfectly timed."

No one ever got hold of me and said: "I want you to be a box-to-box player and I'm going to teach you how to do it." Nor was I given any special coaching, with a view to converting me into a goal machine. It just came naturally and I enjoyed being one of many important cogs in the side that season. When every single player knows his job the way the Ipswich lads knew theirs, it should not be a surprise when everything clicks as it did for us that season. I was no one-season wonder, either, as my record shows, but there is no doubt that the 1980-81 campaign was exceptional as far as I was concerned, the one to remember above all others for Ipswich, and I am certain the fans who were around at the time will agree.

I scored a penalty in our first home game against Brighton, which we won 2-0, and we were the early leaders of the First Division after winning six and drawing one of our first seven games, with me on top of the national goalscoring charts with a tally of six. In one of the early match-day programmes, manager Bobby Robson was featured in an article bemoaning the fact that the standard of English midfield players was on the decline. "I have a thing about midfield players, maybe because I was one," said Bobby. He went on: "We seem to be producing the type of midfield player that is a specialist and when I say specialist don't get me wrong. What I mean is a specialist in just one part of the midfield game. We have players who are creative, that's all they can do. They can't mark or tackle. For example, Trevor Brooking and Tony Currie. I am not knocking these players, just giving them as examples. Then we get midfield players who are good tacklers or markers, and that is all they can do. They do not get involved in scoring or creative team play. Now, to be a world class midfield player, you have to be able to do everything. You must be able to tackle and mark, carry the ball through and therefore be creative, pass and score goals. Those are the requirements for a complete midfield player and the quicker we get down to the job of producing players who can do those things, and do them well and consistently, then the sooner we will be able to compete on equal terms in the world arena." It all made sense but at the risk of blowing my own trumpet, as well as those of Arnold and Frans, Ipswich had three players that I believe fitted the bill.

When supporters are asked to cast their votes in polls to determine the best Ipswich player of all time, the names of Muhren and Thijssen are well to the fore and rightly so. They brought something to Ipswich that made us the envy of every other English club. Just as the fans might plump for one ahead of the other, so the rest of the Town squad at that time also had their favourites. Without a shadow of a doubt, I would nominate Frans. However, pop the same question to my club and country colleague, Alan Brazil, and he will give you a completely different answer. His choice would be Arnold, because he was the player who supplied most of his ammunition. Alan only had to make his move and Arnold would deliver the ball with perfect weight on his pass. They had a wonderful understanding that resulted in a number of goals. Arnold made some goals for me, too, but if pushed to choose one or the other I would go for Frans, who had a unique talent in that nobody could get the ball off him. To this day, Alan and I still have arguments about which player had more to offer and we will never agree. Suffice to say that they both contributed a great deal and each had his own special qualities. After that, it is a question of personal preference.

Arnold had a left foot that was like a magic wand. He was a team player, the main guy who made us tick. He could pass it short or long and while he was built like a long-distance runner who looked as if he needed a good dinner, he could also tackle in his own unique way. We used to joke that he had extensions fitted to his left leg. It was as if it got longer as he challenged an opponent. His tackling wasn't built on strength, but timing, and he nearly always came away with the ball. His balance was such that he looked like a ballet dancer the way he was able to skip through the muddy pitches that we often encountered in those days. There was no more graceful sight than Arnold, with the ball at his feet, selling a dummy and gliding past people as if they were statues. Frans was every bit as effective but in different ways. He looked as if the ball was stuck to his boot as he twisted and turned away from opponents. He would often turn 360 degrees, controlling the ball with the inside and the outside of his right foot, and because he was so good at retaining possession he was the first player the rest of us looked for if we were under the cosh. If we needed a breather Frans would oblige by hanging on to the ball as opposition players became increasingly frustrated at their failed attempts to win it off him. In fact, Frans often did things that deceived us, his team-mates.

There were always jokes about Arnold's kit not having to be washed after games, a reference to the fact that he always looked so cool and unflustered. If you wanted an example of a player who made the ball do the lion's share of the work, Arnold was your man. Frans, on the other hand, would like nothing more than to go off on a mazy dribble past four or five players as his close control, plus an ability to check and change direction, seemed to mesmerise them. They were chalk and cheese as individuals and players, but equally effective and inspirational. The move to Ipswich worked well for them, too, as both were recalled to the Dutch international squad after lengthy absences and in Arnold's case he was still playing for Holland when they were crowned European champions in 1988. They defeated the Soviet Union 2-0 in Munich and it was Arnold who sent over the deep cross from which Marco van Basten scored a tremendous volley. He was 37 by then, so all those 'economical' displays in the Ipswich midfield clearly benefited him as much as they did the club. I would even go as far as to say that Arnold and Frans were better than any of the current Dutch midfielders and they must rank as two of their country's all-time greats. My slight preference for Frans is because he was only too willing to undertake the 'ugly' side of the game when necessary, but in common with all the other Ipswich players – and supporters – of that era I cannot thank them enough for their contribution. Having said that, I am sure they would be the first to acknowledge that they were helped by the fact that they were playing alongside so many good British players and that the two styles complemented one another.

It was a goal from Frans Thijssen that enabled us to beat eventual champions Aston Villa at Portman Road in September and that was the first of three victories over them that season. We knocked them out of the FA Cup at the third round stage and then went to Villa Park in April, just three days after an FA Cup semi-final defeat by underdogs Manchester City, and gave our title hopes the kiss of life. Unfortunately, however, our workload was spread too thinly across a squad that simply couldn't cope. While we struggled to maintain a challenge on three different fronts, Villa were focused on the League Championship from January onwards – after we had done them a favour by eliminating them from the FA Cup – and they achieved their lone target using just 14 players, seven of whom were ever-present. It was a fantastic achievement and a year later they won the European Cup. We knew it could have been us going from one major success to another. I think we proved a point in beating Villa three times but the record books will always show that is was them, not us, who won the title. We paid a huge price for not being sufficiently well equipped to cope with the demands of chasing three top prizes and I am tempted to suggest that most teams, even now when squad rotation is in vogue, would have come up short. The games came so thick and fast that it averaged out at one every four days.

Even our successful UEFA Cup campaign was fraught with danger right up to the final few minutes in the Olympic Stadium in Amsterdam. Our journey started comfortably enough at home to the Greek side Aris Salonika and I scored four of the goals in our 5-1win, including a hat-trick of penalties. Ironically, I was the one Ipswich player who knew the exact location of Salonika and I could even claim to have been there for a holiday the previous year. My first wife's mother was Greek and had been born and brought up there before moving to England. It was during my trip to Salonika that something very, very strange happened. I had played for Scotland against England at Wembley that year and by an odd coincidence the game was being shown on Greek TV. The local papers got to hear I was in town and came along to interview me and take a few pictures. I also had a visit from another two men who said they were from the club and asked about the possibility of me playing for them. I said that wouldn't be possible but they persisted and even opened up a briefcase that was full of money, clearly hoping that might change my mind. It was a very odd episode and I never gave it a second thought until the UEFA Cup draw paired us with Aris.

It was certainly an eventful first leg. By half-time we were 3-0 ahead, all the goals having been scored by me inside the first 30 minutes, and the Greeks were also down to 10 men. Eric Gates was causing havoc and the Portuguese referee showed a lot of bottle to punish those who continually fouled Gatesy. Aris were awarded a penalty just three minutes into the second half and they duly converted it, but Paul Mariner made it 4-1 to us and I completed my hat-trick before the end. The Aris players were far from happy as the final whistle sounded and made it clear to us that in their minds the tie was still far from over. Two weeks later we saw what they meant. The atmosphere was hostile, to say the least, throughout our three days there. We had about 200 fans gatecrash our training session and because it was known as bandit country we had an armed guard to accompany us everywhere we went. Local fans had been brainwashed into thinking that Ipswich had bribed the referee in the game at Portman Road and that fairly stoked up the atmosphere against us. We were 3-0 down after 65 minutes and on the brink of a humiliating exit. They tried everything to intimidate us, including spitting in our faces, and knock us out of our stride, and it seemed to be working until Gatesy scored a valuable away goal. We still had to survive for a further 17 minutes to avoid the possibility of extra time but even after the final whistle sounded our ordeal was far from over. There was no hot water in the dressing rooms so Bobby Robson ordered us on to the bus and said we could shower back at the hotel. As the bus pulled away it was attacked by an angry mob of supporters and a brick came flying through a window, missing George Burley by inches. That was the signal for everyone to get down on the floor until we managed to shake off the hooligans.

Our next opponents were Bohemians of Prague and again we were at home in the first leg. They included the midfield player Antonin Panenka, who had won the European Championship for Czechoslovakia four years earlier. They played West Germany in the final and it ended 2-2 after extra time, meaning a penalty shoot-out was required. It was Panenka who decided it with one of the cheekiest penalties ever, coolly chipping the ball down the middle of the goal as the keeper, Sepp Maier, dived to his left. It was still goalless at half-time against Bohemians but I scored twice within the space of seven minutes soon after the interval, then Kevin Beattie came off the bench and scored a spectacular third from a free-kick. They hit the bar near the end or we would not have had a 3-0 lead to take over there for the second game – and, as things turned out, we needed it. We made the worst possible start, conceding a goal inside the first three minutes, and we were 2-0 down in the 53rd minute when their best player, Panenka, converted a free-kick from about 25 yards. We were without Paul Cooper, Frans Thijssen and Paul Mariner for a game played in sub-zero conditions and I have rarely been more relieved to hear the referee blow his whistle to signal the end of the game.

We again scored five – and this time without reply – in the first leg of our third round tie. The visitors to Portman Road were the Polish side Widzew Lodz, who had beaten Manchester United and Juventus in the early rounds to emerge as favourites to win the competition. I scored another hat-trick, but this time none of the goals came from the spot, so I went home with another match ball. More importantly, though, we established a bigger lead than we had dared to hope for beforehand. Skipper Mick Mills was carried off five minutes before the end after an accidental clash with Terry Butcher and went to hospital to have eight stitches inserted in a leg gash that was to keep him out for six games, including the return in snow-covered Lodz. Ground staff had cleared inches of the stuff off the pitch but it was only because we had a 5-0 lead that Bobby Robson agreed to the game taking place. The goalmouths were frozen with snow on top and only down the sides of the pitch was there any give. It was minus 10 when the game started and it got even colder before it finished. We lost 1-0 but there was never a single moment when we were worried about being pegged back and the Poles had as much difficulty in coping with the conditions as we did. Three days later the same side took to the field for a home league game against Liverpool. The gates were locked half an hour before the start and it ended 1-1, just as the corresponding fixture at Anfield had done a couple of months earlier.

We were beaten 5-3 at Tottenham the following midweek and Gatesy was sent off for retaliation after being fouled by Steve Perryman and then trampled on by Graham Roberts. It meant we had won just three times in a 12-game sequence, although by drawing seven times we had only lost twice. But it didn't stop the media asking 'Has the Ipswich bubble burst?' in the build-up to our next game at Birmingham, five days before Christmas. We delivered the perfect response with a 3-1 win and picked up another win at home to Norwich on Boxing Day. When we drew 1-1 at Arsenal the very next day it meant I had scored in three successive games, but I went on to better that a few weeks later when I scored in four on the trot, including FA Cup wins over Shrewsbury and Charlton that set us up for a quarter-final clash at Nottingham Forest. We saw off Villa in the third round, but before we could think about the possibility of going all the way to Wembley for the second time in three years we had to overcome a major obstacle in St Etienne, who Bobby Robson rated as better than any other side Ipswich had previously faced in Europe. I missed our 4-0 win at Coventry four days earlier but I was passed fit for the game in France and able to play my part in what must be one of the very best performances by a British club in the history of European competition. We even recovered from the shock of going behind to a goal by Dutch star Johnny Rep in the 16th minute to completely overwhelm them 4-1. It was only the third time in 31 games that St Etienne had been beaten at home in Europe and I was delighted to weigh in with our fourth goal to round off one of the best – maybe even the best – team displays in which I ever took part.

Three days later we were at the City Ground, Nottingham, for another pulsating game. We were 2-0 ahead but pegged back to 2-2 by half-time and when my international pal John Robertson converted a penalty just six minutes into the second half we were really up against it. But Frans Thijssen earned us a replay nine minutes from time and three days later it was Arnold Muhren who decided the replay with a goal midway through the second half – and with his right foot! We avenged our earlier defeat at White Hart Lane by thumping Spurs 3-0 at home and then completed the formality of sending St Etienne, for whom Michel Platini was the biggest name, packing from the UEFA Cup. I scored penalties in both games and apart from staying on course for the league title we were also through to the semi-final stages of two cup competitions. Sadly, though, having been beaten just twice in 32 games in all competitions, we suffered three successive away league defeats and that meant our trip to face our main rivals, Aston Villa, was being billed as a title decider.

Before we could even think about that one, however, we were at home to Cologne in the first leg of our UEFA Cup semi-final when my headed goal, my first in four games, was all that separated the sides. I felt I could have had a hat-trick on the night, but there was no time to reflect on what might have been, not with an FA Cup semi-final and the league game at Aston Villa to come in the space of the next six days. We were firm favourites to win the semi against Manchester City and we might even have fancied our chances to the extent that we took our opponents a bit lightly. Another major factor in our 1-0 extra-time defeat was that City boss John Bond sent his team out to bully us. I didn't blame him for that because in a straightforward football contest we would have triumphed every time, so he had to devise some way of improving his team's prospects. The combination of us not being properly switched on, plus City's success in quelling players like Arnold and Frans, contributed to our downfall. We were also unlucky to lose Kevin Beattie to a broken arm, but had we been able to try again after it ended 0-0 at 90 minutes I am convinced we would have booked our place at Wembley. Unfortunately for us it was the first year that the Football Association had decided against replays at the semi-final stage and we were undone by Paul Power's free-kick 10 minutes into the first half of extra time. We had a bad day at the office and would have put it right in a replay, but on this occasion there were no second chances. We knew we had not performed on the day and in the case of some players they were so below-par that it meant we were carrying passengers, which is a recipe for disaster. I was also livid about the decisive free-kick because it looked a harsh decision to punish Terry Butcher for his challenge on David Bennett. With so many things conspiring against us, the outcome was entirely predictable and I was absolutely gutted to come away with our hopes of going to Wembley well and truly dashed.

We returned to Ipswich afterwards but within two days we were back in the Midlands to prepare for the important league game at the very same venue. It said a lot for the character of the team that we hauled ourselves off the floor to defeat Villa in a game so appealing that it attracted more spectators than the semi-final had done. Alan Brazil scored after just four minutes and Gatesy made it 2-0 in the 80th minute. Gary Shaw pulled one back for Villa but we fully deserved both points. That put us one point behind leaders Villa and with a game in hand. We had five games left to their four, and although the first football treble was no longer possible we remained upbeat about our chances of winning the other two competitions. However, the workload was beginning to have a detrimental effect. We played Arsenal at home and lost, went down at Norwich two days later and had just over 48 hours to drag ourselves off the floor for the return game in Cologne. The schedule was so hectic that we didn't even have time to go home after the Easter Monday defeat at Carrow Road. Instead we were driven to Norwich Airport and flew to Germany. Bobby Robson surprised us when he said he had arranged a visit to a huge fun park called Phantasialand the next day and we had a brilliant time. Maybe the manager felt we needed a break – and full marks to him for his decision – but there can't be many teams who have spent the day before a European semi-final on the log flume and other rides. It seemed to work because we had another 1-0 win over Cologne thanks to Terry Butcher and could look ahead to the final.

Our title hopes were hanging by a thread at this stage and we returned from Germany to keep them alive by defeating Manchester City at Portman Road. With a full week in which to prepare for our penultimate fixture at Middlesbrough, who were just above the relegation places, we still had a chance to pip Villa, who had to go to third-placed Arsenal. The title could still be ours and when we were leading 1-0 at Ayresome Park, and Villa trailing 2-0 at Highbury, it was very much on the cards. While Villa's season was about to end, we still had a game in hand at home to Southampton and as things stood that was looking like the one that could clinch us the Championship. Sadly, though, we conceded two goals to Boro in the second half, which meant that Villa were able to celebrate because despite losing to Arsenal they were four points clear at the top and we only had one game left to play. Our only hope of landing a trophy, therefore, was to defeat AZ Alkmaar, the newly-crowned Dutch champions, in the UEFA Cup Final.

The Ipswich directors decided to cash in on the occasion by increasing ticket prices for the first leg of the final and it appeared to backfire when less than 28,000 fans were present. But those who stayed away missed seeing us establish a handsome 3-0 lead – my penalty sent us on our way – to take with us to Amsterdam a fortnight later. By the time that one came round we had been beaten at home by Southampton in our last league game, a result that mattered more to them than us as it meant they clinched a UEFA Cup place for the following season. So our hopes of ending the campaign with a trophy came down to our 66th, and final, game. There were around 8,000 Ipswich fans in Amsterdam, which proved a handy venue for them, and we were determined we were not going to let them down. The news that both Arnold and Frans had passed fitness tests meant we had our strongest available side. No George Burley, of course, because he had been out since January when he tore his cruciate ligament at Shrewsbury. It was Frans who put us 4-0 ahead on aggregate within three minutes of the kick-off, but AZ quickly replied and then took the lead. I scored my 14th UEFA Cup goal to equal a record set by Brazilian striker Jose Altafini as he helped AC Milan to win the European Cup 18 years earlier, but again AZ came back to lead 3-2 at half-time. They scored again with 16 minutes left on the clock and we were only too aware that if they scored another two the trophy would be theirs. That didn't happen, though, and we finally had something to show for our efforts. Suffice to say, we celebrated into the early hours and there were plenty of sore heads around when we eventually surfaced the next morning.

While we had 'only' won the UEFA Cup we completely dominated the individual honours. I won the PFA Player of the Year award, with Frans Thijssen and Paul Mariner second and third respectively, while Frans was crowned Footballer of the Year ahead of runner-up Mick Mills and yours truly in third. It was the first time one club had occupied the top three places in both polls and to the best of my knowledge it has never been repeated. I also won the Young European Player of the Year accolade, which was organised by an Italian magazine and involved me going to Italy to collect it as part of an all-expenses-paid holiday close to Florence. In two of the previous three years it had been won by Jimmy Case of Liverpool and Nottingham Forest's Garry Birtles, so I completed a British hat-trick. The Dutch player Ruud Krol, who was playing in Italy with Napoli, won the senior award and the organisers were superb hosts to Toula and me.

BEFORE THE 1981-82 season got under way the club secured their first-ever shirt sponsorship deal with the Japanese hi-fi giants, Pioneer, and as part of the arrangement they provided 24 stereos for management, players and officials. Bobby Robson was told before training one day that the kit was on its way and would be delivered within a couple of hours, but he said training was more important and the stereos could wait. The session was in full swing when we caught sight of the Pioneer truck reversing down the driveway towards the club offices and that was enough for the manager to call a halt. We adjourned to the car park, where the equipment was unloaded from the truck and transferred to our cars. What was that about the training taking precedence, boss?

One of the highlights of my career occurred in the pre-season of 1981 when I had my first and last opportunity to play at Ibrox. I was delighted when I heard we had arranged a game against Rangers and even more chuffed that I scored both our goals, one a penalty, in a 2-1 win in front of 30,000 fans. It was a day when most members of my family didn't know whether to laugh or cry. Some of them, including my mother and my uncle Hugh, sat in the directors' box, which meant he hid a carry-out of beers in the toilet and picked it up again before he left. Also, one of the Rangers board said to my mother: "We tried to sign your son, Mrs Wark, a few years ago." It was news to mum because she was well aware that I had wanted nothing more as a youngster than to play for Rangers. She replied: "You couldn't have tried very hard."

The 1981-82 season was the first to award three points, rather than just two, for a league win so it wasn't particularly clever of us to start with two draws. But if defeating Manchester United and Liverpool in successive games put our First Division campaign back on track, we were in for a nasty shock as UEFA Cup holders when we were unable to maintain our grip on the trophy beyond the first round. We were seeded and paired with Aberdeen, whose manager Alex Ferguson was still five years away from taking charge of Manchester United, and after a 1-1 draw at Portman Road we were dumped out of the competition by a 3-1 defeat at Pittodrie. I could sense a feeling in the camp that some of the players were perhaps under-estimating our opponents and I recall mentioning more than once that Aberdeen would be fired up for what they would see as a mini Scotland versus England clash. I would not want to take anything away from Fergie and his players – they were an excellent team – but I was angry that we gave such a poor account of ourselves over the two games.

We at least managed to progress further than ever before in the League Cup, but Liverpool were too good for us in the semi-final. Although we managed a 2-2 draw at Anfield, our 2-0 first leg defeat was always going to make our task a near-impossible one and at one stage we were trailing 4-0 on aggregate before late goals by Eric Gates and Alan Brazil added a touch of respectability to the result. Our interest in the FA Cup was ended at the fifth round stage by Shrewsbury, so it was the title race that represented our best chance of success. We had taken 17 points from a possible 21 to lead the table and when I scored after just 12 seconds against Southampton at The Dell things were looking good. It was the fastest-ever goal there and we had a 3-1 lead after 34 minutes, yet less than half an hour later we were trailing 4-3 and that was how it remained to the end. Bobby Robson called it his worst result in 10 years and although we recovered to beat Wolves – Kevin O'Callaghan scored the only goal, his first for the club – the manager criticised me afterwards in the papers when he claimed I was playing and thinking like a striker instead of a midfield player. The manager felt I was too enthusiastic in heading for the opposition box and reminded me it was my timing that had been instrumental in earning me so many goals the previous season.

A run of just three wins in nine games early in 1982 saw us drop down as low as seventh in the table before four successive wins saw us climb to second and that was where we remained until the end of the season. John Jackson, who was 39 at the time, and had not appeared in a First Division fixture for eight years, played his one and only game for Ipswich against Manchester United at Portman Road. Although John Gidman fired the visitors ahead, I managed to score twice to turn things round. When I put us in front against champions Aston Villa it was Ipswich's 1,000th in 17 seasons as a First Division club and the one I put past Jim Platt at Middlesbrough was my 100th for Town. But none of that really mattered when we finished the season four points adrift of champions Liverpool.

I missed two penalties that could have been worth five points so how do you think I was feeling? The one at Tottenham was so bad that Ray Clemence was almost lying on the ground waiting to collect it. I was having a stinker at White Hart Lane and shouldn't have taken it. If anyone else had volunteered to take it I'd have stepped aside. I kicked the ground behind the ball and my kick had no power – probably the worst I ever took for Ipswich. My other miss was against Manchester City, just nine minutes from the end of a 1-1 draw, when I sent my kick over the bar. Two costly misses, but I liked the way Bobby Robson defended me. He said: "Does Jack Nicklaus always sink the 18-inch putt? Is every round a clear round for Harvey Smith? Professional sportsmen make mistakes – it is part and parcel of the game." I ended the season with 23 goals and 18 of them came in the First Division, exactly like the season before, and because 14 of my 36 in the 1980-81 season had come in Europe I had actually surpassed my domestic tally.

Finishing as First Division runners-up for the second season in a row wasn't too bad an effort, but the news we were dreading eventually surfaced when it was confirmed that Bobby Robson would succeed Ron Greenwood as England manager. Bobby was the longest-serving manager in the country at the time but there was no way we could expect him to turn down the England job the way he had rejected the many club offers that had come his way. While he went with our best wishes, no one was sorrier to see him depart than me. In my nine years at Portman Road he had been like a second father to me. Bobby's last job was to recommend that his right-hand man, Bobby Ferguson, should succeed him, but Ipswich were powerless to prevent Arnold Muhren leaving on a free transfer to join Manchester United. He was the first of our UEFA Cup-winning team to leave the club and although we didn't realise it at the time, the exodus was to continue at a fairly rapid rate.

We started the 1982-83 season without a single win in our opening six games but at the seventh attempt we not only won but created a new club record, the

6-0 thrashing of Notts County at Meadow Lane being the club's biggest away win since joining the Football League 44 years earlier. The following week we ended Liverpool's 23-game unbeaten record at Portman Road, but we were still only 16th in the table. I was finding goals harder to come by, thanks in no small way to the fact that we were not awarded a single penalty in the league all season. By the time we faced West Bromwich Albion I had only scored four in 15 games in all competitions, but in the space of just 41 minutes against the Baggies I added four more as we won 6-1. We climbed to seventh place in December and in February 1983 I scored what was probably my favourite goal of all time for Ipswich to put us ahead in the 1-1 home draw with Manchester United, although my feeling at the time was that I had no right to score it. Alan Brazil crossed from the right, Paul Mariner headed back into the middle and because I had timed my run a fraction early the ball was slightly behind me. I had no choice but to go for the overhead kick. I made a good contact with the ball and as I landed on my back I looked up to see the ball sailing past Gary Bailey and into the net. The papers talked about it as a Brazilian-type goal and that was good enough for me. We were 13th in the table after that game and climbed to sixth in March, but a run of just two wins in our last nine games saw us drop down to ninth by the end of the campaign. The smallest Portman Road league crowd for 10 years saw a goalless draw with Notts County and the departures of Alan Brazil to Tottenham and Frans Thijssen to Vancouver Whitecaps were further signs that we were in danger of becoming also-rans in the top flight, which was very difficult to accept.

GOODBYE ROBSON, HELLO WARK

IT WAS IN OCTOBER 1983 that I came to the conclusion – reluctantly I might add – that I would have to leave Ipswich. In some ways, thinking as a husband and father, it was the last thing I wanted to do. My son, Andrew, was only four months old. With Toula's parents resident in Ipswich, and keen to do their fair share of babysitting, why would we want to leave? As a professional footballer, however, I felt I had no alternative. Initially, I asked for a wage rise, predominantly because I was lagging way behind players at other clubs. Future England manager Glenn Hoddle, for example, signed a new deal worth £75,000 a year at Tottenham and my annual salary at the time was £48,000 – which, I might add, was not the basic figure but with all bonuses added. As I readily admitted, Hoddle could run rings round me in terms of his ball skills, but when it came to overall effectiveness I would back myself against him any day. I felt I deserved to be paid more but Ipswich, who were really feeling the pinch, refused and that prompted me to ask for a transfer. The headlines about me were misleading. They asked why I was unable to survive on £1,000 a week, which I accept must have seemed a fortune to the ordinary working bloke, but at no time did I say my salary wasn't enough to make ends meet. That wasn't my argument at all.

At the same time as I was considering my future at Portman Road, my friend and team-mate Paul Mariner was in exactly the same boat. Indeed, little more than 24 hours after I submitted a written transfer request, Paul did exactly the same. His argument was similar to my own – he was keeping Tony Woodcock, who had moved to Arsenal from Cologne, out of the England side, yet he was earning about half as much. Our combined actions led to us being labelled pay rebels and after our stance made headlines in the national, as well as local, press it wasn't long before the letters started to arrive at the club, accusing us of being greedy. We received some terrible flak and in my own case one supporter wrote to me and described me as a rat leaving a sinking ship. But the way I saw it, if I had really been the greedy so-and-so people saw me as, I would have been on my bike years earlier. My stock was particularly high in 1981 when I was the Professional Footballers' Association choice as Player of the Year but never at any point did I contemplate a change of club. I was happy at Ipswich, we had a team full of international players and after winning both the FA Cup and the UEFA Cup with them I was looking to add at least one League Championship winner's medal to my collection.

Two years on, sadly, it was a very different Ipswich. Bobby Robson had departed to become manager of England – a major blow on its own – and Arnold Muhren, Mick Mills, Frans Thijssen and Alan Brazil had all joined the exodus. In other words, the guts had been ripped out of the side and the club was going through a transitional period as it looked to rebuild under a new boss. Bobby Ferguson, who had previously been second in command, was recommended for the job by the outgoing manager. With cash in short supply, Fergie couldn't replace those international stars that had departed with players of a similar standard and he had no choice but to promote kids from the reserves to plug the gaps. No disrespect to them, but the plain truth was that the team was becoming weaker. We started the 1983-84 season convincingly enough, with a 3-1 home defeat of a star-studded Tottenham side that included both Hoddle and Brazil, in front of a crowd of over 26,000, but things were to change for the worse in the weeks and months that followed.

By the time we played bottom club Leicester towards the end of October 1983, a lot of supporters appeared to have deserted us. The crowd for a goalless stalemate was under 15,000 and it was after that game that PM handed in his transfer request. His action resulted in him being stripped of the captaincy, which he had been given by Fergie following the sale of Mick Mills to Southampton less than a year earlier. Despite the disappointing result against Leicester we remained fifth in the table, but after winning just one of our next eight games we dropped to third from bottom and had to face facts – we had a relegation fight on our hands. After a board meeting decided that neither PM nor I should be awarded a wage rise, another get-together of the directors about two months later saw our transfer requests granted and we were both officially made available for sale. Chairman Patrick Cobbold announced at the time: "We can't give money we haven't got. Nobody wants to lose international players, but we have to have in mind the welfare of the club in general." I understood where he was coming from but at the same time I felt I had to look after the best interests of me and my family.

Despite both PM and I repeatedly trying to justify our position, it would be fair to say that there was no sympathy coming in our direction. As much as we argued that we were being under-paid in comparison to others, many of whom were not as highly rated as players, it wasn't a view with which the fans could identify and I accepted that. However, there was to be no turning back. I was adamant that I was prepared to move, even if the domestic upheaval wasn't something to which I was looking forward. My career had to come first and, much as it hurt to admit it, I was going nowhere fast with an Ipswich team struggling to survive in the top flight. PM made a similar stance and, as things turned out, he was the first to move. He scored our first goal in a 3-1 home win over Coventry most memorable for the introduction from the bench of Jason Dozzell, at the time still attending Chantry High School and who went on to rewrite the record books as he netted our third goal in the 89th minute. That made him, at 16 years and 57 days old, the youngest-ever goalscorer in the English top flight. As Jason announced his arrival on the scene, PM said his farewells and signed for Arsenal in a £150,000 deal, the fee saying more about Ipswich's financial predicament at the time than PM's ability. When we went to Highbury the following month PM scored twice in the Gunners' 4-1 win, with another ex-Ipswich player, Brian Talbot, also on target.

I played just two more games for Ipswich after that. There was constant speculation as to whether I would depart ahead of the transfer deadline towards the end of March but up to then the only club that had declared a firm interest was West Bromwich Albion. They showed their hand months earlier, even before my transfer request was granted, but it wasn't something that appealed to me. It was also reported that Manchester United were keen to sign me. "Goodbye Robson, Hello Wark" screamed a *News of the World* headline on a story suggesting that I was headed for Old Trafford to replace United and England skipper Bryan Robson who, it was claimed, looked certain to move to Italy. Of course, nothing of the sort happened, and instead I was to join United's arch-rivals Liverpool, whose interest was confirmed on the Sunday as Toula and I were preparing to leave the house to have lunch with friends. The phone rang and when I picked it up the voice on the other end said: "Hello, is that John? It's Joe Fagan here." My first thought was that Gatesy was playing another of his practical jokes and I nearly said something I would definitely have regretted. Joe went on to explain that the clubs had agreed a fee and we arranged that I would head for Liverpool the very next day – but not before a brief, and extraordinary, contretemps with Ipswich manager Bobby Ferguson.

Talk about everything happening at once. The transfer deadline was looming and the *News of the World* asked me if I would 'write' a two-part feature intended for use once I had moved on, as everyone seemed to anticipate I would before the deadline. Unfortunately, they published both parts while I was still an Ipswich player and as soon as I saw it in print I knew it would cause problems between me and Fergie. Not only was I critical of the decision to sell skipper Mick Mills – I actually described it as one of the biggest mistakes in the club's 97-year history – but I also had a dig at Fergie and the sub-heading on the story said it all. It appeared alongside a picture of him and read: "I often get the feeling that Bobby Ferguson will crack any minute." I was simply illustrating my point that while Fergie was a brilliant coach, which I was keen to acknowledge in the article, I had never felt that he fitted easily into the role of manager. I said younger players were a bit frightened of him and I took the mickey by relaying the story that he drank calamine lotion after suffering from sunburn on an end-of-season trip to Martinique. But at least I finished on a positive note by stating: "Joking aside, he's a good bloke whose heart has always been in the right place."

As I read through the piece, which had been 'ghosted' by reporter Alan Stephens following a chat between us, I had to agree that it was an accurate account of what I had said. But at that precise moment, had I been pressed, I would have had to concede that agreeing to do the article was not one of the best decisions I had ever made, even if I was being paid a decent fee by the paper. Had it appeared after my departure from Ipswich I could have lived with it, but when it was published earlier than originally scheduled I knew I would have a problem. Sure enough, on the Monday morning Fergie summoned me to his office and after I went inside he not only slammed the door shut but also locked it, which I found rather disconcerting. I was stunned when he stood facing me just inside the door and said: "Go on, hit me." I actually looked behind me to see who he was talking to before I realised it was me. Fergie was a former army physical training instructor, very fit for his age, and he was wearing a look that confirmed he was deadly serious. There was no way I was going to hit him. Had I done so, it would have escalated into something that both of us would have regretted. "I can stop you going," he repeated several times, but I knew that was a bluff. It was no secret that Ipswich were skint and needed the cash. I didn't blame them for holding out for the best possible offer, having originally placed a fee of £750,000 on my head, but as the deadline approached it was clear that any clubs interested in me were also playing a cagey game of cat and mouse and Ipswich would be guided by their bank, not football, manager.

Given the scale of the club's financial woes, it became pretty obvious to me that I would be going. The only question that remained to be answered was where, and for how much, but Liverpool were firmly in the driving seat. Two days earlier we had been on Merseyside for a game against Everton at Goodison Park that we lost 1-0. Had I not missed a decent chance and had Mark Brennan's shot that struck one post before running along the line to hit the other gone in, we might actually have earned ourselves a valuable point, perhaps even all three, despite the fact that we couldn't claim it was a great performance. I learned afterwards that I had created a new club record of 162 consecutive appearances. We were third from bottom of the First Division after that game, in which Frank Yallop was the latest young player to make his senior debut. Having been alerted to Liverpool's interest, and knowing the transfer deadline was the following Thursday, I half expected to be staying up there for signing talks. However, absolutely nothing was said to me about a possible transfer and I returned to Ipswich completely in the dark about my future. But less than 48 hours later, having survived the altercation in Fergie's office and had the call from Joe, I was heading for Merseyside all over again after Ipswich accepted Liverpool's £450,000 offer and gave me permission to talk to them.

I was accompanied on the train from Ipswich by my wife and my financial adviser, John Hazel, who sadly passed away a few years ago. Flattered as I was by the fact that Liverpool wanted me to join them, the one thought going round and round in my head as we made our way north was, 'Will I get a game every week?' Liverpool were the reigning champions and going for a hat-trick of successive league titles, so of course I wanted to join them. After all, the fact that Ipswich were no longer contenders for the major prizes was one of the reasons I was keen to move on. I wanted to win things. But throughout the journey I tortured myself with the thought that I might go there, fail to hold down a regular place and miss out on the very thing that was driving me – success. But another voice in my head was at complete odds with the first one. It was reminding me of what I had achieved thus far in my career and that to join a club like Liverpool was an opportunity I had earned – and one I should most certainly grasp.

A meeting had been arranged at the St George's Hotel in Liverpool city centre and we duly checked into the room that Liverpool had reserved for us. In the ten minutes or so before our scheduled appointment, I found myself talking to Manchester United chairman Martin Edwards. United had declared an interest in signing me but had not followed up with a firm offer. John Hazel rang Old Trafford to see if he could ascertain their position and was put through to the chairman, who in turn asked to speak to me. "John," he started, "I just wanted to let you know that we won't be pursuing our interest in you." He went on to explain that Bryan Robson was not going to Italy and so there was no need to look around for someone to replace him. Our brief conversation over, I replaced the receiver. Instantly, it rang again, and the hotel receptionist informed me that the Liverpool FC representatives were waiting for me. I went downstairs to be met by a three-strong deputation that comprised chairman John Smith, manager Joe Fagan and chief executive Peter Robinson.

Joe virtually grabbed hold of Toula and said: "Let's go and get a cup of tea." As they wandered off John Hazel and I were escorted into a meeting room for what we thought would be a round of hard bargaining. Nothing could have been further from the truth. Peter Robinson produced a document from his briefcase and slid it across the table to where I was sitting. "We have prepared your contract," he said in matter-of-fact fashion. "Could you please check it, make sure you are happy with it and then sign it." I kid you not – that was what passed for negotiating between the two parties. I spotted the weekly figure of £851 – don't ask me why it was such an odd sum – and if my calculator is working properly that equates to an annual salary of £44,252. Since it was not a great deal more than I was already on at Ipswich, it crossed my mind for a split second that I should ask for more. But to be fair, the bonuses for league wins and success in the cup competitions were far more generous than I was used to. There was real potential to earn a lot more and another thing I noticed was that the cup bonuses referred in the main to actually winning the tournament, whereas at Ipswich we were rewarded for progressing from one round to the next. Liverpool were only prepared to pay big money for success in the form of sticking a trophy in the cabinet. Part of me wanted to try to push up the basic wage, but I was so aware of the way the contract was presented, not to mention that the deadline was creeping up on us, that I felt I had virtually no choice but to accept or it would mean staying put at Portman Road.

There was one minor stumbling block regarding an ex-gratia payment of £25,000 that I was due from Ipswich as part of my contract with them. It wasn't a deal breaker, but bearing in mind we were now within 72 hours of the transfer deadline it was something that had to be resolved to my satisfaction. It was left to Liverpool to contact Ipswich and work out a resolution, while we sat and waited, the boredom only being broken by endless cups of tea. Basically, as is often the case in situations of this type, which tend to crop up fairly regularly when a player is moving clubs, Liverpool agreed to up the fee to £475,000 to cover the money I was due, which was later paid to me by Ipswich. I signed and the formal part of the business was concluded, although it was made clear to me that everything hinged on me being able to pass my medical. Suddenly, I was concerned that I would fail. I could think of no logical reason why I should after scoring 131 goals in 383 games for Ipswich, but the doubt must have crept in because there was so much riding on it. Had I known what form the medical would take I would have known there was absolutely no need to be concerned.

The Anfield boot room had a reputation second to none. Rather than the luxuriously appointed upstairs boardroom, it was where all the big decisions were made. Yes, the directors ran the club, but the small, rather cramped boot room was where Bill Shankly would hold court in his time as manager, his trusty lieutenants by his side. It was renowned throughout the game. When Shankly quit he handed over to Bob Paisley. Next in line was Joe Fagan and in later years Roy Evans would continue the dynasty. Despite its place in the game, the area in question was not the least bit glamorous. It was actually scruffy, a bit of a workman's hut, and it was hard to believe that this was the hub of what most people regarded as the best club in Europe, where a succession of managers and coaches would sip from mugs of tea as they discussed the team and tactics. It was also where the Liverpool staff entertained their opposite numbers after home games and I spotted a modest fridge in the corner. Toula stayed at the hotel while I was driven over to Anfield to have my medical. Joe Fagan took me into the boot room, where we were joined by Tom Saunders, who was known as the club's top spy as a result of his detailed dossiers on opposition sides, mainly those drawn to meet Liverpool in Europe. Ex-teacher Tom had also been the club's first youth development officer and was responsible for the progress of many a household name all the way from schools football to the first team. He was so highly regarded at the club that he later accepted an invitation to join the board.

Joe explained that the doctor was on his way and I was rather taken aback when he entered the room a few minutes later. He was small in stature and a lot older than I had somehow imagined. Also, I could not help but detect the smell of alcohol on his breath as he introduced himself to me. I was even more surprised when he announced we would stay put to conduct the medical examination. I had imagined moving on to a well appointed treatment room, but instead the doctor opened his bag and produced the equipment I instantly recognised as that to ascertain my blood pressure. I removed my jacket, rolled up my shirt sleeve, and he attached the apparatus before squeezing on the rubber ball to pump up the tube round my arm. Seconds later he looked at the reading and muttered "That's fine." Then something happened that to this day I still cannot get over. He asked me to bend down and touch my toes. Trying not to show my surprise, I did exactly as he asked and as I lifted my head he spoke again, this time to announce "You've passed." That was it, my Liverpool medical. Can you blame me for having a smile on my face as I watched David Beckham undergo what appeared to be a series of stringent tests when he moved from Manchester United to Real Madrid a few years ago? Blimey, it was deemed so important that it was beamed live across Spain by the television cameras, whereas mine was over in a flash.

That wasn't my last surprise, either. After Joe and I met a few press lads to give them some quotes, the club ordered me a taxi to travel back to the hotel. As I made my way to the main entrance there were a number of supporters milling about, something to which I was to grow accustomed during the remainder of my time as a Liverpool player. One guy made straight for me. If I say he was a typical Scouser I think you will know what I mean. He asked if I had signed, I confirmed I had and he winked as he said "I've got something for you." He gestured me towards a white van parked no more than 20 yards from the main entrance and since there was still no sign of my taxi I followed him over to the vehicle. I couldn't believe it when he threw open the back doors to reveal an Aladdin's Cave of household items. There were television sets, videos, stereos, microwaves, toasters, kettles and other bits and pieces, all in their original boxes bearing some familiar manufacturers' names. "What would you like?" he asked and I had to decline. "I can't do anything at the moment," I told Merseyside's answer to Arthur Daley, but I had to admire his nerve, particularly as a couple of policemen in full uniform were nearby, presumably to control the crowd that had gathered to greet Liverpool's new signing.

My first training session as a Liverpool player was another eye-opener. I had heard tales about them placing the emphasis on working with the ball, with a minimum of running, and that appealed to me. We were divided into two teams for a small-sided game under the supervision of Ronnie Moran and Roy Evans, who also joined in. "Two touches, lads" they shouted as the game kicked off. Soon after the start I struck this absolute peach of a pass, the ball travelling about 60 yards and landing right on the foot of its intended target. I was thinking to myself 'How's that for a pass?' when Ronnie bellowed at me. Realising that I was standing there admiring my pass, he shouted "Move your f***ing arse," and I did. They encouraged players to pass and move, preferably first time but certainly not taking more than two touches of the ball. It was drummed into us all the time and it had been that way for many years since Bill Shankly had come on the scene in the 60s.

I loved the training because it consisted of five-a-sides and more five-a-sides. Even the pre-season stuff had very little of the stamina work I had grown accustomed to at Ipswich. We did six-mile runs there and it was a real slog. Lads like George Burley, Russell Osman and Tommy Parkin were always out in front, I would be somewhere in the middle and the likes of Alan Brazil and Eric Gates would be towards the back. As for Allan Hunter and Kevin Beattie, they hated it and would disappear out of sight. They would stroll in long after the rest of us and I even recall one occasion where we were in stitches as a milk float drove in and they jumped off the back of it. I was amazed at how easy the training was at Liverpool – Big Al and Beat would have loved it!

My arrival coincided with Liverpool's preparations for the Milk Cup Final clash with Everton at Wembley. I actually trained at Portman Road for the rest of the week and then travelled down to London to watch the game on the Saturday. When it ended 0-0 after extra time it meant our midweek scheduled league game three days later against Norwich at Anfield, in which I was hoping to make my debut, was postponed in favour of a replay at Maine Road when a Graeme Souness goal was enough to earn victory for the Reds. I couldn't play in either game against Everton because I was cup-tied, having represented Ipswich in the same competition earlier in the season. I had a fair bit of success, too, with three goals in the first leg of our second round tie against Blackburn, another in the return at Ewood Park and then two in our third round home win over QPR. That increased my all-time tally in the League Cup under its various guises to 12 and made me the highest Ipswich scorer in the history of the competition. Unfortunately, in round four we lost 1-0 at home to Norwich – just four days after I netted in our 1-1 league draw with Liverpool at Portman Road. At that point of the season I had scored 11 goals in 18 games, not a bad return and the perfect answer to those people who felt the fact that I was on the transfer list was affecting my form, although it is only fair to point out that I didn't scored again in my next 20 appearances before joining Liverpool, so maybe my critics had a point after all. There was no escaping the irony of joining Liverpool with a reputation as a high-scoring midfield player but after one of the leanest spells of my senior career.

With the Milk Cup in the bag, Liverpool resumed their Championship challenge with a visit to Watford, who had been runners-up to them the previous season. Joe Fagan announced to the press that I would make my debut at Vicarage Road so I made arrangements for Toula and her father to attend the game. Joe even stated that I would replace Craig Johnston and claimed it was the first really tough decision he had been required to make since taking the job. In his programme notes for my home debut against West Ham the following week, Joe said that Craig accepted his decision "with dignity" but I'm afraid that isn't how I remember it. Craig had collected a Milk Cup winner's medal and was none too pleased at being dropped. He actually took out his frustration by refusing to speak to me and that was the case for some weeks before we eventually became quite close. His daughter, Chelsea, attended the same pre-school playgroup as my son, Andrew, and we lived in the same area. It wasn't until 1.45pm at Watford that Joe confirmed the starting line-up and I was handed the number 10 shirt. Given a choice I'd have plumped for number seven, which I had worn at Ipswich, but I could hardly expect to prise that one away from Kenny Dalglish, who had inherited it from Kevin Keegan.

I noticed a big difference between the side I joined and the one I left behind. Liverpool were sharper in all departments, a split second quicker to react, and it was obvious from the word go. Joe Fagan's team talk beforehand could hardly have been briefer or more straightforward. He told me to pass and move, and he must have repeated himself half a dozen times. He said I would get plenty of scoring chances if I got myself into the box. I could not have wished for a better debut as I scored our first goal in a 2-0 win. It was made for me by Kenny and he later did the same for Ian Rush to score our second. The papers made a big thing of the fact that it was my first goal since I scored for Ipswich against Liverpool four months earlier but I knew that if I couldn't bag a few with my new club I'd be as well packing it in. Liverpool played it simply but it was extremely effective. It was about making the ball do the work. Players were constantly on the move, exploiting space, and I quickly learned that you had to be on your toes all the time. If you weren't doing the business you would be out of the side, with several international players waiting in the wings for their chance to show what they could do in your place.

I was on a high after the game at Watford and travelled back to Ipswich with Toula and my father-in-law. The Sunday papers made great reading and Joe Fagan was quoted as saying: "Nobody's fit when they join a new club. The strain of the move takes it out of them. So he was a yard short, as we expected, but I'm pleased with him." Joe had also said some nice things once my move to Anfield was finalised. The reporters lapped it up as he told them: "I'm glad to get the pest after the way he has played against us in the past. I don't know how many goals he scored against us but we thought we would sign him to put him on our side. I think he will be an asset to the club because he's one of the few players who has the ability to score regularly. Goals from midfield was one of the areas we needed to improve and John knows when to move into areas to score. We've tried to legislate for him when we've played Ipswich in the past, but he still caused us problems. We are always trying to get quality players. There are not many around – but he is one."

Scoring on my debut was the best thing that could have happened to me. I had not found the net in 20 games for Ipswich and the last thing I needed was to go on a similar run with Liverpool. To break my duck at the very first opportunity was a mixture of joy and relief. It had been a difficult few months after I decided to ask for a move. I stuck it out but there were times when I felt really low. I occasionally wondered if it might be best to come off the transfer list and instead see out my Ipswich contract, which ran through to end of the following season, and then enjoy the testimonial to which I was entitled. In the end, however, I opted to remain on the list and landing a move to Liverpool convinced me I had made the right decision. It was still a wrench to leave Ipswich, though, and my delight at joining Liverpool was definitely tempered with regret at leaving a club that had been such a major part of my life for 11 years. At the same time, since they signed me for nothing and I had given them 11 good years, they were being handsomely rewarded at a time when their financial situation was reportedly at an all-time low.

Another reason why I wanted a fresh start was that I had been given the cold shoulder by Scotland boss Jock Stein, who stuck firmly to his policy of not selecting any players who were transfer-listed or in any sort of dispute with their clubs. I had won 26 caps by the time I moved to Anfield and only managed to add three more, although I was back almost straight away when I was not only named in the squad for both the Hampden clash with England and the trip to France, but played the full 90 minutes on each occasion. Jock Stein commented at the time: "I've seen Wark three times since he joined Liverpool and there is a new spring in his step." It was clear that the transfer had benefited me. Apart from rescuing my international career, it also earned me a League Championship medal. I only appeared in nine games, but the club successfully applied for me to be awarded a medal, which sits nicely alongside those I collected for winning the FA Cup and UEFA Cup with Ipswich.

Of more pressing concern was that fact that Liverpool were due to face Ipswich at Anfield just a few weeks later and while I knew where my priorities lay I worried frantically that I might help to send them down, which was the last thing I wanted to see happen. On the Monday before we faced them I actually watched Ipswich beat Norwich at Portman Road, making it seven points from their last three games, and then went out for a bite to eat with some of the lads. It was almost surreal to be lining up against them because I had only ever known Ipswich until moving to Liverpool. I had been ineligible for a European Cup-tie – I hadn't signed in time to beat the UEFA deadline – but I was recalled for the suspended Graeme Souness and we fought out a 2-2 draw. I dummied a Sammy Lee cross for Ian Rush to score and Gatesy was on target twice for my old mates, one of his goals an absolute scorcher of a shot to beat Bruce Grobbelaar. Ipswich went on to win at Manchester United, whose title challenge had faded, and avoiding defeat in their last seven games – five wins and two draws – saw them survive in the top flight, eventually finishing 12th in the table, which had probably been beyond their wildest dreams just a few weeks earlier.

TOP OF THE KOP

DURING THE SUMMER OF 1984 Liverpool suffered a huge, but not entirely unexpected, blow when they lost the services of captain Graeme Souness, who signed for Italian club Sampdoria, and I was given the job of replacing him. I even heard that Graeme had recommended me a few months earlier when I was signed from Ipswich. Maybe I wasn't quite as aggressive as Graeme, nor did I possess his passing ability, but I was no slouch in either department. I also had other qualities, mainly my ability to contribute goals from the middle of the park, while I felt I was better than my fellow Scot when it came to heading the ball. I did so well in the 1984-85 season that I even outscored Ian Rush with my tally of 27. It was reminiscent of four years earlier when I bagged 36 for Ipswich. My haul included both the goals as we defeated Ipswich 2-0 at Anfield, one a shot and the other a header from a delicate chip into the area by Kenny Dalglish. Out of respect for Ipswich I kept the celebrations very brief.

Ironically, though, it was when Joe Fagan decided to play me a bit deeper, sitting back and coming through in the way I had done so effectively at Ipswich, that I rewarded him with the first of my three hat-tricks for Liverpool. It came in the second leg of a European Cup-tie at Anfield against the Polish side Lech Poznan. Liverpool were European champions and the first leg a fortnight earlier signalled the start of their defence of the famous trophy. We won that game 1-0 thanks to my goal midway through the second half – Kenny was the architect with a tremendous ball to the far post – but I probably should have netted two, and perhaps even three goals based on the number of chances that came my way. The second leg was like a dream as we put the Poles to the sword. I scored our first two goals in the 13th and 18th minutes, then after Paul Walsh, another Anfield new boy, added a third I had to wait until three minutes from the end to complete my hat-trick, heading in from Walshy's excellent cross after he spotted my run to the back post. My other hat-tricks came in a 5-0 league win over West Bromwich Albion at The Hawthorns and a 7-0 trouncing of York in an FA Cup fifth round replay after they held us to a 1-1 draw at their place.

The change of role certainly agreed with me. The four goals I scored over two games against Lech Poznan took my all-time European tally for Ipswich and Liverpool to 22 from 27 games, a pretty good strike rate for a midfielder, and a lot of complimentary comments were made about me as I appeared to offer a solution to the team's biggest problem at the time, namely a lack of goals from midfield. By the end of the season I shared the runners-up spot in the European Cup goalscoring chart. While Michel Platini of eventual winners Juventus netted seven, the same number as Gothenburg's Torbjorn Nilsson, I was on five alongside my Anfield colleague Ian Rush and another Juventus player, Italy's World Cup winning striker Paolo Rossi. Disappointingly, however, after the treble-winning achievement of the 1983-84 season, of which I only caught the tail end, one year on we didn't win a single thing. Most frustratingly, Everton emerged under Howard Kendall's management to become the champions, with us 13 points back in second place. Suddenly, from winning the League Championship, League Cup and European Cup the previous season, we were only second-best in England. In fact, we were not even the best team on Merseyside.

My time with Liverpool was certainly eventful, as much for what happened off the pitch as on it. We lived in a nice neighbourhood but we were burgled twice and I also had my car nicked twice. Our home was in College Court, Sandfield Park, West Derby, and it was a popular area with a number of the players, including Graeme Souness, Sammy Lee, Craig Johnston and Bruce Grobbelaar. It wasn't too far from our Melwood training ground, but it was actually closer to Everton's training HQ at Bellfield. When I first joined the club I couldn't drive and I would scrounge a lift from any of my colleagues, who were all very obliging. I often got dropped off near my house and close to a bus stop, where I regularly saw a lad who was clearly one of the kids at Everton. It was only years later, when we became team-mates in my third spell at Ipswich, that I discovered he was called Ian Marshall.

I had survived without a driving licence in Ipswich but I started to take lessons fairly soon after arriving on Merseyside and I was delighted to pass my test first time, although I have a confession to make. I must have had close on 30 driving lessons but my instructor was still of the opinion that I wasn't yet ready to take my test. You will have gathered I was no natural behind the wheel but the test was booked and I could see no point in not taking it, even if my instructor's lack of faith meant I was hardly full of confidence on the day. When I met the female examiner the first thing she said was that she was a Liverpool supporter. This, I decided, was my chance. "If you ever want a couple of tickets," I told her, "just give me a call." Only she would be able to state whether or not the availability of much sought-after seats at Anfield had a bearing on her decision to pass me, but let's just say that both me and my instructor were very pleasantly surprised at the outcome.

I felt my emergency stop and the routine of reversing round a corner were less than convincing. I even stalled twice, but I wasn't going to argue with the expert. When she called on a few occasions to ask for tickets I was only too happy to supply them. But to this day, I have to confess, I'm not confident when called upon to use reverse gear.

Stupidly, though, I had only been on the road about six months when I was promptly off it again for two years. I am ashamed to say I was caught for drink driving. It was my 28th birthday and I foolishly got behind the wheel after a session with some of my Anfield team-mates. We had gone straight to the pub after training and it was after 10pm when I left to go home. I had driven for more than 10 minutes and was within 100 yards of my front door when I was pulled over and failed the breathalyser. I was arrested, taken to the police station and a second test showed I was three times over the limit. I spent the night in the cells and in the morning the police said I was allowed a phone call, so I rang Kenny Dalglish to tell him what had happened. He was not amused but said he would speak to the club's solicitor. There was nothing to do, of course, but take the punishment. I was spared the embarrassment of having to appear in person when the case came to court, and once a verdict had been reached my solicitor called me. "Do you want the good news or the bad news?" he asked. Since it was an open and shut case, I wondered what the good news could possibly be and when I asked him the solicitor replied: "It won't be in the papers." I then asked for the bad news and he told me I had been banned for two years. I couldn't resist telling him: "I'd have swapped my name in the papers for a one-year ban." In all seriousness, though, it was a very valuable lesson learned. It makes me feel no less guilty that I was one of about eight Liverpool players who failed breath tests that year. I coped with being off the road by utilising the services of my mate Billy Williams – I called him Mr Fix-It – who was given the keys to my car and became my chauffeur.

The ban was over by the time I returned to Ipswich in January 1988. I recall meeting people who were flabbergasted that I was driving. They were only too aware that I had shown neither the inclination nor the ability when they had known me years earlier, and they admitted they never expected to see me behind the wheel. I was even given a sponsored car, a Mini Metro, during my first spell at Ipswich and before the official hand-over on the main pitch, prior to a home game, I whispered to the garage representative, "Did you know I can't drive?" It was too late to do anything about it then, but to be fair to the company who supplied it they were as good as gold. The car had my name plastered all over it, which gave them the advertising plug they wanted, and it seemed to matter little that my wife, rather than me, would be driving it.

The first time I had my car stolen in Liverpool it was from the drive in front of the house and, would you believe, I was at home at the time. Toula was bathing

Andrew and I was in the kitchen, totally oblivious to the fact that someone was in the process of hot-wiring my car and making off. The first I knew about it was when there was a knock at the door and I answered to find two policemen standing there. One asked if I owned a red BMW and I said I did. I took a step outside and was going to point to it when all I could see was the space where I had parked it earlier. The policeman explained that it had been written off as a result of crashing into a tree three miles away and four young lads, one of whom was wearing an Everton top, were seen running off. I did what the policemen could never have expected me to do and burst out laughing. A strange reaction, I admit, but since we lived in a well lit cul-de-sac of just four houses I almost admired their nerve in carrying out what I thought was a pretty daring raid. Thankfully, when we were burgled we didn't lose anything of sentimental value and the house wasn't turned upside down. Televisions, videos and stereos can be replaced. But each time it happened I was away with the team, so the spate of thefts from players' houses in recent years, when they have been on Champions League duty abroad, is not an entirely new trend.

On the other occasion my car was stolen – by this time I was driving a sporty, two-seater BMW – I went to Sainsbury's and emerged with a trolley full of shopping. At first I thought I had simply forgotten where I had parked, but after searching high and low it dawned on me that the car had been taken. I reported it to the police, called a taxi to take me and the shopping home, and my car and I were never reunited. Before I passed my test, I was given a sponsored car. It was an Audi 90 and when Toula wasn't driving it I let my friend Billy have it on the proviso that he was available to take me from A to B when required. Billy, a convivial, jack-the-lad character, had known Liverpool players for years, going back to the days of Jimmy Case and Ray Kennedy. We got along like a house on fire and nothing was too much trouble for him. He had two mates, Alfie and Kenny, who were also pals of mine. Alfie would supply fish to both Graeme Souness and I, while Kenny would do my gardening and take my dog, Bodie, for walks. Payment was easy and no money changed hands. It was amazing how valuable a currency two tickets for a home game proved to be. Billy was rarely without a wad of notes. I was the professional footballer earning a top salary, but Billy always put me in the shade when it came to the amount of cash he had in his pocket. Billy used to claim that if he couldn't get hold of something I wanted, he invariably knew someone who could, and he proved it more than once.

I had only envisaged staying at the St George's Hotel for a few weeks but because we had trouble selling our house in Badger's Bank, Ipswich, it was nine months later that I eventually moved out. If you said I was in no hurry to exit the hotel I wouldn't argue. Appropriately enough, I occupied the Anfield Suite and very nice it was too. Toula would return to Ipswich with Andrew at regular intervals to spend time with her parents and her sister, but I was never lonely. Other new signings, Jan Molby and Paul Walsh, were also staying at the same hotel but their accommodation was pretty basic by comparison. They were both single and it was because I had my wife and baby son staying with me – well, most of the time – that saw me upgraded to the Anfield Suite. Being single they were always keen to have a night out and in the periods when I was on my own in the hotel I didn't need a lot of persuading to join them. Jan may be Danish but he mastered Scouse in no time at all and definitely long before he could speak English. He had trouble keeping his weight down and there's a classic story about when Graeme Souness was the manager at Anfield and Jan was nearing the end of his time there. Graeme decided to weigh all the players when they reported back for pre-season training and before it was Jan's turn Graeme asked him how much he weighed. "Fifteen stone," said Jan confidently, just a few seconds before stepping on to the scales a few feet away. They showed his true weight to be 17 stone and Graeme laughed: "I've never known anyone to put on weight like you. You've added two stone just walking over here!"

In all seriousness, however, Jan was a superb player. He could pass the ball up to 70 yards with either foot and in that sense covered for the absence of Graeme Souness. We became firm friends in our time together at Anfield and we still speak regularly.

I had heard tales of Bill Shankly labelling injured players as malingerers during his time in charge and nothing much had changed by the time I checked in at Anfield. If you were crocked you were blanked. When we were taking part in an obstacle course one day I damaged the Achilles tendon on my left foot and told Ronnie Moran I thought it was serious. He suggested that I should visit the specialist but also said I should take my training kit with me so that I could return in the afternoon. I booked a taxi to take me to the Accident and Emergency department, where I joined the queue with all the other patients. I had changed into my civvies but, bearing in mind what Ronnie had said, I made sure I had my training kit under my arm. I was in for a shock when the doctor told me it was a good job I hadn't delayed my visit. The doctor explained that the tendon was very close to splitting and, had that happened, I would have been ruled out for several months. A snapped Achilles is still regarded as one of the worst injuries a player can suffer. I was put in plaster, handed a pair of crutches and sent on my way. When I arrived back at Melwood I came across Ronnie and upon seeing me encased in plaster, and walking only with the aid of crutches, he shrugged and said: "Oh, so you were injured after all, were you?"

Once I returned to action after recovering from the Achilles injury I was quickly ruled out again, this time with a broken right ankle. It happened during a game when my studs caught in the turf and as I went to move one way I felt it give way. I came off straight away but while it was extremely sore I decided to go ahead with a night out with friends. It wasn't until the Monday, by which time the pain was intense, that I decided it would be best if I sought medical advice. You can imagine my utter amazement at being told it was broken, as I had been walking on it over the weekend. That was my season finished. Apart from my torn hamstring in 1977, and the Achilles and broken ankle in the 1985-86 season, I have been lucky with injuries. But I missed out when Liverpool won the League Championship and FA Cup double in 1986. At Wembley they recovered from Gary Lineker's opening goal for Everton to triumph 3-1 and it was the first final to feature a team without any English footballers. Although Mark Lawrenson was born in Preston he played for the Republic of Ireland. Liverpool's only other English-born player was substitute Steve McMahon.

Demand for FA Cup Final tickets always exceeded the Wembley crowd limit of 100,000 and although injury prevented me from taking part I was still entitled to a full ticket allocation. Eight years earlier it was an entirely new situation for Ipswich players but Liverpool were past masters in the art of ticket distribution and I recall how a group of us – minus a gun thank goodness – went to a hotel to meet a ticket tout and swap our tickets for his cash. The tout had all his money spread over the bed in his room. I remember one of the lads, who said he only needed two tickets for his family, came out of there with £15,000 in notes. The all-Merseyside final created huge demand and led to astronomical prices, which was reflected in the money we received for our tickets. I'd have willingly handed it all back if I could have played in the game but I was forced to settle for a seat on the bench. I recall two players from each club were injured and on crutches, and once the teams had emerged from the tunnel we had to make our way round the track to the half-way point. Encouraged by the crowd in that area of the ground, all four of us took part in a 'race' to see who could reach their seat first. There are pictures of the victorious squad and I'm on the end with my crutches showing. I could at least attribute my absence from the side to injury, but what I wasn't to know at the time was that my best days at Liverpool were already behind me.

You might think that a club like Liverpool would have had the finest treatment room that money could buy – I know I did – but nothing could have been further from the truth. It could hardly have been more basic and the equipment was antiquated with some of it even held together with sticking plaster. I remember Paul Walsh suffering an ankle injury that dragged on for months with very little improvement and the manager and his staff were not slow in making their frustration clear to him. Day after day they gave him ultrasound treatment, rubbing gel over the affected area and then massaging with the handset, but there was no response and they were all scratching their heads at Walshy's failure to respond. Only when a maintenance guy turned up to service the equipment did they learn the truth, that the machine had been out of order all along.

It looks more like a skating rink but this is where Ipswich played the second leg of our UEFA Cup third round tie against Polish side Widzew Lodz. We lost 1-0 but held a 5-0 lead from the first game, in which I scored a hat-trick.

Spot-on! This is me scoring Ipswich's second goal from the spot as we beat St Etienne 3-1 in the second leg of the UEFA Cup quarter-final at Portman Road.

Action from the first leg of the tie in France, which we won 4-1, as I hit the deck surrounded by St Etienne players.

(Left) I am almost revealing a bit too much as I celebrate with goalscorer Terry Butcher after Ipswich's 1-0 defeat of Cologne in the second leg of our UEFA Cup semi-final in Germany.

(Below) My Ipswich team-mate, Arnold Muhren, looks on as I let fly with a shot during the second leg of the 1981 UEFA Cup Final against AZ Alkmaar in Amsterdam.

My goal against AZ Alkmaar in the second leg of the UEFA Cup Final, number 36 for the season, makes it 2-2 on the night.

Here's the proof that it wasn't alwa
in our 1-0 defeat against Tottenham
divot travelled further than the ball.

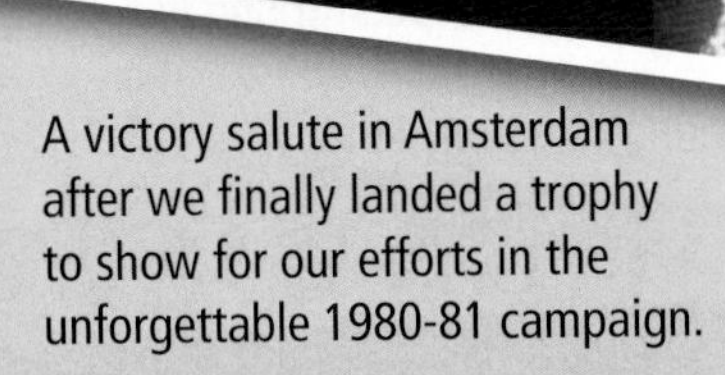

A victory salute in Amsterdam after we finally landed a trophy to show for our efforts in the unforgettable 1980-81 campaign.

That's me outjumping
Lawrenson during Ips
home win over Liverp
Road in October 1982
Steve McCall and Live
Souness are also in th

Me, Paul Mariner and Alan Brazil on the open-top bus ride through Ipswich as we headed for the Town Hall and a civic reception to mark our UEFA Cup win.

Thousands of Ipswich fans fill the Cornhill as me and Paul Mariner show off the UEFA Cup.

That's Andrew trying one of my Scottish international caps for size.

An *Escape to Victory* special. Top left, I am taking a break from filming with Bobby Moore and Mike Summerbee. Top right, that's me with Michael Caine and Sylvester Stallone. Middle left, me and Maurice Roëves. Middle right, me with Mike Summerbee and Pele. Right, a scene from the film as some under-nourished Prisoners of War arrive at the camp.

I mark the occasion of my European a

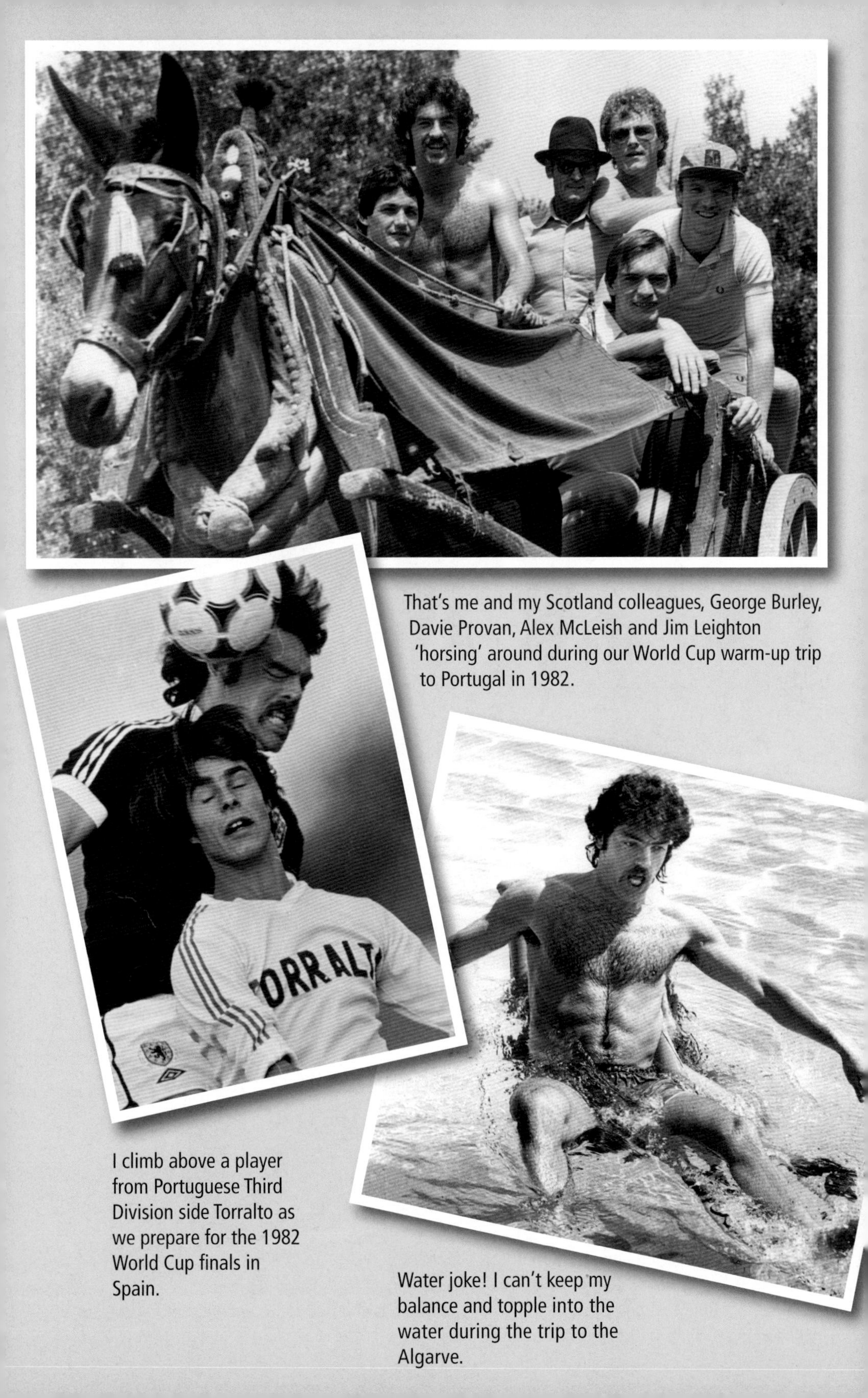

That's me and my Scotland colleagues, George Burley, Davie Provan, Alex McLeish and Jim Leighton 'horsing' around during our World Cup warm-up trip to Portugal in 1982.

I climb above a player from Portuguese Third Division side Torralto as we prepare for the 1982 World Cup finals in Spain.

Water joke! I can't keep my balance and topple into the water during the trip to the Algarve.

Here I am in action for Scotland against New Zealand in the first group game of the World Cup finals in Spain in 1982. I scored twice in our 5-2 win.

The Scotland team line up for the national anthem prior to our 2-2 draw against the Soviet Union in the 1982 World Cup finals that saw us fail to qualify on goal difference. Left to right, Graeme Souness, Alan Rough, Frank Gray, David Narey, Gordon Strachan, John Robertson, Joe Jordan, Steve Archibald, Alan Hansen, me and Willie Miller.

Liverpool's motto back then was to play – and party – well. Some years earlier they had been one of the first clubs to organise a Christmas fancy dress party. I say 'one of' because it had a lot to do with Mark Lawrenson being transferred from Brighton, where the fancy dress idea caught on, and when he mentioned it at Liverpool the lads really went for it. Not only was it a permanent fixture, the aim at each year's event was to try to outdo the previous one. At Ipswich the lads just went round a few of the pubs in town, which was no different to what we did every other week during the season, but Liverpool's event was much more elaborate. It was always held on a Sunday and it was open to all the professional staff.

We were also able to invite three or four mates to join us. Everyone visited a fancy dress shop in the city to pick out their costumes and the party started at lunchtime with a visit to Sammy Lee's wine bar. The evening activity was at Tommy Smith's night club and part of the entertainment comprised every one of the new signings, as well as any young lads who had signed their first pro contracts, climbing onto the stage to sing a song. The food was buffet style and it soon became apparent why. I managed to get through a version of Frank Sinatra's classic My Way and even earned a ripple of applause. But there was no escape for Paul Walsh, who picked a Cockney-type song borrowed from Chas and Dave. He was duly pelted with sandwiches, sausage rolls and other items of food. The party even had its own dedicated photographer in Craig Johnston, who was pretty useful with a camera.

At my first party I plumped for a fat clown costume, only for the decision to rebound on me throughout the day as I struggled to get through just about every door I encountered. Phil Thompson was a very convincing Boy George and when Kenny Dalglish turned up in a Liverpool shirt with a hump in the back, looking like Quasimodo, we were struggling to identify his character. After lots of guessing he said he was Peter Beardsley – and no one laughed louder than Peter. Craig Johnston looked like Fred Astaire from the front but from the back he was more like a dancer from the Folies Bergere, all stockings and suspenders. As you can imagine, the party carried on into the wee small hours and no one had much sleep before reporting for training the next morning when, thankfully, the staff took pity on us. Once we had run twice round the pitch at a leisurely pace we were dismissed to return home and sleep off the effects of the night before. Craig lightened the mood somewhat by turning up in his costume and when he joined us on the run it was definitely the funniest sight I ever saw during my time on Merseyside. That first Christmas party with Liverpool certainly opened my eyes. Kenny wasn't a big boozer but someone spiked his drink and he was in such a bad way that he had to be carried to a taxi to be taken home. I never saw Kenny at another Christmas party because by the time the next one came round he had taken over as manager and the event was off limits.

Joe Fagan, who signed me from Ipswich and was only in charge during my first season at Anfield, appeared to be like a favourite grandfather the way he always seemed to have a smile on his face as he went about his business. Liverpool lost very few games as they won the treble that season so we rarely saw Joe in a bad mood. But he would occasionally show a tough side to his character in order to stamp his authority on the squad and put them in no doubt as to who was the boss. I have to admit I crossed him once but it was not intentional and it only came about because Bruce Grobbelaar tried to pull the wool over his eyes. Bruce rounded up Alan Hansen and I to accompany him to Belfast and attend a couple of supporters' club functions. What we didn't know was that when Bruce had sought permission from Joe it was immediately refused, but our eccentric and stubborn Zimbabwean goalkeeper thought he would go ahead anyway. Bruce assured us everything was taken care of, so after a Saturday home game we headed for the airport and had a bumpy flight to Northern Ireland in a tiny plane. Relieved to land in one piece, Bruce had a car waiting to pick us up and take us to the hotel where we were staying and where the first event was also taking place. What he didn't mention was that our overnight base was to be the Europa, known as the most bombed hotel in the world after numerous attacks by the IRA. Thankfully, we had a couple of bodyguards with us all the time, even when we went to the toilet, and nothing untoward occurred.

On the Sunday we moved to another hotel before we attended the second fans' function close to Shankhill Road, which is a predominantly Protestant area. Bruce's friends provided a car with a driver and a minder, and the venue was nothing more than a glorified tin hut. After a while the supporters were not only singing Liverpool, but also sectarian, songs. When it was time to leave we got into the car to be informed that in order to reach our hotel we would have to pass the Falls Road, which is synonymous with the Catholic community, and as the driver said "I hope we don't get stopped" I saw him reach down by his side and touch a revolver. The trip passed without incident but our plan to catch an early flight back to Liverpool the next morning, and go straight to training, was scuppered by the weather. Belfast Airport was fogbound and our flight cancelled. Bruce rang Joe and both Alan and I listened as he tried to play it down. "You know that trip to Belfast that you refused to give me permission to attend?" he started. "Well, I'm actually in Belfast now and I've got Alan Hansen and John Wark with me." Bruce put the phone down and said: "Joe says it will cost us a week's wages," which it duly did. Never mind that we had ventured into Belfast at the height of the Troubles, from being in profit thanks to the organisers giving us a few bob to attend the events, the fines instead meant we were operating at a loss. I still see a lot of Bruce as we both play for the Liverpool Legends and he remains one of the most extrovert characters I have ever met. During our time at Anfield together he used to go through a pre-match ritual that would drive us mad. There was a light switch on the wall and Bruce would try to switch it off and on by kicking the ball at it. His success rate made it easy to see why he had become a goalkeeper. There are times when I can still hear the constant bang, bang, bang of the ball against the wall. Bruce had another habit – he would go along to the Holiday Inn in Liverpool city centre every Friday night before a home game and tuck into a meal of steak and chips.

But when it came to eating all the wrong things, Steve Nicol was in a league of his own. I roomed with him on away trips for a while and wouldn't have believed what he ate unless I had witnessed it myself. We would join the rest of the lads in the hotel restaurant for dinner but we were not long back in our room when Steve would announce "I'm a bit peckish" and call room service to order a snack, more often than not a club sandwich with all the trimmings, including a portion of chips. Once he had scoffed that lot you would think he would be done for the night. But no, when the hunger pangs returned he would unzip his holdall and delve into his own emergency supplies. He carried chocolate bars, crisps and fizzy drinks, and only after he'd had some of them would he finally be ready to turn in for the night. There were even times when Steve would produce a couple of cans of lager from his bag. That was his way of beating the Liverpool booze ban; the club made sure that when we checked into our hotel players were never given the additional key required to open the fridge in our rooms. That was of little concern to those who fancied a bevvy because they simply supplied their own. Mind you, the same Steve hardly under-achieved. He was one of the fittest guys around and looked as if he could run non-stop for the entire 90 minutes. He won everything there was to win with Liverpool and in 1989 he was even crowned Footballer of the Year, an accolade bestowed by the Football Writers' Association. First awarded in 1948 to none other than Stanley Matthews, the most recent winner was Cristiano Ronaldo, so he's up there with the very best of them.

Liverpool had a weekly Tube of the Week award that would go to the player who said or did the most stupid thing. I played a part in instigating it because I brought a whole new vocabulary with me to Anfield by referring to people I didn't hold in the highest esteem as tubes and numpties. There were times when I almost won it myself and maybe I would have done but for Steve, who collected it most often. I remember one occasion when somebody asked me if I'd had a drink the previous evening. I replied "No" and then, after a pause of a couple of seconds, I added "Just a bottle of wine." That put me in the running. One day in the dressing room a number of players were handed brown envelopes and Steve clocked what was going on. Thinking they contained cash, he decided to seek out the manager and ask why he had not received one. "Think yourself lucky," he was told. The truth was that they were letters from the Inland Revenue detailing how much income tax certain individuals owed. Stevie was also the butt of several practical jokes that some of the senior players played on him. On one occasion, he was travelling with Graeme Souness, Kenny Dalglish and Alan Hansen to join up with the Scotland squad when it started snowing near Gretna. Graeme was driving and pulled over. He asked Stevie to do him a favour and clear the back window. As soon as he was out of the car Graeme drove off. Stevie only had a short sleeve shirt on and ran after the car until Graeme stopped about 100 yards further on. But just as Stevie reached the car Graeme would drive off again and this happened several times before they allowed him to get back into the car to complete the journey.

Stevie is now coach of MLS side New England Revolution and his assistant is none other than my former Ipswich team-mate Paul Mariner. Because of the Ipswich connection, I had a call from Steve to tell me he was thinking about appointing Paul and I couldn't have provided a better reference. My phone often rings and I find myself having a three-way chat with the pair of them in Steve's office. We spend a lot of time taking the piss out of each other – typical footballers, really. Steve had the nickname Chops in his time at Anfield – not, as you might think, because of his odd eating habits but for his Ayrshire accent and the way he pronounced his favourite food, chips. We all liked chips and with no canteen at Anfield we would often send out to the local 'chippy' after training. It seems strange now that he is the Ipswich manager, but one of the apprentices who ran errands for us, and also used to clean my boots, was Jim Magilton. I managed to come up with my very own nickname at Liverpool. We were playing cards one day when instead of saying "Three Jacks" as I produced my hand, a slip of the tongue saw it come out as "Three Jinks." As a result, Alan Hansen quickly christened me and I was known as Jink throughout my time at the club.

At the end of my first full season as a Liverpool player – the 1984-85 campaign – I was to achieve an ambition to play in a European Cup Final. For younger readers, that's how the competition now familiar as the Champions League was known following its inauguration in 1955, all the way through to 1992, when the new format was introduced. There was one major difference in that each country only had one representative, namely the domestic champions, and any player worth his salt wanted to play in the final. Liverpool had a special affinity with the tournament. Not only were they the reigning champions, they had also won it on three earlier occasions. But when I look back on my time in football, and in particular my appearance in what is unquestionably the biggest club game of them all, it is as if I am staring at a blank page in a book. What I had hoped might mark my greatest achievement in club football is instead a nightmare memory of one of the game's very darkest episodes.

It was not my first visit to the Heysel Stadium in Brussels, nor was it any more favourable than when I was there with Scotland in 1979 and again in 1982 for European Championship qualifying games. I had hoped it might have been given a makeover but, once again, it was a huge let-down. I could not help questioning whether it was fit to stage such a prestigious game. Surely the European game's ruling body, UEFA, had got it wrong. Upon disembarking from our bus and entering the dressing rooms I saw no need to alter that view. I had played at some of the top grounds in Europe and this wasn't fit to compare. The rest of the players were similarly unimpressed with the ramshackle surroundings. I even thought to myself 'They could have filmed Escape to Victory here' because they would not have had to alter its appearance one jot in order to go back in time to the Second World War. It was important, however, not to dwell too long on the surroundings and to instead concentrate on the game. It represented Liverpool's only chance to end an otherwise disappointing season with some silverware. Not just any silverware but the most prized club honour of them all. We had won it the previous year and no champion wants to relinquish a title. And if all of that was not sufficient incentive, victory would give Liverpool permanent possession of the famous trophy.

A great deal of the talk beforehand was of the news that our manager, Joe Fagan, would probably be in charge for the last time. There was a report that morning on an English television channel that we were able to receive in our hotel and we knew it was true when we had a team meeting after lunch and the manager said: "After tonight you can call me Joe." Maybe it wasn't such a good idea that the news was reported when it was; on the other hand every single one of us was determined to give the boss the best farewell gift of them all. Our hotel was besieged by groups of fans, which was exactly what we expected. They always seemed to find out where we were staying, so it was normal practice and in no way disruptive because our preparations were over by then and all that remained, or so we thought, was to play the game. For all our determination to retain the trophy, our opponents Juventus were just as single-minded about recording their first such success, which would make them the first club to win all three European competitions. We had also read thousands of words about them having their best-ever team. Their time, they believed, had come. On the short trip to the ground we saw fans of both teams drinking together at local bars, which we welcomed but which gave us entirely the wrong impression about what was to follow.

We were sitting in our fairly cramped dressing room with about 45 minutes to go until kick-off when we heard a loud crashing sound. We had no idea then of what it was, but later on, once we were aware of the terrible tragedy unfolding outside, it was clear that the noise we had heard was a concrete wall collapsing. The first real inkling that something was seriously wrong came when several riot police burst into our dressing room and out again. A few minutes later an official entered and said that due to some crowd trouble the kick-off would be delayed but he was not specific as to how long. We were still relaxed but the mood quickly changed when someone in a UEFA blazer came in and asked Joe to accompany him outside to appeal for calm among the crowd. The next thing we knew the man from UEFA was asking our captain, Phil Neal, to use the PA system and broadcast a message to the fans asking them to behave. When Phil returned to the dressing room the look on his face told us something terrible had happened and he was adamant that we would not be playing. At that point someone put his head round the door and said some supporters had been killed. Within a few minutes he reappeared to tell us the death toll had risen and we saw him several more times as the number of casualties rose.

By this stage it was pandemonium. There seemed to be a constant procession of people coming in and out of the dressing room. Naturally, we sided with Phil and decided not to go ahead with the game, although we sat there in our kit in a state of complete shock not doing anything. Eventually, after what seemed a lengthy wait but was probably no more than a few minutes, we were told the game would go ahead. Phil and some others repeated that they did not want to play but it was explained to us that to postpone the game might spark a full-scale riot and put more lives at risk. It seemed we had no choice and when we eventually emerged from the dressing room it was around the time the game would have been close to finishing had it kicked off as scheduled. All the enthusiasm of two hours or so earlier had drained from each and every one of us. We were about to play the European Cup Final – the dream final as it had been tagged beforehand – but it was played with all the fervour of a pre-season friendly or a testimonial game.

The record books confirm that Juventus won the game 1-0 and the only goal was scored by Michel Platini from the spot after 58 minutes. Their Polish player, Zbigniew Boniek, who was a member of the Widzew Lodz side Ipswich defeated en route to the UEFA Cup triumph four years earlier, was caught by Gary Gillespie as he raced towards goal and the referee awarded a penalty. There was no argument that Gary had brought him down but it was clear the incident had taken place outside the area and television replays later proved the point. We didn't even bother to protest. In the circumstances it didn't seem appropriate. I had one chance to score when Kenny Dalglish set me up and I tried to side-foot the ball into the net, only for their keeper to make a fantastic save. If I am honest, that near miss and the decisive penalty are the only two incidents I can remember of the game itself. Instead I think of the 39 people who lost their lives and I cannot help but wonder if the disaster that occurred could have been avoided had UEFA not selected a stadium clearly not up to the job of hosting a game of such importance. We were on a £6,250-a-man bonus to win that game but the fact that we only came second, and instead pocketed £2,500 each, was of no concern to any of us. Our thoughts were elsewhere.

It was just as terrible an experience for our wives and girlfriends as for us. They were safe and well, but it later transpired when we were reunited afterwards that

Toula and Paul Walsh's girlfriend had been in a toilet when they looked outside and saw bodies being piled on top of each other in a makeshift morgue. Walshy's girlfriend was only a teenager at the time and that grotesque image must have stayed with her for the rest of her life. It was no way for Joe Fagan to bow out, not only from two years in charge of the club but after a lifetime devoted to football. His reason for retiring at the age of 64 was that he was tired and needed a rest; after what he had to endure that would undoubtedly have been true. I shared a room with Kenny Dalglish on that trip and upon hearing that Joe's departure was imminent we speculated as to who might succeed him. Upon arrival back in Liverpool the airport was teeming with journalists and photographers after news had broken of Kenny's appointment as the new manager or, to be precise, player-manager. Only then, once the secret was well and truly out, did he break his silence. "Sorry Warky," he said, "I've known for a few weeks, but I couldn't say anything."

It was in the early stages of my Scotland career that I started to room with Kenny and I have to say it was an education. The very first time it happened I was in for a shock when we returned to the room in the afternoon of an evening game. We had been for lunch and then Jock Stein wanted a meeting with everyone. After that it was free time until the pre-match meal at about 5pm, so I was looking forward to watching a movie on the box. When I got into the room the first thing I did was switch the TV on. But Kenny had other ideas and began to issue his instructions. "Telly off, Warky, and close the curtains. We're going to sleep," he said, and at first I thought he was joking. Not a bit of it. He quickly added: "Take the phone off the hook as well. We don't want to be disturbed." Kenny valued his sleep and, since the room was virtually in darkness, I had little option but to follow his lead. I also roomed with him in my time at Liverpool and by then he was even more into his kip. The lesson served me well, in fairness, and especially later in my career when I needed as much rest as possible between games, so I thank him for that.

There was always a high level of expectancy at Anfield, hardly surprising given their many years at the top, not just of the English game but in Europe. Due to the fact that I suffered the Achilles injury and also broke an ankle, I was unable to make much of a contribution during the 1985-86 campaign, when Kenny made history as the first Liverpool manager to land the League Championship and FA Cup double, an amazing feat to mark his first season in charge. It was a terrific achievement to go straight from playing to become such a successful manager. Kenny changed, for the simple reason that he had to. He was no longer one of the lads, we had to address him as Boss and he had difficult decisions to make regarding a number of ex-colleagues, including yours truly. I was fit and playing regularly in the reserves when an injury to Steve McMahon let me back into the first team. We beat Oxford United and I scored twice, so I was hopeful that I would keep my place the following week. Unfortunately for me, Steve was recalled and I went to see Kenny to discuss my future at the club. He sympathised and understood my concern, but he floored me when he added: "I have picked what I consider to be my strongest team." Clearly, in the manager's eyes, I was a fringe player, someone to plug a gap now and again rather than a regular choice. I had played against Steve at his previous clubs, Everton and Aston Villa. I think he wanted to appear hard but it didn't wash with me.

It was one night at Grimsby that I came to the conclusion that I had to leave Anfield. I was one of eight international players in the Liverpool reserve side and for some reason Grimsby put out most of their first team, which helped to swell the crowd. It was a real mismatch – we beat them by several goals – and I realised my time was up. Phil Thompson, a player when I arrived from Ipswich, had taken over as reserve coach and I had gone to him to see if I could play at the back. My thinking was that if I couldn't hold down a place in midfield, maybe I could force my way in as a central defender, and Phil was happy to oblige when the time was right. I was named as a substitute for the 1987 League Cup Final against Arsenal and although I put in an appearance when I replaced Steve McMahon it was so late that I don't even remember coming into contact with the ball. We lost 2-1, Charlie Nicholas netting twice for the Gunners after Ian Rush had put us ahead. Hard as it was to depart Anfield – Kenny made it clear the decision was down to me and certainly didn't push me out – I knew it was the right thing to do. Many other players have been in the same situation and while some might have hung around to pick up the money, I wanted to play to the extent that I agreed to a substantial drop in wages in order to move on.

I remain a Liverpool fan, just as every player who represented the club probably is, but the club has clearly changed a great deal since my time as a player there. I am just as frustrated as the most loyal supporter that they lag behind Manchester United and have never once captured the Premiership crown. The last time they were English champions was 1990, having won the title 11 times in the preceding 17 years and, quite frankly, I have been embarrassed by some of their displays in recent seasons. I was asked by Radio City to fulfil the role of summariser when they played at Tottenham in the Carling Cup in November 2008 and it was hard to believe I was watching my old club. In the time I was there we, the players, would have died for one another, but I saw no evidence of a similar team spirit at White Hart Lane as they went down 4-2 to a Tottenham side struggling in the league and not even at full strength. Neither Jamie Carragher nor Steven Gerrard was in the Liverpool side and I doubt I would fancy their chances of beating anyone without those two. There has been an influx of foreign talent since Rafael Benitez took charge, but how many of them have made a worthwhile contribution? Take away Xabi Alonso, Martin Skrtel, Daniel Agger, Fernando Torres and Javier Mascherano, and you are talking a massive waste of money. The night I saw them at Tottenham they fielded full-backs Andrea Dossena, who cost £7 million from Udinese, and Philipp Degen, and I wouldn't want either of them for my Sunday team. David Ngog and Leiva Lucas also played against Spurs, and again they were well below what I would expect of Liverpool players. Suffice to say that none of that lot would have been considered good enough in my time at Anfield – in fact they would have struggled to get a game in the reserves.

THE BOOZE BROTHERS

IF THERE HAD BEEN a League Championship for drinking in the 70s and 80s, Ipswich Town would have been among the major contenders. Even in the 90s, by which time there was an influx of foreign players and their more disciplined approach was said to be rubbing off on the Brits, it was still rife. That's not a proud boast, more an admission of guilt, I suppose, that the booze culture of that era did not pass me by. There may have been a misconception among the public that a club's on-the-field success was a sign of players behaving impeccably off it, but from my experience every club was the same and I found absolutely no difference after I was transferred to Liverpool in 1984. They were a match for anyone when it came to knocking it back. At each of my clubs, players broke the rules right, left and centre, and when I reflect on my lifestyle in those days I can hardly believe what I achieved, both individually and as part of some very good teams.

I had never been attracted to the drink, nor even set foot inside a pub, back home in Scotland. But after I headed south to join Ipswich that all changed. In my youth team days, when I was still below the legal age of 18, I am afraid I developed a taste for it. However, my modest consumption then was in line with my modest wage packet, and nowhere near what it became once I was established in the first team. I was not alone, either, and none of the lads needed to have their arms twisted to join in. There was only one notable exception at Ipswich, because Arnold Muhren was a teetotaller and showed absolutely no interest in our favourite extracurricular activity. We respected that and thought nothing less of him for it. Arnold was an extremely valuable player and a model professional, something that I'm afraid few of the rest of us could claim.

When I was still a teenager and playing regularly in the Ipswich first team there were very few days when I didn't drink. Typically, if we were at home on a Saturday, I would start as soon as possible after the final whistle. We had a lounge at Portman Road, which was also open to friends and visiting players, but we often bypassed that and went straight to the pub. The Blooming Fuchsia in Foxhall Road, Ipswich, was one of our favourite haunts. It was close to where a lot of players had been in digs in their youth team days and not too far out of town. The landlord, Jack, and his wife Jean, used to accommodate us in a lounge at the back and there were times when supporters would come into the front lounge, spot us and do a double take. More than once we were asked: "How come you got here before us?" To borrow a well-worn football saying, I think we wanted it more than they did. The next landlord at the Fuchsia was Joe, a fellow Scot and Celtic supporter, and that made for some good banter between us.

By about 8pm we would often meet up with wives and girlfriends, although not all the time, and move into the town centre. We would go to different bars and inevitably end up in a nightclub. Ipswich wasn't the liveliest spot back then and there wasn't a great deal of choice. It tended to be a club called Tracy's in our younger days and then we frequented the First Floor Club, which had an older clientele. It was about as far removed from a trendy West End nightspot as you could possibly imagine. It hosted afternoon bingo sessions but beggars couldn't be choosers. We were welcomed with open arms and had no need to either queue or pay, because the managers and owners knew the one thing we weren't short of was disposable income. It would be the early hours of Sunday morning before I got home and I would have consumed goodness knows how many pints of lager. I was never counting but it would easily have been into double figures and sometimes as many as 20. What I found was that the more I drank, the more my capacity increased and that meant I was caught in a vicious circle.

A popular Sunday routine was to go out for lunch and because I lived in Badger's Bank, almost next door to the Belstead Brook Hotel, and knew owner James Hatfield, it was the perfect venue. We would be joined by other players and their partners. Russell Osman, Terry Butcher, Eric Gates, Alan Brazil and Kevin O'Callaghan all lived nearby and needed little encouragement. Paul Mariner was a little bit out of the way at Upper Layham but he wasn't going to let that stop him, although in fairness to him he didn't drink as much as we did on those occasions because he had to drive home. We may have turned up for lunch but it was usually tea time before we departed. We still weren't finished, though, because I would pop out again in the evening and although I would tell my wife I was going out for 'a drink' that was never the case and I would sink as many as half a dozen pints before returning home after 10pm.

We would be in for training on Monday and our thinking was that we would sweat the alcohol out of our bodies – only to replace it with more in the afternoon. Sessions were not necessarily planned, but often off the cuff in as much as someone would ask "Who fancies a drink?" and we'd be off again. Tuesday was a day when we did a lot of running and the players hated it. As soon as that finished we were demob happy – Wednesday was more often than not a day off – so we weren't in again until Thursday, and with the Saturday fixture looming up the training sessions became less demanding to avoid the risk of injuries. We would call into the Sporting Farmer, the pub nearest the ground, for starters. Its main attraction, apart from its location, was that it had both a pool table and a juke box. After a few there we would wander into town and move from one bar to another. As a non-driver, I always booked a cab to get me home, but some of the lads risked their licences by driving. In Clive Woods' case, he had to travel up the A140 to Newton Flotman, just a few miles short of Norwich. There were no speed cameras around at the time, but there is no way he would have survived a breathalyser.

The Tuesday session was usually pretty heavy, for the simple reason that there was no training the next day, but rather than use the time to recover and relax we saw it as the perfect excuse to drink virtually all day. The horse racing fraternity might head for Newmarket, either to celebrate with champagne if they backed a winner, or to drown their sorrows if they were parted from their cash. There were still enough of us left behind to have 'a spot of lunch' which was our way of inviting each other to an extended drinking session that often didn't end until closing time. With Thursday night being pretty lively in Ipswich – at least at certain pubs – we would be out again for more of the same. It didn't matter if we were playing at home or away on the Saturday, we often still abused the club rule of not drinking on a Friday night. Put it this way, we may not have gone overboard but it was never quite a total abstention.

More often than not, because of the distance involved, away games involved an overnight stop and that required a bit of forward planning on our part. We wanted to be sure we had the supplies for the coach journey home, so we took them with us. I would put half a dozen cans of lager in my bag and PM would have a couple of bottles of wine in his. There were even times when we couldn't wait and would open them in the hotel room on the Friday night. PM said it helped him to sleep and it seemed to work for me as well. In my time at Liverpool, we would have a visit from Ronnie Moran and Roy Evans. "Anyone want a sleeping tablet," they would say, while at the same time having a nose around to make sure we weren't infringing the Friday night rule. There were no such checks by either Bobby Robson or any of his staff at Ipswich, but I am convinced they must have known about our drinking habits. However, if they did, they were inclined to turn a blind eye. I suppose the bottom line at any football club is the results and we didn't often let the manager down in that department.

The angriest I ever saw Bobby Robson was on the bus going home after we had suffered a defeat that he felt could have been avoided. Sometimes, not very often, we just had to admit that we had been second best on the day and had lost to a better side. But there weren't many sides better than us and if we had taken a beating from an outfit below us in the table, for example, it would be hard for the manager to accept without reacting. The players' attitude, to be fair, was 'We can't do anything about it now, let's move on'. But the manager would play it over and over again in his mind, trying to figure out if it was something he had done wrong. Had he picked the wrong team or opted for the wrong tactics? Or was it perhaps more a case of players not doing their jobs, generally under-performing and letting the side down? As he was musing, if he heard laughter from the back section of the bus it would wind him up until his patience snapped and he barged through the dividing door to have words. He would find us playing cards and drinking, with the stereo blaring, and after a few sharp words he would return to the sedate atmosphere of the front section. That was where Arnold parked himself for every journey. He was the only player alongside the manager, coach, physio, directors and other club officials. Fellow countryman Frans Thijssen, though, was one of us, in that he loved his drink and was a mean snooker player. We called him Sam because we felt he looked like Sam McCloud, as played by Dennis Weaver in the popular American television series McCloud, which was on our screens at the time. He and Arnold were pals, and their families were close – they were neighbours in the Rushmere area of Ipswich – but they were worlds apart when it came to boozing.

George Burley liked a drink, too, but he wasn't one of the hard core. George would often become a bit aggressive if he had one too many. I was the opposite and would just get silly. As for skipper Mick Mills and Allan Hunter, they were a bit older and would be a bit choosier about when they enjoyed a drink. Steve McCall, who had a big part to play in the 1980-81 season after George was injured in January and missed the rest of the campaign, was another more casual drinker. For me, Russell, Terry and PM it became a way of life.

You must surely be thinking by now 'What a bunch of piss-heads' and you would be right. Apart from the booze we took on board the bus for the journey home from away games, we would also stop en route at a hotel for dinner, and the manager would tell us: "Have a drink in the bar but don't overdo it." Then it was back on to the bus for more drink. When we pulled into Portman Road and the back door opened, there was an avalanche of dozens of cans and bottles, and it was left to Trevor Kirton, who doubled as driver and kit man, to clear up the mess. Meanwhile, we were off to one of the nightclubs for more drink and so the weekly cycle continued. It became the norm to ring home from the hotel where we stopped off for dinner – no mobiles back then – and make up some excuse for our estimated time of arrival being put back, so buying us more drinking time at the end of the night.

The heaviest – and by far the most expensive – drinking session in which I ever indulged came after the Professional Footballers' Association Awards Dinner at the London Hilton in 1981. We were regulars at the annual bash and the club looked after us really well by booking a room for everyone who attended, but they exceeded their generosity on that occasion. Or rather one of the directors, John Cobbold, who had stepped down in 1977 to allow his brother, Patrick, to take over as chairman, did. We started that day at 12 noon when we left Ipswich with a carry-out on board the bus and by the time we reached London we had run dry. Russell Osman knew the manager of a hotel in Mayfair, so we headed over there in the afternoon and had one cocktail after another until we had worked our way through the card. There was barely time to get back to the Hilton and put on our dinner suits before we had to be taking our seats in a huge function suite that must have sat about 600 people, mainly footballers of course. To be blunt, most of us were pissed as the event kicked off.

We had been told that the main award, the PFA Player of the Year, had been won by an Ipswich player. Three of us were among the six nominees and when they announced that PM had finished third in the voting, clearly the top prize was going to either Frans Thijssen or me. When Sam was named as runner-up I had a few seconds to compose myself before my name was announced. As I made my way to the stage most of the Ipswich party were standing on their chairs shouting and applauding. I received the magnificent trophy from Sir Stanley Rous and although it was football's Oscars I had not bothered to write a 'just in case' speech. I kept it very brief, thanking my colleagues for making it easy for me to win it, praising Bobby Robson and the coaching staff for their assistance, and said it was a pity that my father, who had died the previous year, wasn't alive to see me now because he would have been a very proud man. I somehow managed to avoid slurring my words, which was just as well with millions of television viewers looking in, but had I not been half-cut I probably would have done, if you follow my warped logic.

Because PM and I were sharing a room we invited people to our private party and there must have been about 30 people there. I rang room service and ordered so much drink that when the guy arrived with it all on a trolley he looked as if he had just emerged from the cash and carry. You name it, we had it. Apart from the other Ipswich players, we were joined by my Scotland colleagues John Robertson, Asa Hartford and Kenny Burns. There is a strict black tie dress code but although Robbo conformed he still looked like a tramp. He's one of these blokes that could be kitted out from head to toe by Armani and still look scruffy. His bow tie was hanging loose and the top two buttons of his dress shirt were undone, plus he was also smoking as he nattered away. Suddenly, I noticed he had dropped his cigarette down the inside of his shirt. Robbo took a few seconds to catch on, but as smoke began to puff out the top of his shirt he started jumping up and down, first having to locate the cigarette before he could put it out.

Every drink was consumed before PM and I finally flopped into bed at 5am and the next thing I knew he was waking me up to go downstairs before they stopped serving breakfast. I wanted to turn over and go back to sleep but instead I accompanied him to the restaurant and while he scoffed a full English, I couldn't face it and made do with some tea and toast. When we had finished we made for reception to pay the bill and while they retrieved it I asked him how much cash he had on him. "Seven pound fifty," he replied. "Well," I said, "I think we're in trouble because I've only got a fiver." The receptionist put the bill in front of us and we saw that it was £510. At that precise moment, as we both had our heads in our hands wondering what to do, Mr John walked past. "Anything wrong, boys?" he asked. When we explained our dilemma he just smiled and said: "Leave it to me." As we thanked him and walked off he called after us to add: "Must have been one hell of a party – why wasn't I invited?"

Later that day, once we were back in Ipswich, PM gave me a lift home. I can't remember what type of car he had – a something cabriolet – but as we came along Belstead Road and turned into Badger's Bank we had the roof down and I was standing up with the PFA Player of the Year trophy above my head and he was beeping the horn non-stop. It was something worth celebrating but a lot of neighbours probably didn't have a clue what was happening. It's when I look down the list of players to have won the award that I realise its significance. Liverpool and England star Steven Gerrard was the 2006 winner and I met him soon after he had been crowned. I was in Liverpool for a game at Anfield in support of the Marina Dalglish Appeal. Kenny's wife was diagnosed with breast cancer in 2003 and after she succeeded in beating it they pledged to do all they could to raise money and help find a cure. There was a reception after the game and I went to the bar around the same time as Steven. I congratulated him on winning the PFA award. "I won it in 1981," I told him. He replied: "You must have had a good season." When I told him I'd scored 36 goals from midfield he said: "Oh my God!" Then he promptly ordered a bottle of champagne and presented it to me. It was a terrific gesture and I took it back to my table, where Bruce Grobbelaar, Alan Hansen and Bob Bolder helped me to drink it.

In my time with Liverpool I cannot deny that I also drank to excess. One incident that immediately springs to mind actually made it into John Aldridge's autobiography because he was so impressed by my powers of recovery. I was in Sammy Lee's wine bar, Rumours, one Sunday – I was out 'for lunch' but by this time it was around 5pm – when Aldo called and invited me over to his dad's birthday party, which was taking place in a social club close to where he lived. Every inch a Scouser, it wasn't until the beginning of 1987 that Aldo joined Liverpool from Oxford United and he remained as down to earth as he had been as a supporter on the Kop many years earlier. If I remember correctly, Paul Walsh was with me and we decided to pay Aldo, his old man and the rest of the revellers a visit. The party was going with a real swing when we got there and I hit it off with Aldo's dad. He could play the spoons, so he entertained a group of us, and the drink was flowing to the extent that I quickly lost all track of the time. It got too late for Aldo, who said his farewells around midnight. Walshy had long since disappeared – after two lagers I put him in a taxi – so I was on my own with Aldo senior and a few others. It wasn't until 2.30am that I departed for home and when I reported for training about seven hours later, Aldo wasn't his usual chirpy self. Both he and Walshy looked hung over, but I was feeling fine and put in a good shift. It wasn't until later, when Aldo still wasn't feeling right, that he learned from his old man what time I had left the social club. At first, I don't think he could believe it, but the longer he spent in my company the more he realised what I was like. Mark Lawrenson referred to me as "our champion beer drinker" in his autobiography published in 1988 and Jan Molby talked about me having "hollow legs" when his life story went to print a few years later. One day when I was visiting the Ipswich training ground, Charlie Woods suggested I should sue over such slurs to my reputation. "I can't do that," I explained, "because they're true!"

My 36-goal feat was also mentioned when I represented Ipswich at the handing over of the UEFA Cup in Manchester ahead of the 2008 final between Zenit St Petersburg and Rangers. I found myself in top-class company at a glittering event at which the trophy was presented back to UEFA by Seville, who had won it in each of the previous two seasons. It took place at the City of Manchester Stadium and I was able to have a quick chat with UEFA president Michel Platini, who was in the St Etienne team beaten by Ipswich at the quarter-final stage in 1981. "Ah, yes, I remember you beat us," said Platini. "No, Michel, we battered you – 4-1 at your place and 3-1 at ours," I said, which made him laugh. Denis Law, one of Scotland's all-time greats and someone I idolised when I was a kid in Glasgow, came up and gave me a hug. They showed clips of Ipswich winning the trophy and Peter Reid, the ex-Everton and England midfielder, and former Sunderland and Manchester City boss, asked how many goals I scored that season. When I said 36 he was clearly impressed and turned to other guests like Phil Neal, Peter Barnes and Garry Owen to tell them: "Warky got 36 goals that season, you know!"

Mention of St Etienne reminds me how we regularly let our hair down on trips abroad. The manager would often allow us a free afternoon the day before a game to go shopping, which was a nice touch. Rather than spend all our time looking for presents to take home, however, we would invariably adjourn to a convenient bar. In St Etienne we found a small, friendly place called the Toby Jug, which was tucked away in a back street and we got so settled that we failed to return to the hotel for 6pm as agreed. We were only 10 minutes late but Bobby Robson was far from pleased as we trooped in. "I can smell booze so you're all fined," he said. Nothing more was said and the next day we turned in one of the best-ever displays by an English club in Europe to win 4-1. We are still waiting for the fine to be deducted from our wages. There was another amusing story that followed an incident in Innsbruck, where some players broke a curfew and went out for a drink the night before the game. Allan Hunter and Paul Mariner were involved and were caught red-handed when Cyril Lea, the first team coach, spotted them in a bar close to the team hotel. What Cyril didn't realise was that Paul Cooper was also there but he legged it back to the hotel and jumped into bed, fully clothed. When Cyril got back he went round all the players' rooms to see if anyone else was out on the town and when he checked on Coop he appeared to be fast asleep so nothing more came of it. Bobby Robson announced that the four players would each be fined £250 and that seemed to be the end of the matter. We managed to get through against Innsbruck and the next day we flew back to Heathrow, where a bus picked us up for the last part of the journey to Ipswich. It brought the house down when Big Al got on the microphone to entertain us as we headed home, especially when he announced: "Is there anyone interested in joining the two-fifty club? If so, please see Bobby Robson for further details." Even Bobby was laughing at that one.

Another European trip that I cannot forget was to Zeist, the headquarters of the Dutch Football Association, where they had excellent training facilities. It was an ideal place for pre-season training and we were not the only English club who went there. It is located near Utrecht and the idea was to train and prepare there for a series of friendly games. It was on our last night that things got out of hand and led to Ipswich being told they were no longer welcome. A group of us went down to a local pub and while some travelled on foot, others borrowed some of the many bikes that were available. By the time we decided to return to the camp we were the worse for wear and both Bobby Robson and Bobby Ferguson were waiting for us. The area was surrounded by a huge wood and while some of us made it back to our beds others decided to hide in the darkness of the woods, making what they thought were passable impressions of owls that would throw the manager and coach off the scent. The next morning, of course, Bobby Robson had worked out exactly what was going on and who was involved, but because we were on our way home he was prepared to overlook the fact that we had stayed out longer than we should have done. We were putting our stuff on the bus when someone from the complex demanded to see the person in charge. The manager went inside with them and later emerged to say he was going to impose a blanket fine on every member of the squad. A room had been completely trashed and although Russell Osman and Terry Butcher owned up to being the culprits, the manager decided we would all share the cost of compensation. The people who ran the complex had threatened to report the matter to the press unless the club paid up in full and I think you will find Ipswich have not been back there since.

To finish on a humorous note, Paul Cooper reminded me recently about his home debut for Ipswich in August 1974. He had been on loan from Birmingham towards the end of the previous season and his first game was in a 3-2 defeat at Leeds. He was then signed permanently in the summer and his first game at Portman Road was against Burnley. About an hour or so before kick-off he wandered up the corridor outside the dressing room and through to the reception area, where he was leaving tickets for family and friends. Mr John was just about to go upstairs to the boardroom and invited Paul to join him for a glass of wine. "I'm playing in an hour," said Paul. "Good," said Mr John, "you've got plenty of time." No one liked his alcoholic refreshment more than Mr John and maybe it isn't so surprising that so many of the players followed suit.

BACK HOME

WHEN THE TIME CAME to leave Liverpool I had to choose between three clubs – Ipswich, Coventry and Watford. The initial approach from Ipswich came via Charlie Woods, who had been my youth coach when I first arrived at Portman Road in 1973. At the time he was assisting manager John Duncan, who had only been in charge for about six months, and it was good to know they wanted me back. Watford were managed by Dave Bassett and I have to confess I wouldn't have minded playing for someone with such proven man-management skills. The trouble is, when I went to Vicarage Road I found it rather depressing and that was what put me off the idea of joining the Hornets. As for Coventry, they were managed by John Sillett and we got along like a house on fire when I visited him at his home, where he had a lot of horses in training. I left after more or less promising him I would sign, but I still hadn't properly explored the possibility of returning to Ipswich at that time and in the end my heart ruled my head. There were family reasons, too, because Toula wasn't happy in Liverpool and was actually spending more and more time back in Suffolk. In fact, we were apart at the time I decided to leave Anfield and although there had been no talk of a divorce at that stage it was clear to both of us that if we were going to make a go of our marriage it would have a far better chance of surviving if we were back living in the Ipswich area. I also sought the advice of my former boss, Bobby Robson. While the Ipswich move seemed to make perfect sense, theirs was actually the lowest of the three financial offers I had received, although Bobby merely endorsed what I was thinking when he told me: "Money isn't everything – go where you will be happiest."

It soon became evident that I was not rejoining the club I had left four years earlier. If things were on the decline when I left to join Liverpool in 1984, they were a lot worse now. For a start, Ipswich were a Second Division club, having been relegated 18 months earlier. The directors had given Bobby Ferguson another year to see if he could regain top-flight status at the first time of asking, but although he led the club to a fifth-place finish, which secured a play-off place, defeat by Charlton prompted a managerial change. John Duncan had arrived from Chesterfield – it was reported that the directors sensed a similarity with Bobby Robson when he had taken charge in 1969 – and when we lost each of my first four games back at the club, to Aston Villa, Blackburn, Leeds and Plymouth, we were sitting 15th in the table. I missed the next game, a home defeat by Leicester that attracted an attendance of just over 11,000, and then I returned for a 3-2 win at Barnsley. I was injured again and only managed a substitute appearance in each of the last two fixtures, and by the end of the season we were eighth, 11 points worse off than fifth-placed Blackburn, who occupied the last play-off berth. In the first half of the season Ipswich had won 11 home games in a row but we were blighted by inconsistency after my return and because of injury I had not made anything like the contribution expected of me.

Just as the club had changed in my four years away, it was the same for me. I was four years older and couldn't kid myself that I was still the same player I had been in the club's halcyon days. I played alongside world-class colleagues in my first spell at the club, but without being disrespectful to my new team-mates, clearly that was no longer the case. On my first day back on the practice pitch at Portman Road I was surprised to see John Duncan referring to a piece of paper as he put us through our paces. That was something I had never seen before and it suggested to me that perhaps he was out of his depth. He was a decent man but in the two and a half years that I worked for him I was rarely convinced that he had what it took to get us back into the First Division. There were some useful players in the squad but I sensed they did not fully respect the manager, which is a problem at any level of the game. My experience taught me that you didn't actually have to like the man in charge, but if you had no respect for him you could forget about being successful. From a personal point of view, my relationship with John Duncan was fine, but I felt he lacked the wow factor to take the club on to the next stage and become a top manager. Perhaps it was unfair of me to compare, but alongside other managers for whom I had played – Bobby Robson, Joe Fagan and Kenny Dalglish – he was someone who still had a great deal to prove.

In the summer of 1988 John Duncan spent a club record £300,000 to buy David Linighan from Shrewsbury and, pound for pound, he turned out to be one of Ipswich's best-ever signings. At that time I was playing in midfield but in my third spell at Portman Road, by which time I had sensibly decided to revert to my original role as a central defender, I partnered Lini at the back and we became quite a double act – in more ways than one. Here was a player who could hardly believe his good fortune at being paid to play the game he loved. He had experienced the other side of the coin, serving his apprenticeship as a joiner before turning to football, and appreciated the opportunity he had been given. There was no more wholehearted or committed servant to Ipswich Town. He knew his limitations and he pushed himself to the very max. There were times when I winced at his bravery and others when I was certain he was stark raving bonkers. In Lini's case there was a very thin line, but he was the type of guy you would want alongside you in the trenches and John Duncan deserves credit for bringing him to the club. His successor, John Lyall, was certainly pleased to have Lini to call upon and both men rated him highly enough to turn a blind eye to his number one weakness, booze.

There were very few days when I did not smell alcohol on Lini's breath when we were in the dressing room preparing for training. It was no secret that he was a drinker, but managers preferred to judge him on his performances for the team and if there was one player who could be relied upon to sweat blood for the cause it was the big lad from Hartlepool. When I look back on our time together at Portman Road I remember some comic moments – pure slapstick – as he looked anything but an accomplished footballer. But I also recall games in which he stood firm and refused to surrender. I had played alongside some of the world's finest, but I found him to be an inspiration for his never-say-die attitude. He was an outstanding character, even if there were times when he was, to borrow the phrase Bobby Robson coined about Paul Gascoigne, daft as a brush. In our 1991-92 Second Division title-winning campaign, and the three backs-to-the-wall years that followed in the Premier League, he was a tower of strength. I can't speak highly enough of the big fella.

Lini had a dog the spitting image of Bullseye, the bull terrier in the film version of Oliver Twist. He was his best pal and would often accompany his master when Lini ventured into Hadleigh, where he was based, for a drink. The dog would be tied up outside the first pub Lini visited and when he moved on to the next he would often forget to take his canine friend with him. His memory only deteriorated as the evening wore on and many a time he was alerted by a call from the landlord at pub number one, which meant Lini going to retrieve the dog – but not before he had one for the road, presumably. The dog even slept in Lini's hotel room one night before an away game. The reason I know this to be true is that I was sharing the same room. Lini wanted the dog with him as he was intending to stay up north after the game, but there was no way that John Duncan would allow it on board the team bus. Arrangements were made for Dave Allard, one of the local press guys, to drive Lini's car with the dog in the back and then hand it over at the hotel. So far, so good, but when I wanted to answer a call of nature in the middle of the night I forgot about the dog's presence until it bared its teeth and let out a frightening growl. I tried to waken Lini but he was snoring away, so because the dog was between me and the toilet I decided not to bother and lay awake in some discomfort. What made it even worse was that the dog frequently broke wind and the smell in the room was close to unbearable. It wasn't until Lini stirred in the morning that he saw to the dog and cleared the way for me to relieve myself.

It was only years later, after Lini had departed and probably even retired, that I discovered the truth about his escapades. I moved to Hadleigh on a short-term basis and the locals didn't take long to enlighten me. I was told he would often spend the Friday night before home games at a Colchester night club, for example, and that explained a lot in my book. There were times when I tried to have a quiet word on the side about his boozing. Years earlier I could have given him a run for his money when it came to sinking pints, but time had caught up with me and I had cut right back. "You should cut back," I would tell him, trying to give him the benefit of my own experience, but he was having none of it. "Who do you think you are, my dad?" he would respond. Lini was a law unto himself and in no mood to change. His football career over, he has picked up the tools again and lives in Preston. He did a lot of work a few miles along the road, putting the finishing touches to the City of Manchester Stadium. In the bars, I would bet.

We started the 1988-89 season with a seven-game undefeated run that reaped 17 points from a possible 21 and took us to the top of the table. It included a 5-1 away win at Shrewsbury, who were clearly missing a certain Mr Linighan, but we were unable to sustain our impressive early-season form. We suffered our first defeat at Crystal Palace, recovered to beat Manchester City at home – despite having David Linighan sent off – but then lost five on the trot to drop down into mid-table. That was the pattern for the remainder of the campaign. I did not manage a goal until my 13th appearance of the season, when I converted two penalties in a 3-1 home win over Walsall. When I headed our opening goal in another 3-1 win at Portman Road, this time in March, it was my 144th for Ipswich and it took me ahead of Tom Garneys into third place behind Ray Crawford and Ted Phillips in the club's all-time scoring charts, a position I still occupy to this day. We knocked on the door to the play-offs, and even gatecrashed the top six for a time, but we eventually came up short. Inconsistency was our biggest problem. We finished with five straight wins, not even conceding a goal in the last four, which was part of an unbeaten seven-game run, but prior to that we had lost four in a row. It was that sort of season, one week promising so much and the next showing we were simply not good enough. Despite collecting seven points more than in the previous campaign, we again finished eighth, but this time we were only three points adrift of sixth-placed Swindon.

I felt John Duncan's failure to control certain players was a key factor that contributed to our failure, albeit narrowly, to qualify for the play-offs. Dalian Atkinson was the major culprit and although he incurred a £500 fine for his contribution to a newspaper article in which he stated 'Play me or sell me' he could have been in hot water on several other occasions too, as a succession of Friday night curfews were also broken. Powerfully built, lightning-quick and an immensely exciting prospect, Dalian was his own worst enemy. He hit a number of spectacular goals, including a fabulous hat-trick in April 1988 against Middlesbrough. England manager Bobby Robson was at Portman Road that day to have a look at Boro central defender Gary Pallister, who was partnered by Tony Mowbray, but it was unquestionably Dalian's day. His ability was there for all to see, but his attitude wasn't the best and he lacked discipline. There were times when I tried speaking to him, only to realise I was wasting my time. I don't blame John Duncan, but other more experienced managers would have coped better with him, to their mutual benefit. Dalian duly departed to Sheffield Wednesday in the summer of 1989 and the £450,000 fee was made to look even more of a bargain by Ipswich's failure to insert a sell-on clause in the deal. Owls' boss Ron Atkinson later confessed he was surprised that Ipswich did not insist on such and Ipswich were made to suffer financially when Dalian was sold to Spanish club Real Sociedad just one year later for a whopping £1.7million.

Big Ron, who by this time had taken charge of Aston Villa, proved himself a shrewd judge when he brought Dalian back to England in 1991. Everyone remembers the goal he scored for Villa against Wimbledon, when he started in his own half and waltzed round several players at top speed before chipping the ball over the keeper and then, as if the whole thing had been rehearsed, grabbing a spectator's brolly for the celebration that followed. That won him the BBC's Goal of the Season accolade and he also scored Villa's opening goal in the 1994 League Cup Final win over Manchester United at Wembley. Throw in a Turkish League Championship with Fenerbahce in 1996, and several England Under-21 caps, and it wasn't a bad career, but I am not the only one who felt that he under-achieved. There was a bit of Cyrille Regis and Emile Heskey about Dalian and he should be disappointed he didn't go all the way and win full England honours. It was a terrible waste of ability.

I actually finished joint leading goalscorer for Ipswich in the 1988-89 season – me, Dalian and Jason Dozzell scored 13 – and I also collected the first of my four supporters' Player of the Year awards. That season also saw the emergence of Chris Kiwomya, whose arrival on the scene probably had a lot to do with the club's willingness to sell Dalian, although the cash on offer was another major factor. Chris, different to Dalian in that he was keen to listen and soak up advice, netted his first two career goals that season in successive league fixtures at Walsall and at home to Stoke, a game significant for marking the debut of Sergei Baltacha, English football's first import from the Soviet Union. An international sweeper, he arrived from Dynamo Kiev at the age of 30 and before the game at Walsall he presented us all with a pennant from his former club. Mick Stockwell suffered a leg fracture in our 4-2 win at Fellows Park and it must have been a huge shock to Sergei when he was asked to replace Stumper on the right of midfield the following week. In true fairy tale fashion, Sergei made light of the fact that he was playing in an unaccustomed role. After a goalless first half he opened the scoring as we went on to beat Stoke, managed at the time by ex-Ipswich skipper Mick

Mills, 5-1. Sergei and his family were very popular in and around Ipswich, and while Sergei Jnr went on to play professionally, daughter Elena took up tennis and graduated all the way to become British number one in 2003, although injury problems have held her back in recent years. It should be no surprise that Sergei's children excelled at sport because apart from his own background, their mother Olga represented the Soviet Union in both the pentathlon and heptathlon at the Olympic Games. I had no reason to think in 1982, when Scotland played against the Soviet Union in the World Cup finals in Spain, that their sweeper and I would eventually become team-mates at Ipswich.

John Duncan had a tough time of it in the 1989-90 season. Results, always the barometer by which a manager will be judged, simply were not good enough and the Ipswich supporters could not take to the direct approach he championed. Had it been paying off, it would have been a different situation altogether, but a combination of what the paying customers deemed to be dull football and a clear lack of success proved his downfall. It was not a very uplifting experience for the players, either, to be playing in front of such small crowds, their enthusiasm often sapped by the inferior quality of the football they were paying good money to watch. No season ever hinges on one result but the New Year's Day defeat at Port Vale was doubly disappointing, not merely for the 5-0 scoreline but the fact that I was totally unprofessional for what I consider to be the one and only time in a career that spanned more than 20 years and almost 900 games for club and country. No matter that it was a rare occasion, however, because to act as I did just that once was once too often. Nor did the fact that I was merely one of several players to step out of line make it any more acceptable.

We checked into the Post House Hotel at Newcastle-under-Lyme on December 31, 1989 – or, as they say in my home country, Hogmanay. We were unbeaten in 11 league games, a terrific run that had taken us from 17th in the table – the lowest Ipswich had been in 25 years – to fifth. But we were to come crashing back to earth with an almighty thud in front of fewer than 9,000 fans at Port Vale as a result of a humiliating 5-0 defeat. To those Ipswich supporters in the crowd, I would like to offer my sincere apologies. After our evening meal at the hotel, John Duncan told us he would have no objection, bearing in mind the time of year, if we came downstairs for one drink. "One drink only," he said, several times, but on reflection he would have been better confining us to our rooms, although he was entirely blameless for what ensued. It had come to our attention as we checked in, and more so when we had dinner, that the hotel was especially busy with a number of seasonal parties. When we later came down for the drink that the manager had sanctioned, both Lini and I decided to have a wander round the hotel and before long we were entering into the spirit of the occasion. It was the early hours of the morning before we got to bed, much the worse for wear after we overdid the New Year celebrations.

It later emerged that both Jason Dozzell and Chris Kiwomya had also stepped out of line. Being that much younger, they jumped into a taxi and headed for the bright lights of nearby Stoke-on-Trent and the first nightclub they could find. Again, they had more drink – and too little sleep – than was good for them. Naively, though, Jason, Chris, Lini and I still thought we had managed to keep our misdemeanours sufficiently quiet so as not to arouse suspicion in the manager. How wrong we were. Before the game, John Duncan made us aware that he knew exactly what had occurred, and if he hoped we would make amends on the pitch he was in for a huge disappointment. I am ashamed to admit that I was in no fit state to play. I was booked inside the first two minutes for a foul on Robbie Earle and if he had decided it warranted a red card I honestly believe the referee would have been doing us a favour. Alongside me, Lini said his legs felt so heavy that it seemed as if he was walking in quicksand. Messrs Dozzell and Kiwomya were not at their liveliest, either, and we were simply carrying too many passengers to make a proper game of it. To make matters worse, the Vale Park pitch is one of the widest in the country – or so it seemed – and at 5-0 we were let off lightly. John Duncan was livid and rightly so and threatened to fine us – yes, the whole team – for an embarrassing display. The damage was done, of course, but we at least managed to partially redeem ourselves five days later when we won 1-0 at Leeds in an FA Cup third round tie. Leeds won the Second Division that season and it was like the Alamo as we defended our slender lead thanks to Jason Dozzell's goal. The manager fielded the very same team that had been thumped at Port Vale and he got the reaction he demanded as we at least restored some professional pride.

One of John Duncan's ideas was to introduce a new Friday night diet before away games that involved an overnight hotel stop. He was adamant that we should not eat steak but switch instead to things like pasta, and while some players were happy to embrace the change both Lini and I were reluctant. We hatched a plan to take our own steak with us, smuggle it into the hotel kitchen and hope that when it arrived on our plates the manager would not notice. We got away with it for a few weeks, but inevitably he found out, although to be fair to him he allowed us to continue. I preferred a normal-sized fillet but Lini opted for a huge T-bone that just about filled the plate. On one occasion we were travelling north when we were held up in fog and arrived hours late at our hotel. We were too late for anything other than sandwiches, we were informed, but Lini and I just smiled. We asked to have our steaks cooked and the kitchen staff agreed, leaving the other lads – and the manager – to look on enviously when they were delivered to the table and we tucked in.

It was during the 1989-90 season that I had a brief run as a makeshift striker alongside Chris Kiwomya. We worked on our partnership in training and I told him, "Let's be like Toshack and Keegan. I'll head them on for you to chase." It needed a bit of fine tuning, that move, because Chris was so quick that he would often set off too early and run into an offside position. But we persevered and I thought we were a lethal combination while it lasted. I managed to score four times in my five games up front, yet I had mixed fortunes with penalties. My first goal of the season came from the spot, in the 2-1 win over Newcastle that ended a nine-game barren spell. But I ended up missing half the spot-kicks I took, although to give that statistic some proper perspective I had better point out it was actually two from four. I was again voted Player of the Year by the supporters, an achievement that rewrote the record books because I was immediately reminded that I was the oldest-ever winner.

There was no escaping the fact that the fans wanted a change of manager. We did reach the dizzy heights of fifth place at one stage, but that no-show at Port Vale was followed by another seven league games without a win. It was a run that turned up the heat on John Duncan, with supporters calling for his head at every one of the last eight games of the season. In the end it didn't matter how we fared, the manager seemed a dead man walking. We won three of our last four fixtures, including visits to Middlesbrough and West Brom, and a home game against Blackburn, and the one we lost, at Hull, saw them score in the 89th minute to sneak a 4-3 victory. But it didn't matter a jot because in the eyes of the supporters John Duncan had to go. It started with shouts of 'Duncan out' and there were the usual boos and slow handclapping, but in the end it became necessary for the police to cordon off the directors' box as the angry brigade got on to the pitch at the end of a game.

The police presence was increased for the last home game and some fans even burned an effigy of the manager to reinforce their view. I remember going into the White Horse in Capel St Mary, the manager's home village, one night with a friend and I asked the landlord: "The boss comes in here, doesn't he?" The chap nodded and pointed to the corner of the room, where a figure was slumped forward on his seat with his head and arms on the table in front of him. It was John Duncan and he appeared to be fast asleep. When the end came, just three days after the season was over, I didn't know whether to feel sorry or relieved for him.

His successor was John Lyall, who needed no introduction after his success at West Ham. He was surprisingly sacked by the Hammers a year earlier and had been working for Tottenham until learning of Ipswich's interest in reviving his managerial career. I first met him when I was summoned to his office one day to discuss the fact that my contract was up and the club wanted to offer me a new one. From being initially encouraged, I was very quickly deflated by what the manager had to say. He told me what he was prepared to pay, or rather what the club felt they could afford, and I considered it derisory. Yes, I was 33 and there was no getting away from it. But I was delivering where it mattered most, on the field of play, and had just been voted Player of the Year by the paying customers for the second year in a row. Surely, that counted for something. I was not being greedy, just looking for a rise that I felt I had earned, and I reminded him that I had taken a considerable drop in salary in order to return to Portman Road two and a half years earlier. Having proved my worth, I was surprised at the club's reluctance to reward me with an increase. John Lyall had no personal axe to grind with me – I am certain of that – but he made it clear the club would not budge. They either felt I would accept the first offer that came my way, because I did not want any further upheaval in my life and would prefer to remain living in Suffolk, or there was a feeling that I was on my last legs and that one year on I would only be fit for the knacker's yard. Little did they, or me for that matter, realise that I would not cease to be a player for a further six years.

Managers are a wily breed, particularly those of the old school. I likened John Lyall to Bobby Robson in many ways, although I did not get to know him properly until I returned to Portman Road for a third spell later in my career. These guys were clever the way they manipulated situations to their own benefit. There's a great story about Bobby that shows what I mean. Paul Cooper had an appointment to see him one day and knocked on his office door. Bobby called him in and as Coop entered Bobby put the phone down. "I'm trying to sign Bryan King," he said, and in the next breath asked Paul what he could do for him. Coop had only been at the club a year but argued that he merited a wage rise and Bobby replied: "Well, yes, but I'm thinking of bringing Bryan into the club. That might affect you." Bryan King, one of the country's most promising goalkeepers, was at Millwall at the time and subsequently joined Coventry. The news took the wind out of Coop's sails and he emerged from the manager's office having secured a rise a lot more modest than what he was seeking. The flip side of the coin, however, was that later in his Ipswich career he was awarded a rise completely out of the blue, with Bobby Robson telling him: "You deserve it, son."

When I realised I was wasting my time trying to argue my case for an improved deal, John Lyall and I parted company and I honestly believed I might never see him again. I must stress there was no fall-out; he was doing his job in trying to secure me at the best price and I was exercising my prerogative in deciding to look elsewhere. My name was added to the long list of free agents looking for a new club and the first one to show a definite interest was Middlesbrough. I made the long journey to Teesside with my financial adviser, John Hazel, and we met the club chairman, Colin Henderson, chief executive Keith Lamb and manager Colin Todd. Negotiations were very friendly and although nothing was agreed when John and I left to drive back south, we were hopeful that something could be agreed and, sure enough, the following week I was summoned back to Middlesbrough to have a medical at Ayresome Park and sign. To coin a phrase, they made me an offer I couldn't refuse. It dwarfed what was on offer at Ipswich and I would have been a complete fool not to accept, even if it was going to mean spending a lot of time away from home.

My first season as a Middlesbrough player went well. I operated as more of a defensive midfielder, with a game now and again at centre-back. We had a decent team that included Tony Mowbray as captain. Just as you might expect, he was an inspirational figure and it was clear he was a coach and manager in the making. There was no lack of quality, with Stephen Pears, Colin Cooper, Bernie Slaven, John Hendrie, Stuart Ripley, Alan Kernaghan, Mark Proctor and my former Ipswich team-mate, Trevor Putney, also on board. I didn't miss many games and by finishing seventh we made it into the play-offs, where we met Notts County. The first game at Ayresome Park ended 1-1 and I was completely taken aback when Colin Todd told me prior to the return leg at Meadow Lane that he was leaving me out. He said: "I thought you would be a bigger influence in the dressing room." I was furious and hit back: "F*** off, that's your job." Generally speaking, I didn't have a lot to say for myself in the dressing room at any of my clubs, but at the same time if I felt I was a victim of an injustice I would soon speak up. Todd was a great player in his time with Derby and England – he was the PFA Player of the Year in 1975, six years before I won it – and to be honest I was excited at the prospect of working for him. But my level of job satisfaction was quite low in my year with Boro. I thought some of the Brian Clough magic might have rubbed off on him, but nothing could have been further from the truth. Whereas Clough was a larger-than-life character, I found Todd to be almost devoid of personality and I found him to be a complete let-down. Notts County beat us by the only goal in the second leg and while they went on to defeat Brighton at Wembley and book their top-flight return, I thought I would be playing out the second and final year of my Boro contract in the Second Division.

When Colin Todd departed to be replaced by Lennie Lawrence my world was about to be turned upside down all over again. Lennie made it clear at his first meeting with the players that he was expecting everyone to live within an hour of Ayresome Park. There was no way that could include me, even with my increasingly successful efforts to reduce the travelling time between Teesside and Suffolk. When I originally signed my contract the club agreed that I would be able to train with Ipswich on a Monday and report for duty with Boro on the Tuesday morning. My normal routine was to drive home on a Saturday and to return on the Monday evening, but then I began to spend the Monday evening at home and rise at about 6am to motor up the A1 in time for training at 10am. It was madness in a way because I would climb out of my car and head straight for the training ground in no fit shape, because after four hours in the driving position I was as stiff as a board. I had a very nice apartment in the town and although my alcohol intake had been drastically reduced over the years, I was still up for a night out and some of my team-mates were made of similar stuff. It wasn't all about booze, either, because Bernie Slaven was, and still is, a teetotaller, but he wasn't going to let that stop him having a good time. When I met Lennie Lawrence one-to-one I had no gripe with him and perfectly understood his way of thinking. We had a chat and came to a sensible agreement over the money owing to me for the remaining year of my contract, which enabled us to part company on friendly terms. I thought, at the time, that he had actually done me a favour, but within a few weeks I was forced to think again.

RENAISSANCE MAN

ONCE I SEVERED MY ties with Middlesbrough in the summer of 1991 I faced an uncertain future, but I was unduly concerned since I had read about players being out of contract and how they simply waited for the phone to ring before entering a new chapter of their playing career. In my case, however, there were hardly any calls. Colchester and Orient both rang and said they were interested and I was also contacted by Falkirk, who invited me to go up there for a few weeks on trial. Not wishing to come across arrogant or big-headed, I felt the standard at both Colchester and Orient was beneath me, while Falkirk's suggestion was a non-starter. I felt I had no need to go anywhere on trial and the answer would have been the same to any club coming up with a similar proposal. But that was it, not another single enquiry, and I moped around for a few weeks wondering what I had done wrong. I was convinced I could still play at the same level as I had done with Boro the previous season, but it seemed no one else shared that view. The new season duly started and I virtually resigned myself to the fact that I had reached the end of the road. If my career was over, therefore, it seemed I had no alternative but to 'sign on' and join the ranks of the unemployed. I actually got to the front door of the dole office, decided I couldn't go in and turned back. At that time it was situated at the top of Portman Road, so as I left I turned and walked the few hundred yards to the football ground and wandered in. One of the first people I saw was Charlie Woods and at first he was surprised to see me. I explained the situation and asked if it might be possible to train at the club so that I would at least be fit if and when I got myself a club. Charlie said he didn't think it would be a problem but said he would have to double check with John Lyall and then get back to me. He rang me the next day and said John was happy for me to train with them.

I was keeping myself to myself as far as training was concerned until one day I was asked if I fancied a game for the reserves. I hadn't had a game in months so I was quick to agree and that one game turned into about four or five. Around that time Tony Humes suffered a broken arm at Newcastle and with Ipswich having recently sold Brian Gayle to Sheffield United, they were short of numbers at the back. I was on the bench for a League Cup-tie at Derby and didn't play, but three days later I was again a substitute in the league game at Grimsby and this time I was called upon. The Ipswich fans who were up there gave me a great reception, but the home crowd, and especially those supporters in the area between the dug-out and the corner flag, came up with a few cruel taunts about my age as I warmed up. Not that I ever let comments from the stands or terraces bother me, but there were fewer than 7,000 spectators and I heard every single remark aimed in my direction. The next league game was at home to Oxford and I played from the start, completing the 90 minutes. I was happy to sign on a week-to-week basis at first and I later progressed to a monthly contract before agreeing a deal through to the end of the season. This time I wasn't going to argue about what they offered me and couldn't sign quickly enough. I slotted in alongside Lini at the heart of the defence and played every game through to the end of the campaign, a total of 43, and also scored three goals. The icing on the cake came when we won the Second Division title and again when I was voted Player of the Year by the fans which, given the circumstances behind my return to the club, was really quite remarkable.

Ipswich had been 25-1 shots to win the title, so it was regarded as a magnificent achievement by John Lyall and the players to finish on top of the pile. Lini was a tremendous captain and to be honest I found it fairly easy alongside him. In my second spell at the club under John Duncan I had still been regarded as a midfielder and it was the same at Boro, although I recall filling in at the back alongside Tony Mowbray on a few occasions. Now I saw myself as a centre-back, full stop. I always knew that I was capable of reverting to that role and extending my career, but at the start of the 1991-92 season, when I was without a club, it seemed I was going to be denied the opportunity to prove it. Lini and I had a great relationship at the back, although he made me wince with some of his challenges. He was absolutely fearless and while I never held back throughout my career, I had to admit that he went for the ball on occasions when I might have thought twice. We had a decent side, a nice mix, and a wily manager in John Lyall. Even at that stage of my career, and right up to his departure, he taught me a lot and it would be extremely rare in the world of football if you heard anyone bad-mouthing him. John was the man behind many a successful career, both at West Ham and Ipswich, and I enjoyed working for him.

John Lyall made some good signings for Ipswich on the modest transfer budget he had at his disposal. Steve Whitton, for example, provided excellent value for money and in the Second Division title-winning season he played a vital role for the team, scoring 10 goals from his 50 appearances. He made countless others as part of a triangular move that caught out opposition defences time after time. Left-back Neil Thompson would knock a diagonal ball to him and because he was invariably taller than the opposition left-back, nine times out of 10 he would be able to win his header and knock the ball on for Chris Kiwomya, who was generally quicker than most central defenders. Chris got 17 goals that season and a healthy proportion of them probably came from that simple move. There was a good atmosphere around the club and Chris was eager to improve. He would regularly take up the manager's offer that his door was always open and they would spend a fair time discussing the game and how he could become a better player. John Lyall christened Chris 'Lino' because he thought he spent a lot of time on the floor, but when Chris addressed the manager it was always 'Mr Lyall'. Jason Dozzell had also matured into a quality player and weighed in with 15 goals, while there was no lack of energy in the ranks with workaholics such as Romeo Zondervan and Mick Stockwell beavering away to make things happen.

We also had a settled side, which always helps, and there was a great camaraderie within the group, the kind you always find at a successful club. In my eighth game back, at Leicester, I scored the first goal of my third spell at Ipswich and it also happened to be my 500th appearance. We drew 2-2 that day and it was right in the middle of our worst spell of the season, when we followed five draws in a row with three straight defeats, which left us ninth in the table. Fortunately, we recovered to put together a run of just two defeats in 15 league games, a spell that coincided with us also making progress in the FA Cup. Having beaten Hartlepool the hard way, drawing at home and winning the replay in the North East, and then cruising past Bournemouth in round four, we were paired with my former club Liverpool at Portman Road. It was just like old times with a 26,000-plus crowd and just before half-time I very nearly decided it. It was a lousy day of wind and rain, and when I smacked my header against the bar I remember the rebound clearing the 18-yard box. It remained goalless and 10 days later I was back at Anfield – as far as I was aware it could be my last appearance there – for a replay in which we gave a superb account of ourselves. Ray Houghton's goal was all that separated the sides and when Gavin Johnson scored with a fantastic diving header in the 82nd minute it took the tie into extra time. Jason Dozzell gave us the lead in the 95th minute, only for Jan Molby to equalise three minutes later with a glorious free-kick. It has always been a sore point with me, conceding free-kicks in dangerous positions and having played alongside Jan I actually expected him to score. There simply wasn't anything we could do to stop him. Steve McManaman netted the winner and I actually had to come off about three minutes before the end when I got cramp in both legs. I was lying on my back when they physio came on and I told him I couldn't move. He managed to get me back on my feet but I was as unsteady as a drunk as I took my first few steps. It may not be particularly PC, but if I tell you I was walking like Douglas Bader you will get the picture. To make my way to the dressing room I had to walk along in front of the Kop and they gave me an unbelievable reception. It seemed every single one of the fans joined in the standing ovation and it made the hairs on the back

(Above) Surrounded by opponents during Scotland's European Championship qualifier against Switzerland in March 1983 and, below, scoring our first goal as we recovered from being 2-0 down to draw 2-2.

I scored four of Ipswich's goals – and none of them were penalties – in the 6-1 home win over West Bromwich Albion in October 1982 and, right, that is Irvin Gernon congratulating me.

Me and my sponsored car at Ipswich, which I couldn't drive because I did not have a driving licence.

(Left) In full flight as a Liverpool player.

(Bottom left) Future team-mate Ian Rush crosses my path during a game between Ipswich and Liverpool at Portman Road.

(Bottom right) Kenny Dalglish is first to congratulate me on my debut goal against Watford at Vicarage Road in March 1984.

Celebrating one of my two goals as Liverpool beat my former club Ipswich 2-0 at Anfield in November 1984. It was also my 100th career league goal.

I get in a tackle on Juventus star Zbigniew Boniek during the European Cup Final at the Heysel Stadium in 1985.

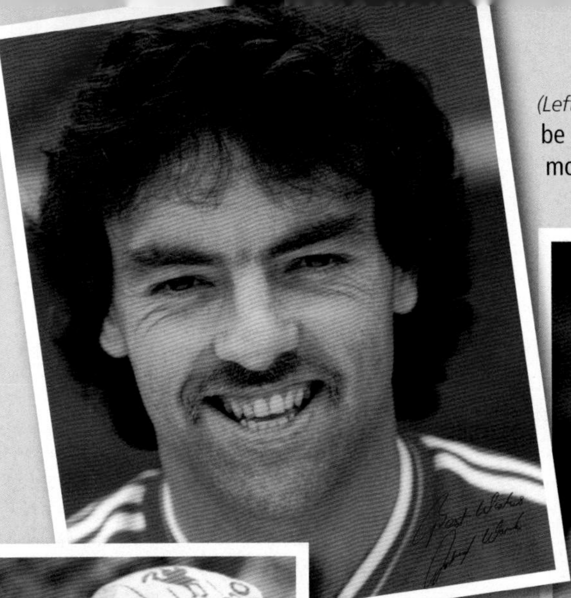

(Left) Smile please! I'm happy to be a Liverpool player after my move from Ipswich.

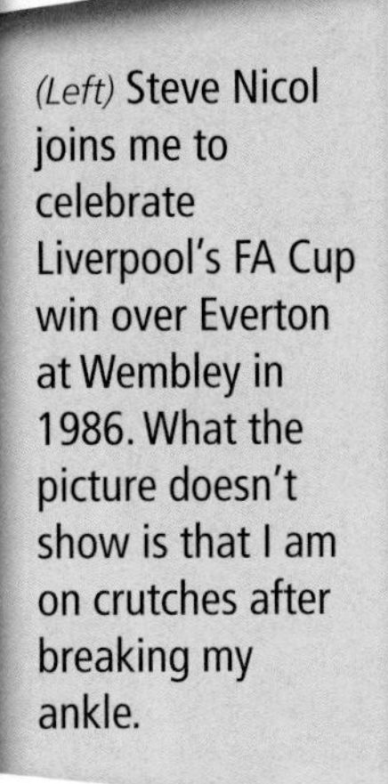

(Left) Steve Nicol joins me to celebrate Liverpool's FA Cup win over Everton at Wembley in 1986. What the picture doesn't show is that I am on crutches after breaking my ankle.

(Above) Niall Quinn is in the background as I take aim during an Ipswich away game at Manchester City.

(Left) Manager John Duncan looks on as I sign on at Ipswich for a second time in January 1988.

(Above) I hold the record of most games and goals in East Anglian derbies and here I am celebrating Ipswich's first goal in a 4-0 pre-season win at Norwich in August 1989.

(Left) I have scored another goal against Norwich, this time from the penalty spot in a 1-1 draw at Portman Road in September 1994.

(Above) My older brother Alex with his wife Morag and children, Alex junior and Allison, during a visit to Ipswich for my 40th birthday in August 1997.

(Left) I put in a challenge on Liverpool goalkeeper Bruce Grobbelaar during an FA Cup clash that ended 0-0 at Portman Road in February 1992.

It seemed like a good idea at the time. I played Santa Claus at the Christmas party for the Ipswich players' kids in 1988 during my second spell back at the club.

In at the start of the Premier League with Ipswich in 1992.

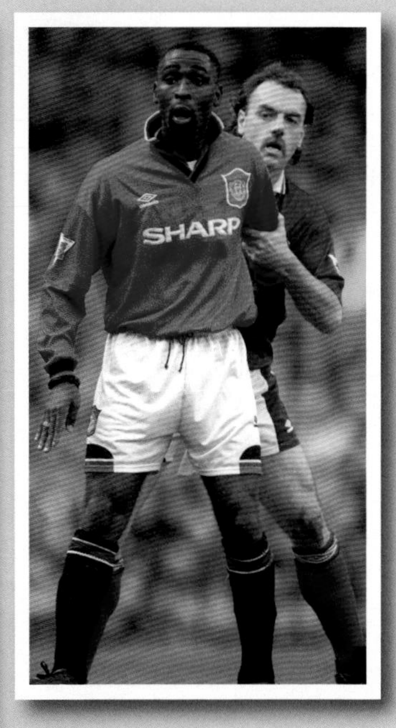

Doing my best to keep an eye on Andy Cole, although he still scored five times for Manchester United as they defeated Ipswich 9-0 at Old Trafford in March 1995. I was feeling rough beforehand with a chest infection and was even worse after that pasting.

Testimonial time and both the Ipswich and Arsenal teams form a guard of honour before my big game at Portman Road in August 1996, which ended in a 1-1 draw.

The old magic's still there as I knock in a penalty for Liverpool in the Masters.

Me and my souvenirs that confirm I had a successful career.

Karen & I have been happy together for more than four years.

of my neck stand to attention. The rest of the ground joined in and they probably felt they had seen the last of me. Although we were sitting second in the table, we still had 15 league games to play and there was no guarantee we would win promotion to join Liverpool in the Premiership. There was more to come, too, because as I eventually reached the dug-out area everyone on the Liverpool bench was giving me high fives. It was very emotional – almost too much to bear – and I can't deny I shed a tear or two.

We were actually top of the table when we had an attack of promotion jitters later in the season, but even taking just two points from four games couldn't knock us off our perch. In the last of the four, which was our penultimate fixture at Oxford, the point we gained was enough to ensure we would go up. Jim Magilton put Oxford ahead in the seventh minute and Gavin Johnson equalised two minutes later. It was like a home game because there were so many Ipswich fans in the crowd and they were in party mood. The local police had to ask John Lyall to address them over the PA system in order to calm things down and send them on their way. It was actually 30 years to the day since Alf Ramsey's team had won the League Championship but we would have to wait another week to ensure we took the title. The biggest home gate of the season, almost 27,000, saw us beat Brighton 3-1 and they were relegated. Steve Whitton scored one of his two goals from the spot after I had stepped down a few weeks earlier when my penalty at Southend came back off the bar. Steve had a 100 per cent record, converting all four of the penalties we were awarded in our last seven games, which was a pretty remarkable statistic.

It was only when I sat down with John Lyall to discuss a new contract that I knew for sure I would be around for the inaugural Premier League campaign. The negotiations were concluded pretty quickly. The club knew I was less than keen to put myself in the same situation I had been in a year earlier and that, together with the extra incentive of playing in the brand new set-up, was always going to keep me at Portman Road. John and I shook hands on a new one-year contract and I didn't even waste my time asking for a longer deal. The summer of 1992 could hardly have been more different to that of 1991 because I was suddenly in demand, rather than being overlooked. When Sky Sports asked the club to send a player down to their studios in London to film an advertisement I was nominated and I have to confess it felt a bit strange being around some of the big-name stars who were involved. I remember having to do a scene where I was lifting weights and sweating profusely, except that the reality of the situation was that there were no weights attached and I was merely pretending, while the 'sweat' was supplied by a girl just out of camera shot who was spraying me with water. It was great fun and as I looked around at the others who were involved it started to dawn on me that I was back in the big-time. I was also Ipswich's representative in a Premier League squad that played West Ham at Upton Park to mark the opening of the new Bobby Moore Stand. The select team was managed by George Graham, the Arsenal manager, and the first words he ever said to me were "Warky, I'd like you to captain the side."

Before we reported for pre-season training we heard that John Lyall's role at the club was to change. He was still very much the man in charge, but coach Mick McGiven, who had been with John at West Ham, became first team manager and John's title was club manager. Mick basically took the training most of the time but the pair would get their heads together when it came to picking the side and deciding on tactics. As far as the players were concerned it was only a subtle change as we had regarded John and Mick as a double act since they had taken charge two years earlier and they were very much on the same wavelength. The Premier League's television deal with satellite broadcaster BSkyB meant the 22 clubs would share a cash jackpot of £37.5 million, depending on the number of live games in which they featured and where they finished in the table. Football was to change for ever on the strength of that tie-up and it was merely the start of a revolution that has seen the game completely transformed by the mountain of cash willingly handed over year on year by the TV companies. But whereas nowadays a newly-promoted club is seen to lavish millions on its squad in an effort to ensure survival in the money-laden Premiership, spending was far more modest back then. Ipswich, for example, may have paid a club record £650,000 to sign Welsh international midfielder Geraint Williams from Derby, but they clawed back some of their investment by selling David Lowe to Leicester. Eight games into the first-ever Premier League season we were the only club still unbeaten after two wins and six draws, and even if that run came to an end in our ninth game at Oldham, come Christmas we were still in the top six, having been beaten only twice. I scored my first Premier League goal against Tottenham at Portman Road, but millions of armchair viewers also saw Jason Cundy level with one of the craziest goals I ever saw. When he came to Ipswich a few years later we gave him some flak for it. He insisted it was intentional but he was alone with that view. Everyone else who saw him thump the ball clear and send it sailing over Craig Forrest knew it was a wind-assisted fluke.

We actually made it into fourth place after we beat eventual champions Manchester United 2-1 at Portman Road in January 1993, ending their long unbeaten run. But after that we somehow managed to go 13 games without a win and gathered just 10 points from the last 48 up for grabs. It was a potentially disastrous spell and even if it was in direct contrast to what had gone before we had to face up to the fact that we might go down. We were jeered off after home defeats and it was just as well that we managed to win two of our last three games. We beat rivals Norwich, who were surprise title challengers that season, and then Nottingham Forest on the very last day in what was Brian Clough's final game in charge, an emotional occasion for him. We finished in 16th place with 52 points, just three more than relegated Crystal Palace, so it was a close shave. I contributed seven goals, six of them in the league. But I also missed a penalty in the home defeat by Arsenal as we saw a point slip away. I had already converted one when we were awarded a second and David Seaman saved it. I was happy to let Steve Whitton take the next penalty we were awarded, in the last-day win over Forest, and it proved to be the clincher. The main thing was that we would still be in the Premier League the following season and I must have done well enough because another one-year contract came my way. We had even enjoyed a couple of cup runs, reaching the quarter-final stage of both the League and FA Cups, so all things considered it had not been a bad season, despite that alarming late slump in the league.

Jason Dozzell departed for Tottenham in the summer of 1993 and a transfer tribunal eventually awarded Ipswich a fee of £1.75 million, a large part of which John Lyall spent to bring in Ian Marshall from Oldham and another Scouser in Paul Mason from the Dutch club Groningen. The Premier League had a 'brand' new name – the FA Carling Premiership – and we could hardly have anticipated a better start. Both the new boys scored in our 3-0 opening day win at Oldham, then Marsh's goals sealed two 1-0 home wins over Southampton and Chelsea, which put us second in the table. But we managed just one win from our next 13 games and found ourselves down in 16th place. I was ever-present in that spell and my only two goals, one from the spot, both came in the same game, a 2-2 draw at Swindon that marked my 600th appearance for the club. We were to win only nine games in the entire league campaign and of our 16 draws seven were achieved by a 0-0 scoreline. We were hanging on grimly at times and as far as a lot of our opponents were concerned we were 'Boring Ipswich' thanks to our defensive tactics. We managed just five home wins all season and that was the club's worst record in more than 30 years. I was not training very much because I tended to use the time between games to recover, rest and conserve my energy. I needed some late fitness tests just to confirm I would be okay to play and they took place in some bizarre places. One was conducted in the hotel corridor, as I ran up and down in nothing but my boxer shorts, and another in a hotel car park. Mick McGiven liked us to have a walk on the morning of away games and I would usually just wear a pair of flip-flops. One day, just as we arrived back from our stroll, he asked if I was going to be okay. He suggested a fitness test there and then so I borrowed his Hush Puppies, ran up and down, twisted and turned a bit and within a minute or two confirmed I would be fine.

When we could only draw 1-1 at home to Swindon, lost 5-0 at Sheffield Wednesday and then went down 2-1 at home to Manchester United, a lot of people probably thought the game was up. All we had left was an away game at Blackburn and we were one of six clubs who could still join already-relegated Swindon in going down. It was another backs-to-the-wall display on a day of incredible drama. They were constructing a new stand at Ewood Park and only three sides of the ground were in use, so the atmosphere was strange. Throughout the game substitute keeper Clive Baker was running up and down the touchline collecting news of how our many relegation rivals were faring. Periodically, having heard the latest from the other grounds, I would hear him urging us forward because at that particular point a goal would have been invaluable. 'Attack, attack' Clive was shouting and I couldn't help but think we had our work cut out defending, so how we were going to summon up the energy to mount an attack? Blackburn were runners-up in the league to Manchester United no matter what happened on the day, but don't let anyone tell you they were unconcerned at the outcome. Believe me, they wanted to win and late on it needed a goal-line clearance by Mick Stockwell to keep them out. Lini and I had our hands full to contain Alan Shearer and Ian Pearce, and as we repelled attack after attack Clive would reappear on the touchline to shout 'Defend, defend' because he had received an update from elsewhere. Clive played an absolute blinder that day.

At the final whistle we didn't really know where we stood for a few seconds but our cheering supporters left us in no doubt that the 0-0 scoreline had been enough, but only because Mark Stein had scored right at the death to earn Chelsea a win over Sheffield United and that goal was enough to relegate the Blades. Had they held on at 2-2 they would have survived and it would have been us taking the drop. John Lyall came on to the pitch and we embraced and I burst into tears with the sheer emotion of it all. But there was no champagne in the dressing room. Instead John came in and said: "You lucky bastards – make sure it doesn't happen again!" As the rest of the lads had a drink in the players' lounge I went to Kenny Dalglish's office to find him reading from the same script as John Lyall. Kenny kept shaking his head as he muttered: "How the hell did you get away with that?" No team could ever have come closer to being relegated and in the end, despite our heroics in keeping Shearer & Co at bay, it was Stein's goal at Stamford Bridge that had kept us up. We were lucky so-and-sos and we knew it, but it was a happy trip home. The newspapers made it clear they would have rather said farewell to Ipswich than Sheffield United, one of them even describing us as 'the most bland and negative waste of space in the Premiership'. Harsh words, but we had to face facts. While we had performed the job required of us as professionals, our defensive strategy had quite clearly bored the pants off a lot of people and they were entitled to their views. Of course, we would have liked nothing more than to turn in an entertaining 90 minutes every week and to have amassed far more points, but the horrible truth was that we had to make the best of what we had at our disposal. Despite the criticism from many quarters, we knew it was a near-miraculous achievement to have booked our Premiership place for another year.

Having been named the fans' Player of the Year for the fourth time in five years at the club, I signed another one-year contract in the summer of 1994 but I was in for a shock when chairman John Kerr approached me out of the blue one day and asked: "Have you ever thought about becoming a manager?" To be honest, the question came as such a huge surprise that I was initially stuck for an answer. I told him I had never really thought about it because I was too busy enjoying my time as a player, knowing only too well that because I was almost 37 my time on that side of the fence was drawing to a close. The chairman asked if I would attend a meeting in the manager's office along with him, John Lyall and Paul Goddard, who had decided to retire from playing. Basically, the outcome was that Mick McGiven was relieved of first team duties and given a new job as football development manager, while John Lyall resumed his role as manager, with Charlie Woods assisting him. Paul was named as first team coach and me as player-coach, but from my very first day in the job I never really felt comfortable. Paul was doing the coaching and I trained along with the others. My afternoons were spent working with Paul on a variety of tasks. We would watch videos featuring possible new signings, discuss other players we might like to bring to the club, plan training sessions and generally chat about the players we had at our disposal and how they might best be deployed. My new role also meant taking in games up and down the country, checking on players who had been recommended to us and deciding whether it was worth our while pursuing an interest in them. It was a massive change for me and to be honest I probably had enough on my plate just being a player. I also found it frustrating that I couldn't tell some of our players a few home truths. Whereas I wanted to rip into them, Paul favoured a more laid-back approach. Paul and I had been told it was our job to select the team, but the reality of the situation was that John Lyall had what you might call the casting vote. We would present our selection and while there were some occasions when he was happy to proceed, there were other times when he would persuade us to change our minds and go with his revised line-up.

Because of the club's narrow escape the previous season, the board of directors came up with the cash to reinforce the squad with four new faces. Defender or midfielder Steve Sedgley cost £1 million from Tottenham, while the equally versatile Claus Thomsen arrived from the Danish club Aarhus and a trip to South America by John Lyall and Charlie Woods resulted in Uruguayan forward Adrian Paz and Argentinian full-back Mauricio Taricco coming on board at a combined cost of over £1 million. We failed to repeat the uplifting start of the previous year and although we defeated Manchester United 3-2 at home just seven games into the season, it was only one of three league victories in our first 17 and we were at the bottom of the table. The 'boring Ipswich' label quickly resurfaced and there was a minor bust-up between John Lyall and Kevin Keegan at the end of our 1-1 draw at St James' Park when the Newcastle manager had a real go at us for our defensive tactics, labelling us 'hoofers'. I had never seen John Lyall as angry as he was that day and it was impossible not to feel sorry for him. He was up against it because we basically weren't good enough and our only hope was to shut up shop and try to pinch points to which we were not really entitled. It was clear the pressure was getting to John and a week later, after a home defeat to Manchester City, he took the decision to resign. I repeat, he resigned. When he died in April 2006 it was wrongly reported in some quarters that he had been sacked by Ipswich, but that was not the case. A very proud man, he stepped down after coming to the conclusion that he could do no more. Over the years I have heard supporters criticise his management, but anyone of that opinion would be well advised to keep it to themselves when they are in my company. I liked and respected John Lyall and no one will ever convince me he was not good for the club.

Paul Goddard took over as caretaker manager for three games, a defeat followed by two draws, until the appointment of my former team-mate, George Burley, who had only been in charge at Colchester for six months. Soon after he took charge we managed a three-game unbeaten run that included a home win over Leicester and an away success at, of all places, Liverpool. I had been to Anfield with some very good Ipswich sides and never managed a victory, yet here I was finally celebrating victory at the tail-end of my career and with a team that was unfit to compare with those that both George and I had been a part of during Bobby Robson's time as manager. That's football, I suppose, but the irony of our achievement was not lost on me. The only goal was scored by Adam Tanner, who had only made his debut the previous week with a goal against Leicester. He looked to have a promising career ahead of him, but two years later he was suspended for three months after a random drugs test found traces of cocaine in his blood and he eventually moved on to Colchester and Peterborough before joining Canvey Island. The game at Anfield started early because the Grand National was taking place that day and when I was in the players' lounge having a drink with Steve Nicol he casually said 'Why don't you come with us?' It seemed like a good idea, so while my Ipswich colleagues headed home I instead jumped on the Liverpool team bus and headed for Aintree. I had no ticket but despite being stopped for so-called security checks at four different points I was allowed through. One security guard even said 'Alright John?' and I wondered if he thought I still played for Liverpool. The Liverpool lads, who had booked a hospitality suite near the finishing post, couldn't believe they had lost to Ipswich and nor could I, to be honest. Lini and I had kept Ian Rush and Robbie Fowler quiet, making it one of the highlights of my career. That night Steve and I went out on the town and I stayed in a city centre hotel before returning by train to Ipswich the next day, complete with yet another sore head.

Although we managed to get off the bottom of the Premiership for a time, we never really looked like escaping the relegation places and the lowest of many lows came at Old Trafford on March 4, 1995 when we were beaten 9-0 by Manchester United, a Premiership record that still stands to this day. I was feeling terrible on the morning of the match and told George there was no way I could play, but he refused to rule me out and suggested we review the situation at lunch. I had to tell him I was feeling no better, but again he wanted me to delay a final decision until we got to the ground. He said I should have a fitness test and it comprised nothing more than running from the Old Trafford tunnel, which is situated in the corner of the stadium, to the half-way line and back again. I felt like death warmed up and told George, but he more or less begged me to play and I agreed because I didn't want to let him or the side down. Never mind that I was lining up against Andy Cole and Mark Hughes, the show had to go on. I had forgotten a lot about what happened that day until I saw the game again recently and I was amazed at how well I did under the circumstances. It was one to forget for everyone involved as United showed us no mercy and instead of showboating they went for the jugular. I'd have done exactly the same so I didn't blame them one bit. We were 6-0 down before the hour mark and when the eighth one went in I asked Lini how long there was left? "About 20 minutes," he said and I honestly thought United would reach double figures. That they didn't was down to some fine saves from Craig Forrest. At one stage I spotted substitutes Paul Mason and Ian Marshall going down the touchline to warm up and when there was a stoppage I could see they were behind an ambulance out of sight of the manager. Marsh later replaced Lee Chapman and Paul was the lucky one because he wasn't sent on.

I was feeling so poorly in the dressing room afterwards that the United doctor was summoned and he gave me some medication. Had I not been feeling so rough I might have taken more part in the discussion, or should I say row, which was erupting around me. George didn't slaughter the team but he directed a few comments in the direction of Steve Sedgley, who reacted to the criticism by chucking the captain's armband at George, who had only appointed him skipper eight games earlier. There always seemed to be some tension between them. I went and saw my own doctor on the Monday morning and was told I had a nasty chest infection for which he prescribed antibiotics and I was absent for the following game, a 3-0 defeat at Tottenham. I returned for the East Anglian derby at Norwich but I didn't even last until half-time because I was sent off for only the second time in my career for bringing down Darren Eadie. The incident took place just inside the Ipswich half and with Darren being one of the quickest players around at the time I felt I had no alternative. The referee was Paul Durkin and he stunned me when he produced the red card. It was my first foul of the game and I felt a yellow would have sufficed since the point of contact must have been about 50 yards from our goal. The game was live on Sky and when I reached the tunnel I could hear Andy Gray commenting on the incident and saying he felt sorry for me, although that was no consolation. Since then I have met Darren on many occasions and there has been some good Ipswich-Norwich banter between us. I certainly couldn't attribute any blame to him for what happened.

I played just one more game before the end of the season and after George could only manage four wins from his 22 games in charge we finished rock-bottom of the Premiership, having recorded fewer victories and suffered more defeats than in any campaign in the club's history. Our leading scorer was Claus Thomsen, who netted five times, and I was second alongside Steve Sedgley on four. Yet again, I signed a one-year contract and in our first season back in the second tier we only just missed out on the play-offs, finishing in seventh place. I scored a couple of goals, including a penalty at Carrow Road, in my 19 games and I would have played more regularly had it not been for a troublesome foot injury that flared up for a second time when I thought it had been cured. At the end of the season I more or less decided that it was time to retire and I took on a role as a match-day host to sponsors, as well as working with the club's Football in the Community department, although I stayed registered as a player – just in case I was ever needed. The club awarded me a testimonial and it was my intention for Ipswich to play Liverpool at Portman Road. Provisional arrangements had been made but Liverpool were forced to withdraw because of other commitments. My next choice was Rangers and I even went to Ibrox to speak to Walter Smith, but the police were not in favour and so I was left in the lurch and forced to think again. It was at this stage that Ipswich did me a huge favour because they had Arsenal lined up for a pre-season friendly and they agreed that I could have that game as my testimonial. There was a crowd of around 17,500 and one of the things I remember was hearing manager Bruce Rioch and Ian Wright having an almighty row in the away dressing room. Put it this way – I wasn't surprised when I heard that Bruce had been sacked just two days later.

I came out of semi-retirement on three occasions in the 1996-97 season, for a League Cup tie at Fulham that ended 1-1, a 1-0 home win over Queen's Park Rangers and at Tranmere on St Andrew's Day for what was my very last game in an Ipswich shirt. We lost 3-0 and my former Liverpool team-mate John Aldridge, with whom I was pretty close during our time together at Anfield, scored two of the goals. I also recall a young lad called Ian Moore, who was 19 years my junior, running past me so quickly that he was a blur and I knew my time had come. I spent the remainder of the season assisting chief scout Charlie Woods, attending games and filing reports on players, and I thoroughly enjoyed what I was doing. When Charlie decided to leave and take up a similar post with Tottenham, I made it clear I would like to succeed him. I thought I was the obvious choice since I had learned the ropes from him and knew exactly what the job entailed. I had served my apprenticeship, I knew our network of scouts up and down the country, I knew the game and I loved the club. Plus, I was known in the game and I felt I could open doors. But when I went to see George Burley about it he said: "I can't give you it. I'm looking for somebody experienced." If George had turned round and said he was giving the job to Dave Sexton or Don Howe I would have understood, but instead he told me he was going to appoint Colin Suggett and I hit the roof. His mind was made up and I was so incensed that as I left his office I told him to f*** off. I walked along the corridor and knocked on the chairman's office door. I was summoned in and expressed my disappointment at being overlooked for the chief scout's job. "George makes the football decisions," said David Sheepshanks, who had said in a newspaper article that year that I would have a job for life at the club. Again my temper got the better of me and I left the chairman with the same two-word farewell.

The club's job offer to greet sponsors and work in the community department, which I felt was glorified babysitting, wasn't what I wanted. I wanted to be involved in football but I had always made it clear I did not want to be a manager. Scouting suited me far better and I believed I was good at assessing players' strengths and weaknesses, as well as compiling 'How to beat them' reports on future opponents. I took the decision to leave Ipswich and a few weeks later I received a call from Alan Ball, the manager of Portsmouth, who asked me to go down to see him at Fratton Park. He was the thoroughly nice guy I had heard he was and he offered me the job of chief scout, which I accepted. Alan insisted he only wanted to see me a couple of days a week and the rest of the time I was doing the rounds of games, not only at first team level, looking for players. Unfortunately, Alan left in December 1999 and was replaced the following month by Tony Pulis. I continued as normal and on Friday, March 3 2000, the night before Portsmouth were to play Ipswich at Portman Road, I arranged to meet him for dinner at the Five Lakes Hotel near Maldon in Essex. I also handed over my 'How to beat them' report on Ipswich and when we finished our meal he delivered the news that I was being sacked because he had someone else lined up for the job. Less than 24 hours later, Pulis sent his team out to play exactly as I had suggested in my report and they won 1-0 through a Steve Claridge goal.

A few months elapsed before I heard from Gordon Strachan, manager of Coventry and my former Scotland colleague. I went up to see him – I clocked the journey and it was much quicker than getting to Portsmouth – and after a brief chat he offered me the job of chief scout. I was delighted to accept and I started back at what I knew best. Gordon wanted me to come up to the training ground every Thursday and eventually he asked me to join their five-a-side team to play the youngsters, one of whom was Gary McSheffrey. I enjoyed the scouting but that hour or so was the highlight of my week. Again, however, it didn't last as long as I would have liked. Gordon was under pressure from above to trim costs and I was one of the victims. I loved that job. One day I would be watching a Premiership game and the next I would be sitting in the stand at a reserve game with 30 other scouts looking at kids who were going to be released. That job was my last in football.

SCOTLAND THE BRAVE

I BELIEVE I CAN lay claim to a record as the only Scot to have rubbed shoulders on the field of play with both Pele and Diego Maradona. Furthermore, when you consider that I was a member of the same team as the legendary Brazilian it is without question a unique achievement. So what if it was during the filming of Escape to Victory and it wasn't a real game? Okay, let's get serious. A year before my temporary stint as a movie star I was one of many Scots given the run-around by the little Argentinian, who for my money is the only other player worthy of being discussed in the same breath as Pele. The friendly against Argentina at Hampden came one week after we were beaten 3-1 by England at Wembley and we lost by the same margin to the reigning world champions. I was a relative newcomer to international football, winning only my fourth senior cap, while Maradona was just 18 and outside South America very little was known about him at the time. But just a few minutes into the game in Glasgow the secret was well and truly out because he put on a show to confirm he was a very special talent and anyone who saw his display would have left Hampden Park knowing they were going to be hearing an awful lot more about the stocky kid who stole the show and was destined to be a world superstar. I could say Scotland fielded a weakened team because there were a lot of call-offs and I could claim we were cream-crackered after a long, hard campaign. But the truth of the matter is that I'm not sure our best X1, in peak condition mid-season, could have coped with Maradona & Co.

He was a right little so-and-so. We all wanted to throttle him, or at least stop him from creating havoc, but none of us could get anywhere near him. Eventually, with half-time just two minutes away and us trailing 1-0, I saw my chance to nail him. I will admit it wasn't the best tackle of my career. I actually caught him above the waist. My challenge had just one purpose – to stop him in his tracks and slow him down. Sometimes you have to resort to that treatment when a player is running riot like Maradona was that day. But not only did he somehow manage to ride the tackle, he even stayed on his feet and continued on his merry way. It didn't matter what we did, we couldn't stop him. He had pace and power, thighs like tree trunks and his close control was something else. We had no idea what to expect. Yes, we had heard bits and pieces about him, but it wasn't until we were on the pitch that we realised how awesome he was. Not having our strongest side, we were up against it from the start and it was sweltering, about 80 degrees if I remember rightly. Maradona was impossible to mark. He would drift out wide, drop deep or play in behind the front two. He had the lot and when I look back I actually regard it as a privilege to have been on the same pitch with him.

My Ipswich team-mate George Burley, who was to become Scotland manager of course, was at right-back that day and I remember he also tried to sort him out with, shall we say, an old-fashioned tackle. Once again, Maradona was having none of it and poor George was just like the rest of us by full-time – almost dizzy. It was close to exhibition stuff and none of us were surprised at what he went on to achieve. We all said he would be the best player in the world, which he undoubtedly was, but I would have to own up and say I was absolutely stunned when I heard Maradona was the new coach of Argentina. Given his chequered history, he never struck me as manager material. It seemed as if he virtually appointed himself, the way he demanded the job and was given it, and that is an indication of the reverence in which he is held. It wouldn't surprise me if he completed the fairy tale and Argentina won the World Cup in South Africa in 2010.

My pride and delight at playing for my country at the highest level of professional football is tempered with genuine frustration that only in a couple of my 29 senior international appearances did I play in what I would regard as my best position. Had I operated in a similar role to the one I occupied for Ipswich, and in which I scored almost 100 goals – 97 to be precise – in four seasons between 1979 and 1983, I am absolutely convinced I would have contributed more than the seven goals I did score on Scotland duty. I certainly don't want to sound arrogant, but I am basing that view on my club ratio. Put simply, if I could score seven times when being played out of position, I believe I am perfectly entitled to suggest I would have improved considerably on that tally had I been given the opportunity to perform in the role to which I was accustomed. That is not meant to be a criticism, either, of manager Jock Stein, who was in charge for each and every one of my 29 games. There was extremely strong competition for places back then, so much so that my ex-Ipswich colleague George Burley probably wishes he had a similar problem now. Unfortunately George's toughest decision is who to select, not who to leave out as it was back then. I am not going to speculate on the reasons why, but Scotland are far worse off these days when it comes to contenders for full international honours, so much so that I doubt if any of the current squad would have been considered good enough to force their way into Big Jock's plans.

Injury put paid to me playing for Scotland in 1977 when Ally MacLeod called me into the squad for a game in East Germany. The whisper was that I would have played in Berlin, but I tore a hamstring in Ipswich's last pre-season game over in Holland and it wasn't until January 1978 that I played my first game of the campaign. Playing for Scotland took even longer and it was almost two years later, by which time Ally MacLeod had made way for Jock Stein, that I eventually made my debut against Wales at Ninian Park, Cardiff. Among the telegrams I received ahead of the kick-off was one from my old secondary school, Victoria Drive, which read 'Orrabest'. Sadly, it was not a debut to remember for either me or my Ipswich colleague, George Burley, on a day when Scotland, unusually, chose not to field a single player from either Rangers or Celtic. John Toshack scored a hat-trick and after a start like that I would be lying if I said the thought of maybe never appearing again didn't cross my mind. Just three days later, however, I started the home game against Northern Ireland at Hampden, although I was replaced at half-time by David Narey. Scotland were 1-0 winners that night.

The following Saturday, the final game in the end-of-season Home International Championship was at Wembley against England. I made arrangements for my parents to fly down from Glasgow and I booked them into a hotel. I wanted them to be there because having played against both Wales and Northern Ireland I was reasonably confident of retaining my place at Wembley. Not only did I start, I also scored the game's first goal after 21 minutes. To say it was a tap-in is an understatement. Kenny Dalglish laid it on a plate for me and when I looked at pictures in the newspapers the next day I noticed that because I had so much time to make sure I didn't miss, I actually had one knee on the ground to steady myself as I used my right foot to roll the ball into the net. By some distance the easiest, most straightforward goal of my career – and at Wembley against England. It was a moment every Scot dreams about, although Kenny quickly brought me back down to earth afterwards when he told me: "My granny could have scored it." Had it been the only goal that wouldn't have mattered, but England staged a stirring comeback and Kevin Keegan was the main inspiration behind their 3-1 victory. The record books show that I scored for Scotland against England at Wembley, but a lot of the gloss was taken off the achievement by England's recovery to win comfortably in the end.

Following the friendly defeat by Argentina we headed for Norway and I came on as a substitute in our 4-0 win in a European Championship qualifier. In September that year I missed a penalty – my first and last for my country – in a 1-1 draw against Peru at Hampden. I could have been a hero if that one had gone in but instead it cost us a victory in a game we very much wanted to win. It was windy and raining in Glasgow that night, and the ball rolled off the spot twice before I could hit it. One of the Peruvians was also mouthing off a bit and although I hadn't a clue what he was going on about it had an unsettling effect on me. Their keeper looked towards one side of the goal so I went for the other side but he saved it. It may have been a friendly, but to my mind it was a disaster that I didn't score. There was a miserable end to the year as I took my tally of caps to nine. We drew with Austria at Hampden and then lost both home and away to Belgium, which put paid to our chances of going to Italy for the 1980 finals. The fact that the Belgians finished runners-up to West Germany was not even scant consolation.

After the agony of Argentina in 1978, then not making the Euro finals, Scotland badly wanted to make it to the final stages of the 1982 World Cup in Spain. The draw paired us with Northern Ireland, Israel, Sweden and Portugal, and it was in February 1981 that I made my first appearance in the qualifying campaign, by which time we had won in Sweden and played out a goalless draw with Portugal at Hampden. I was being labelled the forgotten man of Scottish football by the press after being left out of the squad for the previous year's Home International series and a summer European tour. I was still missing for the game in Sweden and although I was recalled for the clash with Portugal I played no part in it. I had not played for Scotland in 14 months and yet at club level I was having the season of my life for Ipswich, scoring regularly as we closed in on a possible hat-trick of major honours. My eventual recall was for the game in Israel and on the previous Saturday, after I had scored in our 3-1 home win over Wolves, their striker Andy Gray and I travelled by taxi from Portman Road to Heathrow Airport. We were due to meet the rest of the guys in Glasgow on the Sunday and it was such a rush that we showered in record time to jump in the cab at 5pm. Although I felt I was fit enough to start the game in Tel Aviv I suffered a hamstring strain and was replaced at half-time by Willie Miller of Aberdeen, a third central defender to line up alongside his club colleague Alex McLeish and Nottingham Forest's Kenny Burns. It may have seemed that Jock Stein was trying to shore up the defence and hang on for a point, but a goal nine minutes after the restart by Kenny Dalglish, and the reinforced rearguard's determination to keep a clean sheet, earned a very important victory.

The following month, unbeaten Scotland were at home to an Irish side who were the reigning British champions and it was a game of huge significance. Jock Stein had a few harsh words to say about me in advance of the game. In a newspaper interview he said: "I think John has a bit to prove. He took a chance in Israel when he wasn't quite fit – and the gamble boomeranged on him and us. It is natural that players want to play but no one can take fitness chances on himself because it can hurt others." Fair comment by the manager, who had taken me to one side and made his feelings known, and he warned against complacency when he said in his team talk: "They gave us a working over in Belfast last year – make sure it doesn't happen again." Jock was keen to start with the players who had finished the game in Israel but an injury to Graeme Souness forced him into one change and he plumped for me to replace Souey. On the morning of the game I was reading a paper and the reporter wrote: "The midfield is worrying, largely because Wark has still to show his undisputed Ipswich form in a Scotland jersey. But he is burning to play and that is no bad start." The same journalist took a leaf out of the manager's book, adding: "To take Northern Ireland lightly would be the biggest mistake since General Custer peered out over the wagon train and decided not to rate the quality of the opposition." Clever – and very wise – words as it turned out because the Hampden stalemate was broken in the 70th minute by Irish striker Billy Hamilton, whose glancing header was the first goal conceded by our keeper, Alan Rough, in four internationals. To the relief of nearly everyone inside the ground, and millions more at home, I managed to level just six minutes later after a quick free-kick by Archie Gemmill when I hit the ball low past Pat Jennings. It was payback time after I had scored just once in my previous 10 games, a poor return I suppose when compared to my record with Ipswich. I was chuffed to weigh in with a goal – and especially one that was to prove so crucial in the final analysis.

I did not play in the next qualifier, a 3-1 home win over Israel, but I completed the entire 90 minutes when we beat Sweden 2-0 at Hampden in September, which was another giant step in the direction of the finals in Spain. Next in line was the away game with Northern Ireland the following month. Oddly enough, Ipswich again played Wolves at Portman Road on the previous Saturday, so Andy Gray and I followed our 1-0 win that took us to the top of the First Division with another hasty exit and taxi dash to Heathrow in order to join up with the squad the next day. We both had to be content with a seat on the bench at Windsor Park in Belfast and in my case I was not quite right after hurting my groin at Manchester United and not training for five weeks. I got through the Wolves game and was ever-present for Ipswich, but only because I was having treatment, rather than training, in between fixtures. Neither team managed to score but no goalless draw could ever have been celebrated so enthusiastically, as the point earned was enough to guarantee qualification to the World Cup finals. From that moment on I made it my goal to be there representing my country. Scotland failed to complete the group without losing a game when they went to Portugal in November 1981 and were beaten 2-1 but on the same night Northern Ireland secured a 1-0 win over Israel in Belfast to ensure they would also be heading for Spain the following summer.

England also qualified that night with a 1-0 win over Hungary at Wembley, with my Ipswich pal Paul Mariner scoring the key goal. That put an end to the mickey-taking in the Ipswich dressing room because up till then me, Alan Brazil and George Burley had been winding up our English team-mates by chatting about "stocking up on the Ambre Solaire for Spain" and breaking into spontaneous choruses of Viva Espana.

A 3-0 friendly defeat in Valencia to the World Cup hosts hardly sounds like ideal preparation for the real thing in Spain, but despite the scoreline Scotland manager Jock Stein took a great deal of satisfaction from our display. "On paper it looks as if we took a real drubbing," he said, "but we've played a lot worse in the past and won." Even England boss Ron Greenwood, one of many international managers looking on, admitted: "It was cruel luck on the Scots. They deserved to take something from the game." Alan Rough saved a penalty but was beaten by the rebound and it was not until the final few minutes that the Spaniards scored their other two goals, one of them coming from the spot. The Dutch referee was taking charge of his first international, news that didn't surprise us because the two penalty decisions were both a bit dodgy. On a personal note, it was definitely one of my best performances for my country. The manager put me in a central position alongside Graeme Souness and instructed me to get into the opposition box as often as I liked. That was music to my ears and I remember getting in two good headers, one that hit the side netting and another from which their keeper pulled off a decent save. It was going well for over an hour but when Steve Archibald came on for Gordon Strachan we had to change the system. Their second goal killed us because it came at a time when we were looking good for an equaliser.

After the game in Valencia manager Jock Stein had special words of praise for Liverpool defender Alan Hansen when he said: "He (Hansen) was quite clearly the outstanding player on the field." The man they called Jocky at Anfield is obviously better known these days as a *Match of the Day* pundit but back then he was undoubtedly among Europe's finest defenders and he turned in a display against the Spanish in their own backyard that was reminiscent of Franz Beckenbauer at his brilliant best. His Liverpool career included three European Cups, eight League Championships, two FA Cups and three League Cups, yet he won only 26 Scotland caps over an eight-year period. Coincidentally, he made his senior debut on the same day as me, as we lost 3-0 in Cardiff, and his last cap came in 1987, three years after my own. When I went to Liverpool from Ipswich in 1984 it made me even more aware of how good a player he was. Jocky's problem, I think, was that there was a bit of a campaign by the Scottish-based media for the Aberdeen pair of Alex McLeish and Willie Miller to transfer their club partnership into the national team. It could even be argued that the press north of the border were keen to have as many home-based Scots as possible in the squad. Some supporters also had it in for Jocky and he was so affected by the negative vibes that he called off from games claiming to be injured when he was perfectly fit. He clearly didn't fancy it on occasions and made no secret of the fact. The irony is that England, or indeed any other country in the world, would have loved to have had a player of his quality available to them, but for some strange reason his own country was less than welcoming. I remember one day in the

Anfield dressing room when he turned to me and said: "How the hell did you win more caps than me?" I replied: "Because a lot of the time you didn't want to go." He didn't say anything else because he knew it was the truth. Whereas Jocky would occasionally decide he wasn't going to report for duty, I could never have done that and was even guilty of wanting to play when I was less than 100 per cent and therefore unlikely to do myself justice.

The argument about home-based Scots and Anglos never caused a real divide in the squad, but there was an atmosphere at times that suggested the lads playing south of the border were viewed as big-time Charlies. I think a lot of it had to do with the money we were earning – players' wages were a regular topic of conversation when there was time to kill – and it was clear those who played for Scottish clubs, even Rangers and Celtic, were lagging behind. Also, the Anglos would travel up to Scotland on a Saturday and we would have a night out in Glasgow before reporting for duty the next day. It was the same when we played at Hampden on a Wednesday night and the lads from English clubs would be out in Glasgow afterwards, then travel back south the next day. Clearly, there was no need for the Scottish-based players to do any of that and I can recall one or two comments about us being "flash" for the way we did things. Don't get me wrong, we were not at each other's throats or anything like it, nor was it a case of rival cliques causing disharmony within the squad, but I wasn't the only Anglo who detected a bit of an inferiority complex from some of the lads who played their club football in Scotland. The media also seemed more supportive of the home-based Scots but as far as we – the Anglos – were concerned it was no big deal and we considered ourselves every bit as Scottish as anyone else in the squad.

After our rather unfortunate 3-0 defeat in Spain, I played in a 2-1 win at Hampden over Holland, whose side included my Ipswich team-mate Arnold Muhren. Then I scored my third goal for Scotland when we drew 1-1 in the Home International clash with Northern Ireland in Belfast. Alan Brazil's shot was parried by goalkeeper Jim Platt and I was first to the rebound to bundle it over the line. I was unable to play in the other games against Wales and England at Hampden because of an injury that I initially feared might keep me out of the World Cup finals – if selected, I hasten to add. There was absolutely no guarantee that I would make it into Jock Stein's 22-strong squad, but it became even less certain when I was despatched back to Ipswich with a knee problem I had been carrying for about six weeks. A Scottish specialist wasn't too optimistic about my chances when he said I had a cyst that would require surgery, but I sought a second opinion from Cambridge-based David Dandy, who had rebuilt George Burley's knee and saved his career the previous year. He assured me I was okay to continue playing and I returned north to prove my fitness in a practice game in Ayr that was watched by Jock Stein. That was something to celebrate, but nothing to the feeling of elation when I heard the news that I had been picked for the finals in

Spain. I was just as delighted that my Ipswich team-mates, George Burley and Alan Brazil, would accompany me. George had not appeared in any of the World Cup qualifying games, but his timing was spot-on as he proved his fitness as a substitute against the Welsh and then in the 1-0 defeat by England before being named in the squad that night. The squad included two players who had been to the finals in West Germany eight years earlier, Danny McGrain and Joe Jordan, and six who had been to Argentina in 1978 – Jordan, Alan Rough, Kenny Dalglish, Graeme Souness, Asa Hartford and John Robertson.

Jock Stein made a point of telling everyone at Hampden after the game against England and the squad was released to the press that night. I still have the Scottish Football Association letter, dated May 29, 1982, confirming my selection. It starts Dear Sir, is headed up FIFA World Cup – Spain 1982, and reads:

> I would confirm that you have been selected in the pool of players to represent Scotland in this competition and I am enclosing two copies of the general arrangements made by the Association. The playing party will assemble at 12 noon on Thursday, 3rd June at the Macdonald Hotel, Eastwood Toll, Glasgow, and will stay there overnight before travelling to Portugal as indicated in the enclosed instructions. Details of your selection will be sent directly to your club.
>
> Yours faithfully
> E Walker, Secretary.

On the back of the letter, which was accompanied by a detailed itinerary, were the names and addresses of almost 20 family members and friends – my postcard list. We were kitted out in light blue blazers, with the Scotland badge on the breast pocket, and black trousers – it wasn't too dissimilar to what the Ipswich team wore at Wembley in 1978. We flew from Glasgow to Faro on June 4 on a British Caledonian charter flight and until June 11 we were based at the Penina Golf Hotel at Portimao on the Algarve, and then we flew from Faro to Malaga before a drive along the Costa del Sol for about two hours to the Hotel Sotogrande, which was to be our World Cup base. For how long, we didn't know exactly, but the SFA itinerary offered various possible scenarios depending on how far we progressed in the tournament. During our time on the Algarve we played a couple of bounce games against Torralto, a Portuguese Third Division side, but generally speaking the emphasis was on relaxation and if we weren't lazing by the pool we did nothing more strenuous than swim, play cards or enjoy a game or two of tennis.

Sotogrande was a fabulous location but the lads renamed it Colditz because we felt as if we were 'imprisoned' there. There was plenty of time to call our own and

I formed a regular card school with Alan Brazil, Alan Hansen and Davie Provan, the Celtic winger who now works for Sky Sports and was the Scottish PFA Player of the Year in 1980, the year before I won the English award. By far the lowest-paid of our quartet, Davie had such a lousy time that he lost about £500 and because he didn't have the cash to hand we nicknamed him COD – cash on delivery – and he squared up with us the next time we met up. His losses were roughly the same as his fee for the tournament and because he didn't top up his earnings with any appearance money he was actually out of pocket by the time he returned home. High-profile footballers such as Paul Merson, Eidur Gudjohnsen, John Hartson and Matthew Etherington have admitted to losing fortunes and there are no doubt plenty of others with hard-luck stories of their own. Before mobile phones, iPods and personal DVD players, cards was the favourite pastime to while away the hours on the road and to play for cash made it all the more interesting. Bruce Grobbelaar was Mr Unlucky at Liverpool. He formed a school with me, Alan Hansen and Ronnie Whelan and on five-hour journeys from the south back to Anfield he often lost half a week's wages.

I was lucky not to suffer such huge losses but there was a time when gambling had me in its grip. There is no doubt about it, I was addicted. I had a telephone account and tried my hand at football betting. Stupidly, the more I lost the more I tried to recover my money and I was only succeeding in doubling what I owed. I would think nothing of laying out, say, £500 on a 'certainty' to win £200, but for every successful wager there was a more substantial loss and there had to be a day of reckoning. It eventually came when a chap who worked for the bookies rang to ask if I realised I owed his company £4,000. I was taken aback by the extent of my losses and when he said he needed the bill to be settled in the next couple of days I had to borrow the cash from a friend. It taught me a very expensive lesson and while I still enjoy the occasional bet I am pleased to say the stakes are now far more modest. I have never had any fascination with the sport of horse racing, but three of my Ipswich team-mates – Paul Cooper, Alan Brazil and Eric Gates – were into it in a big way. They were regular visitors to Newmarket and we had quite a few owners, trainers, jockeys and stable lads who attended our games at Portman Road. Valuable information regularly changed hands, which enabled my colleagues to win handsomely from time to time, but I think I would be right in saying it was the bookies that came out on top in the end. So keen were Coop, Pele and Gatesy on the horses that they were often up at the crack of dawn on their day off to drive to Newmarket for the early-morning gallops. Also, Bobby Robson often had to delay his pre-match team talk because they were not present. A few minutes later they would appear, having been in the players' lounge to view a race and see if they had won a few bob. The Liverpool lads were also into their horse racing and I remember jockeys Tony McCoy and Kieran Fallon visiting Anfield for games, and popping into the players' lounge for a drink afterwards.

Gambling and Alan Brazil tend to go hand in hand, and one of his biggest successes was to back the 1983 Derby winner, Teenoso, at ante-post odds of 100/1. We were both in the Scotland squad for the Home International Championship that year and Jock Stein, who loved a bet, got wind of Alan's coup. According to Alan, the manager pestered him for a bit of the action but he steadfastly refused. Alan had played and scored in the 2-0 win over Wales on the Saturday and we were due to meet England at Wembley four days later. Alan's goal at Ninian Park, Cardiff, meant he had every right to be confident about his chances of fulfilling a lifelong ambition and playing in the big one. Every time he bumped into the manager, however, the subject of the Derby bet was raised. Big Jock wouldn't take no for an answer – by this time Teenoso was a short-price favourite for the race – and he eventually said to Alan: "You've never played at Wembley, have you son?" Alan took it as a veiled threat that unless he was prepared to give the manager a share in his bet he would be dropped from the starting line-up. He eventually convinced himself that Big Jock wouldn't be so petty, but when we were in the Wembley dressing room and the team was announced Alan's face was a picture. He was on the bench and the rest of the lads, who knew all about the bet and the friction between Alan and the manager as a result, could not help but let out a very brief snigger. It seemed cruel on Alan but not only did he come on as a second-half substitute, as I did, but the horse won to land him a massive win.

Back in the World Cup finals, meanwhile, our first game was against New Zealand in Malaga and I played what I consider to be my best game for my country. Kenny Dalglish put us ahead then I added two more and everything was clicking as we led 3-0 at half-time. By the 65th minute, however, the Kiwis had pulled back to 3-2 and we were glad to see John Robertson convert a terrific free-kick and Steve Archibald added a fifth. As delighted as I was to score twice, I was also kicking myself for fluffing a chance to complete my hat-trick. I was no more than three yards out when a cross came over and I expected to score, but I somehow sent my header over the top. The former Celtic and Scotland captain, Billy McNeill, was commentating on the game and said I would never have an easier chance to claim a hat-trick and he was absolutely right. It cost me a place in the record books, too, and the only crumb of comfort was that it didn't affect the final score. It would have been different had the game been poised at 0-0 with just a few minutes left for play, for example.

When Steve Archibald came off the bench against New Zealand it was to replace Alan Brazil, who had run himself into the ground. Alan was looking forward to getting back to the team hotel and celebrating his 23rd birthday, but instead he was left behind at the stadium, struggling to provide a urine sample after being summoned to the medical centre for a random dope test. He was with John Robertson and two of the New Zealand players but they had no problems coming up with the goods. Poor Alan was so dehydrated that five hours after the final whistle he was no further forward. They tried everything to make him go, including running water and standing him on blocks of ice, but to no avail. It was 3am when he and the Scotland team doctor were allowed to return to Sotogrande and then, after snatching a few hours' sleep, they returned to the stadium the next day at noon. The test was negative but was quickly declared invalid because the rules demanded that he should either have been retained at the stadium or a FIFA official should have accompanied him to the hotel. No blame was attached to Alan, who had still not recovered fully by the time we faced Brazil in Seville three days later.

As any Scot will know, we took the lead against the Brazilians through David Narey. Graeme Souness found me with a 50-yard pass on the edge of the Brazil box and I nodded it down for David to hit a stunning goal. It was a toe-poke according to BBC pundit Jimmy Hill, every Scotsman's least favourite Englishman at the time. But any hope we had of pulling off a tremendous shock disappeared as Brazil hit back to level 15 minutes later and then added three more in the second half. My consolation prize, if you like, was to receive Zico's number 10 shirt from the great Brazilian. He was their biggest name at the time and some of my Scottish colleagues were after his shirt. As luck would have it, though, Zico always insisted on swapping with the opposition number 10 and that was me. As far as the World Cup was concerned, all was not completely lost and we went into our final game against the Soviet Union back in Malaga knowing that a win would take us through to the second stage. It was not to be, even if Joe Jordan gave us an early lead. They didn't level until the hour mark and then, five minutes from the end, a terrible mix-up out near the touchline between Alan Hansen and Willie Miller allowed their striker to race clear and beat Alan Rough. Within seconds, we got it back to 2-2 through Graeme Souness, but we couldn't score again and ended up being knocked out on goal difference. If only we had not allowed New Zealand back into the first game we would have been through. It was the third World Cup in a row that Scotland exited that way. We all felt sorry for our supporters because for the duration of the tournament they had been in tremendous voice. Everywhere we looked during that time we saw so much tartan that we could have been back in Scotland rather than sunny Spain. All our games were like home games and it was sad to think that our adventure was over just three games in.

On the coach journey back to our hotel we passed through the up-market resort of Puerto Banus and somebody came up with what we all thought was a daft idea, to ask Jock Stein if we could get off the bus, have a few drinks and make our own way back to Sotogrande. I think it was Graeme Souness who was nominated to pop the question and to our surprise Stein agreed. He warned us not to overstep the mark and added: "I don't want to be reading about you in the papers." With that, the bus pulled over and 22 players in Scotland tracksuits disembarked. We couldn't possibly stick together and I was in a group with Alan Brazil, Alan Hansen, Kenny Dalglish and Graeme Souness when we wandered into a bar to find Rod Stewart and his wife Alana with a group of friends. Rod, who knew Kenny very well, invited us to join them and it was an amazing night. Within a few minutes word had got out that Rod and some of the Scotland team were in the bar, which prompted a large section of the Tartan Army to take up a position right outside. Rod was in his element and it wasn't long before he leaned over to Alana and said: "Why don't you go back to the hotel. I'm staying on here with the lads." She did exactly that and after an extraordinary singalong – I remember *Sailing* was a particular favourite – we said our farewells to grab taxis for the journey to the team hotel.

The next day, at around lunchtime, we were heading back into Puerto Banus. Big Jock gave his blessing but woe betide anyone who was not up and ready to leave the hotel the following morning at 8am for the journey to Malaga Airport and the flight back to Glasgow. Later in the day, Alan Brazil met up with a group of people he knew and we never clapped eyes on him again. It was nothing to worry about – or so we thought. After another good night visiting the bars we made our way back to the hotel. There was no sign of my room mate but that didn't ring any alarm bells. He would no doubt get himself back in time for a few hours' kip and be ready at the required time. Except that he wasn't. I was up in time to get packed and at 7am there was no sign of him, while his bed had not been slept in. There was no way I was going to say anything to Jock Stein so I chucked all Alan's stuff into his suitcase and got it ready. With no more than five minutes to spare Alan turned up and was like death warmed up. I have never seen anyone looking as ill. He was as white as a ghost and when Big Jock caught sight of him as we climbed on board the bus, all Alan could think to say was: "Dodgy pint, boss."

I had my doubts if Alan was going to make the airport, never mind get back to Ipswich, and things went from bad to worse when he threw up on the bus. There was a terrible mess and Jock Stein went berserk, as annoyed as I ever saw him. A lot of the Anglos had to travel on to Heathrow and when we got there Alan's wife, Jill, was waiting to greet him. I'm not sure Alan even recognised her but I'm told they are now just about back on speaking terms. Once the dust had settled, Alan explained that someone had given him a tablet on his last night in Spain and that was what made him so ill. I think it was Ecstasy but we'll never know for sure. The good thing was that Jock Stein forgave him and he went on to win a few more caps. Big Jock was one of only a few people I encountered who had the presence to walk into a room and it would fall silent. Pele and Bobby Robson were the others, so I think that says it all about him. He gave me some of the very best times of my career and for that I shall always be grateful. He also provided me with one or two of the more amusing moments. I don't know what it is about successful managers but they seem to have an unfortunate knack of getting names wrong. Bobby Robson regularly tied himself in knots during team talks and there was an occasion when Jock Stein was giving a team talk. He was going on: Poland this, Poland that, and how important it was for us to get a result until one of the lads eventually piped up "You mean Russia". We all fell about laughing, including Jock. Another time, we were in the dressing room – I can't remember where, but it was an away fixture – when the manager wanted to get everyone together for a team talk. There was no sign of goalkeeper George Wood and he was tracked down to the toilet. The poor lad was on his hands and knees, and when Big Jock asked him what he was doing, George said: "I've lost one of my contact lenses." The manager had us in stitches when he laughed: "If you can't find your f***ing lenses how will you see the ball?" It was a joke, rather than a slight on the big keeper, who was good enough to replace Pat Jennings at Arsenal, no mean feat.

International football was a big step up from playing at club level and while I am proud to have won 29 senior caps I can't help wondering if it might have been more. I missed out due to injury in the very beginning, when Ally MacLeod gave me my first call-up in 1977, and I had to look on from the outside again when I was on the transfer list at Ipswich prior to my move to Liverpool. In my second full season I was injured and out of contention, and I still find it hard to take that I only added three more caps after my move to Anfield. I felt I had one of my better games, arguably my best-ever, for Scotland in the Home International clash with England at Hampden in May 1984. Jock Stein pulled me to one side in the dressing room and told me to keep an eye on their captain, Bryan Robson, and I felt I came out on top in our personal battle.

ESCAPE TO VICTORY

IT WAS THE SUMMER of 1987 and I was back in Glasgow for a few days with Toula and Andrew. We were in the city centre, flitting from one shop to another, and as we approached a street corner I made eye contact with this elderly chap. He was probably in his 60s and as we got nearer he approached, at which point I thought he was going to ask for my autograph. Instead he took me by surprise when he said: "Bloody hell, John, you really did escape then!" No further words were necessary. We both burst out laughing and within seconds were heading our separate ways. He was referring, of course, to *Escape to Victory*, the film starring Michael Caine and Sylvester Stallone and in which I also appeared along with several other footballers, including the one and only Pele. If you haven't seen it, what planet have you been on? It was Hollywood's first big film about football, although once the publicists got to work the official line was that it was a story 'of the human spirit prevailing against almost impossible odds in a game that is not merely a game'. Put another way, it is a German propaganda stunt that backfires as a group of allied prisoners of war take on a team selected from the German troops and use the game as a means to escape, with help from the French Resistance. It tickles me when people say 'You were in *Escape to Victory*' because they remember me for a fairly minor role in a film rather than for my many football achievements. Back in my early days, an occasional highlight would be a visit to our local cinema, the Grosvenor at Hillhead, and I also thought it strange that my family were going along there to see a film in which I appeared.

The idea of being involved was first put to the Ipswich Town squad towards the end of the 1979-80 season when Bobby Robson gathered us together in the dressing room at Portman Road. He said he had a friend in the film business that was looking to hire a group of players. It would involve about five weeks' filming in Budapest. Was anyone interested? That was it – no mention of Caine, Stallone or the fact that it was going to be directed by John Huston. The same John Huston who won two Oscars – Best Director and Best Adapted Screenplay – for *The Treasure of the Sierra Madre*. Seven hands shot up, including mine. Well,

Toula and I had yet to book a holiday that year, so why not? It sounded like a lot of fun and the money wasn't bad, either. A couple of weeks later Bobby's pal turned up to speak to those who had shown an interest in getting involved. We were going to be in the movies and five of us – me, Russell Osman, Kevin O'Callaghan, Robin Turner and Laurie Sivell – would be involved in the game sequence, while Kevin Beattie and Paul Cooper would be body doubles for Messrs Caine and Stallone.

We were accompanied by wives and partners, and it was only when we arrived in Budapest that we realised there was an awful lot more to it than we had realised. On our first night in the Hungarian capital we met most of our co-stars, including England's World Cup-winning captain Bobby Moore, Tottenham and Argentina star Ossie Ardiles, ex-Manchester City and England winger Mike Summerbee, and internationals Paul van Himst (Belgium), Kazimierz Deyna (Poland), Soren Lindsted (Denmark), Hallvar Thoresen (Norway) and Co Prins (Holland). Then we had a meeting with several big-wigs from the film company and it was only then that the extent of our involvement began to emerge. The next morning a bus picked us all up from the hotel at 7am and we were transported into another world just a few miles away, where a huge Prisoner of War Camp had been constructed on a set covering about three acres at what used to be riding stables on the outskirts of the city. That was when we were introduced to Huston and Freddie Fields, the producer and former agent whose list of clients reads like a Who's Who of Hollywood, and later on we met Michael Caine, Sylvester Stallone and the many other actors involved in the project.

We were each handed scripts as thick as War and Peace and as she distributed them a woman representing the film company kept repeating, "Your parts and lines are highlighted". Lines? Hang on, we thought, none of us expected speaking parts. This was getting serious and we all looked at each other, not knowing quite what to say. I had a quick look at mine and spotted that I had a scene with Michael Caine. 'This wasn't in our script,' I thought to myself. Then we were in for another major shock when we were informed that the barber was ready to see us. We all had long hair, no good for a film set in 1943, and again it was something that none of us had considered. There was no swish salon, just one guy with the bare minimum of tools. He was a local barber who had clearly been given carte blanche to do what needed doing and took the minimum time to do it. We all laughed at each other's new look and wondered what we had let ourselves in for. There was more fun and games as we were sent to the wardrobe department to be measured and fitted with our uniform and football kit, including boots that had been specially made and felt as if they weighed a ton compared to the lightweight ones we were used to wearing.

For the first few days the wives and girlfriends were sufficiently interested to come along and they were made welcome. But the days were rather long – we were still being picked up at our hotel at seven in the morning and not being taken back until 5.30 or 6pm – and more often than not they stayed at the hotel. After about three weeks, my wife went off to Greece to visit relatives because the boredom had set in. In all our time on set we were sometimes only required for half an hour, so there was a lot of hanging about while scenes were filmed over and over again before they were right. There was a canteen we could use for meals and snacks and it felt quite strange sitting there with an actor in full German officer's uniform as we chatted about this and that. I also sat and played chess with Ossie Ardiles a few times, although I have to confess he was a bit too good for me. The real buzz came from being involved in the making of a major movie, seeing how scenes were shot and generally being around all the famous people, who were all easy to get along with. In their quest for authenticity the film-makers also called upon Major Pat Reid, a wartime escapee best known for writing *The Colditz Story*, to add a touch of realism where required. His expertise was crucial and I think his official title was Prison Camp Consultant.

We had to spend time in make-up – some longer than others – but fortunately none of us had a similar experience to that of Deyna, who some fans may remember playing for Manchester City as well as the Polish national team. They wanted him to look as if he had just been released from a concentration camp. That meant three different haircuts in the same day and two hours waiting for his make-up to be applied. Then they decided he wouldn't be needed and it took another hour to remove the make-up. But that wasn't the end of his 'ordeal' because the very next day he was summoned by the director and told there had been another change of plan – they were going to use him after all, so the entire procedure started again. We had to admire his patience.

The fact that we – by that I mean the five of us who had expected to do little more than play a game or two of football – were spending long hours on set, and also had speaking roles, caused a bit of unrest. We kept hearing what other people were picking up for their involvement – things like royalties and other rights were being discussed – and the general feeling was that we had been hired on the cheap. My deal was worth £1,000 per week, which I appreciate was a lot more than most people earned in 1980, but when the other lads asked if I would be prepared to approach Freddie Fields and discuss an increase in our fees I agreed. I knocked on the door of his large trailer, and a voice called on me to enter. When I opened the door he was sitting at a desk, clearly engrossed in something, and he looked up to greet me. I said: "It was our manager, Bobby Robson, who agreed our fees and I have been asked to speak to you on behalf of the players from Ipswich. We came over here expecting to be used as extras in a football match but instead we are finding ourselves far more involved than that. We have had a chat and feel we are worth more money or we will have to consider leaving the film and returning home." Well, that was what I intended to say, but because I was extremely nervous the words would not come out as I had hoped they would. Eventually I got to the end of my brief speech and uttered the words 'returning home' at which point Fields looked me straight in the eye and replied in an American drawl: "Okay, best you f*** off now then." I sensed he was in no mood to re-negotiate our deals and turned on my heels to leave. When I got back to the lads, who were eager to hear his response, I simply told them what he had said and added: "Looks like we're staying."

Many years later, Paul Cooper told me that one of the first things he had done upon arriving in Budapest was to re-negotiate his own fee and that of Kevin Beattie. I suppose they had more bargaining power than the rest of us because they were body doubles but despite my own failure to up the ante I have absolutely no regrets about taking part in the film. It opened doors that would have otherwise remained shut. Would I have met people like Caine, Stallone, Pele etc without *Escape to Victory*? Absolutely not. In fact, to pick up a grand a week for my involvement was a bonus. It was such an enjoyable experience that I'd have done it for less, maybe even nothing. It was worth it for what happened a few years later when Pele was in London for an event that was staged on a boat on the Thames and the Ipswich lads were all invited to attend. The theme for the night was 'Meet Pele' and there were plenty of people prepared to part with a large sum of money for the privilege. When we arrived he was chatting to a number of them but upon spotting us he broke away to greet us and we all sat down together. I was, as they say in Liverpool, made up.

Some of the most enjoyable times during the five weeks we were in Budapest were back at the hotel. Michael Caine was staying there and joined us for dinner a lot of the time. If we didn't eat together, we invariably got involved in a drinking session. Michael admitted to knocking back two bottles of vodka a day back then and he wasn't exaggerating. Just as we were fascinated by his tales about the movie industry, he loved listening to our football stories and those evening sessions were tremendous fun. Sylvester Stallone was nowhere near as sociable. He and his entourage, which comprised several minders, were even booked into a different hotel. Sly had made two Rocky films by then and was a top box office attraction. Our weekends, Saturday and Sunday, were free and while we stayed in Budapest he would jet off to Paris. To make sure the booze didn't affect our performance in front of the cameras, Bobby Moore and Mike Summerbee would lead us on an early- morning run. If that didn't sweat it out of our system, the sit-ups at the end did. Mike used to visit us at Portman Road quite a lot after that. He had a shirt-making business and his gimmick, if you like, was to have your initials embroidered on the breast pocket. He picked up quite a few new customers during his time in Budapest, including Michael Caine.

It was during one such drinking session that Pele got carried away in more ways than one. He wasn't a drinker but one evening he had two or three whiskies and we noticed he had actually fallen asleep. He was sitting on a high-backed, carver-style chair and rather than wake him we picked it up and carried it over to the lift, waited until it arrived and then, once the doors opened, we placed the chair, with him still in it fast asleep, inside. His manager was there and said, "Thank you, I will manage now" as the lift doors closed. Pele displayed his fantastic skills more than once in the film and when he was required to score an acrobatic volley he obliged right on cue. Bobby Moore crossed the ball, Pele threw himself into the air and with a wonderful overhead scissor kick sent the ball high into the corner of the net. One take, job done.

Stallone was coached briefly by Paul Cooper but quickly decided that he could manage without him. The original idea was that Paul would be seen making some great saves and then it would be Stallone in the close-ups. That was how it worked with Michael Caine and Kevin Beattie. You would see Caine standing there panting as if he had run the length of the pitch, but in fact it was Beat who had done the hard work. Actually, there is a scene where if you freeze it at precisely the right bit you can see quite clearly that it is Beat. Apart from deciding he would do all his own 'stunts' Stallone, who had to go on a crash diet and lose about three stones to look the part, also wanted to steal the show at the end. One day, as the closing sequence was the topic of conversation, he said, "How about I go past five guys and score" until it was pointed out to him that he was a goalkeeper and that simply wouldn't happen in any game, not even in Hollywood. In the end he was required to save a penalty and if I have a criticism of the film it is that it is let down by Stallone's unorthodox approach to goalkeeping, although I suppose the fact that he is American, and you remember when the film was set, allows him to get away with it. It is also worth bearing in mind that he had a financial stake in the production and therefore was entitled to have his say.

Our kit also came in for some criticism for being too modern and the shorts not baggy enough. We were given it to keep but I donated it to charity years ago. All I have to remind me of my involvement are a series of pictures that were taken by Toula. When there was a break everyone was only too happy to smile for the camera. I hit it off with Maurice Roëves, who was born in Sunderland but raised in Glasgow, and for several years after *Escape to Victory* was filmed we exchanged Christmas cards. Perhaps one of the strangest things about the film is that it didn't feature one German footballer. The Mr Nasty character, captain of the German side, was played by Werner Roth, who was born in Yugoslavia but emigrated to the USA. He played for New York Cosmos alongside Pele and later the American national side. The rest of the German team were from every country bar Germany. The goalkeeper was our very own Laurie Sivell and Robin Turner played up front, while most of the others were recruited from the Budapest clubs. One of them was Ferenc Fulop, the father of Sunderland goalkeeper Martin Fulop. He played for MTK Budapest and he scored two goals for the 'baddies'.

The balls we used were heavier than what we were used to but nowhere near as heavy as they would have been in 1943. There is a scene when we are required to take a shower and you actually see my bare backside. If only it could have been shot as quickly as the one featuring Pele's great goal. Instead, it needed about 12 takes and what made it all the worse was that the water was freezing cold. The idea was that Stallone's character would use the opportunity to hide and then escape later. Modesty went out of the window and we all stripped off as if we were showering after a training session or a game at Portman Road. But we spotted that Stallone preferred to wear a pair of mini briefs and all these years later I still can't help wondering what 'Rocky' wanted to keep hidden from us.

It was common knowledge that the film had a £5 million budget. That may be small fry compared to today's blockbusters but it was a decent sum almost 30 years ago. And don't forget they had to pay about 20,000 extras, those people who comprised the crowd at the stadium. Maybe that's why there wasn't enough in the kitty to pay the Ipswich contingent a bit more. When we were taken to the stadium for the filming it was an impressive sight. It had been dressed up with huge swastika signs and the attention to detail was amazing. There were rows and rows of German officers who really looked the part and it was quite an eerie atmosphere until you remembered it wasn't real. You could say the same about the game because John Huston more or less let the players get on with it and in our enthusiasm to make it as real as possible the tackles were flying in right, left and centre. I was actually injured by one flying tackle and because of the heavyweight boots we were wearing, which made it awkward to run properly, I went over on my ankle more than once. I was still crocked when I returned to Ipswich and feared Bobby Robson would fine me but I recovered in time to play the first game of the marathon 1980-81season and even scored the only goal of our win at Leicester. Both Russell Osman and I received Good Luck telegrams beforehand from John Huston, a gesture that was much appreciated.

The extras that made up the crowd in what was supposed to be the Stade Colombes in Paris, but was actually the only ground in Budapest without floodlights, could not have been more enthusiastic. They were directed by a chap on the PA system and sang at the top of their voices when asked. As for the climactic scene, when the crowd invade the pitch and the French Resistance put jackets and caps on the players to conceal them, there was an interesting incentive for the extras as they sprinted towards the exit gate. On the other side of that gate there were people handing out pairs of jeans and CDs, neither of which could be easily obtained in Hungary at the time. I found the invasion a bit scary because of the crowd surge and I was pleasantly surprised to hear that no one had been injured.

It was more than a year after filming that we were eventually able to see the film in its entirety and we were completely in the dark as to what had made the final cut. Because of the Ipswich connection arrangements were made for a premiere in the town and we all piled into the cinema wondering what to expect. The Ipswich lads must have been fed up hearing me going on about my speaking part in a major Hollywood film. Now, at long last, they were going to see for themselves that I wasn't making it up. Just one problem – when my big moment appeared it wasn't my voice. My character, Arthur Hayes, said, "I'll take the top bunk" and as soon as I heard the words spoken by someone else I couldn't contain myself. The silence in the cinema was broken as I said "I've been dubbed!" in a louder-than-usual voice. The audience started laughing and I couldn't blame them. I was later told that my accent had been too broad to use because too many people wouldn't have understood it. But in that famous scene when the bath caves in and the players are set to disappear down a tunnel to escape, only for Russell Osman to declare "Hold on, I don't want to go, we can beat them" and prompt them to instead carry on with the game, it really is him speaking.

I AM WHAT I AM

EARLY IN 2005, BY which time I had been married for close on 28 years, I decided to leave my wife, Toula. We had been papering over the cracks for a number of years and it was when I met my new partner, Karen Taylor, that I knew the time had come to bite the bullet. I left home with a suitcase and my head tennis ball, and a lot of people would probably say that sums me up pretty well. We were divorced towards the end of 2007. I bear Toula no malice and I hope she and her new partner will have a happy future together. At the time of writing, Karen and I are planning our wedding to take place in Gretna Green in May 2009. My son, Andrew, is making plans to travel back from Vancouver, where he is living at the moment, and we are planning a quiet affair with family and only a few friends from each side. When I left the matrimonial home in Bucklesham, a village about five miles from Ipswich, I had nowhere to go, so I rang the Ipswich manager, Jim Magilton, and he agreed to put me up. Jim and I go back a long way, to my time at Liverpool when he was an apprentice after joining straight from school in his native Belfast, and it was one of life's amazing quirks of fate that he later joined Ipswich in 1999 before succeeding Joe Royle as manager in the summer of 2006, just weeks after announcing his retirement as a player. It was ironic, I felt, that Jim, who would clean my boots and look after my training gear in his early days at Anfield – in return for a decent tip at Christmas – was still doing me favours around 20 years later. I stayed with Jim and his family for a week and then sought temporary accommodation with another friend, Phil Hullis, who runs a computer software company called SophtLogic. I have been player-manager of his Sunday team of the same name for the past eight years and I am also his personal trainer with a couple of sessions per week. Phil is a workaholic who doesn't switch off as much as he should, and in the time I lived at his house I hardly saw him. When he eventually came home from work he invariably got stuck into more work. Eventually Karen and I rented a house until we were able to buy our current home in the village of Onehouse, near Stowmarket, about 15 miles west of Ipswich, which we share with her black Labrador, Molly. We have settled in well, which has a lot to do with the fact that my local, the Shepherd and Dog, is so welcoming. The couple who run it, Karl and Debbie, have become good friends and I have been only too pleased to support a number of fund-raising events that have taken place there.

Toula and I were married at Rushmere St Andrew Parish Church on July 1 1978, just a few weeks after Ipswich won the FA Cup. We delayed the ceremony when I was named by manager Ally MacLeod in Scotland's initial, 40-strong World Cup squad, although I was not really surprised when my name was missing from the squad of 22 selected to travel to Argentina for that year's tournament as I must have been the youngest of the contenders. Paul Mariner was my best man and a number of my Ipswich colleagues were there, including skipper Mick Mills, George Burley, Roger Osborne and Les Tibbott. Others, including Bobby Robson, attended the evening party. Our son was born in June 1983 and it was when I was transferred to Liverpool the following year that Toula and I first began to experience problems. A long delay before we were able to sell our Ipswich house and buy a new one on Merseyside meant we were in a city centre hotel for nine months – or at least I was. Toula missed her parents in Ipswich and it wasn't easy for her. I was away a lot and it was no bed of roses looking after a youngster within the confines of a hotel suite. From time to time she would return to Suffolk to visit her family and even after we moved into our new home the trend continued until she started going back more and more frequently. Eventually she went back for what we called a trial separation. It lasted about six months and after that I would return to Ipswich whenever possible, but I was also serving a two-year ban for stupidly being caught drink-driving and that didn't make things any easier. I would phone regularly but it was some time later, when I realised I had to leave Liverpool for the sake of both my career and my marriage, that we were reunited and decided to make another go of it.

Two and a half years after I returned to Ipswich in January 1988, however, I was off again, this time to Middlesbrough for a year. We did not move north as a family; instead I rented an apartment there and drove back and forth on a regular basis. I would occasionally take Andrew up to Teesside – he was seven at the time – and one of the highlights for him was to accompany me to a local snooker club. To this day he still talks about it. I rejoined Ipswich after the start of the 1991-92 season and that made life a whole lot easier for all of us, although a lot of factors played a part in our eventual split. Toula's father, Stewart, who had worked as a bank manager, passed away and we were planning to build an extension to our bungalow for Toula's mother, Pepi, who was suffering from breast cancer. We hired a builder, Andy Blasby, who was a family friend, had been best man at the wedding of Sophia, Toula's sister, and was also godfather to Sophia's daughter, Ellie. He asked for payment up front and we handed over thousands of pounds. It later transpired that he owed money elsewhere and was using our cash to prop up his ailing business. The law caught up with him and he was jailed, but to carry on building the annexe for Pepi we had to fork out all over again, which meant in effect that we paid for it twice, although we did retrieve a small fraction of the initial payment to Blasby.

I thought the world of Toula's parents. It was after I met Toula and complained that I was constantly switching from one set of digs to another that I moved in with the family. They treated me as one of their own and I used to tell the other young players how I had finally found the best digs going. The original plan was to stay for a few weeks but instead I moved in permanently, Toula and I were engaged, and I became part of the family. Pepi, who had been born in Greece and lived there for a while before she came to England, was a wonderful cook and she used to spoil me. I couldn't have eaten any better if I'd taken up residence in a five-star hotel. After I first moved in Pepi even turned a blind eye to the fact that I was sneaking through to Toula's bedroom most nights. I remember almost bumping into her in the middle of the night and she put her finger to her lips to suggest I should be a bit quieter, although there was nothing I could do about the creaking floorboards. Everybody loved Pepi, especially at parties, when the Greek in her was well to the fore, and when she died a lot of people lost a very dear friend. I had good reason to be grateful to her for all she did for me and in a way I regarded it as payback time when we overcame our initial difficulties and were able to build the two-room annexe that was to be her home until she passed away.

After Toula and I became engaged we made plans for some members of my family to come south and meet her family. I was a little tentative. Among my clan was my uncle Walter, who was married to my father's sister, Annie. Before the two sides came together I remember telling my lot that Toula's family were 'posh' and I warned them not to let me down. We were sitting enjoying a drink in Stewart and Pepi's lounge, and all was well until the family dog suddenly appeared. It let out an almighty bark, which took Walter by such surprise that he shouted at the top of his voice: "What the f*** was that?" As icebreakers go, it was a belter, and we still talk about it. Our wedding reception was at the Copdock Hotel, just four miles out of Ipswich on the London side, and the Glasgow contingent, wary of the bar prices, visited a local off-licence beforehand. They came armed with their very own carry-outs, which they tucked under their tables, much to the embarrassment of yours truly, but thankfully there were no repercussions. Either the hotel management let it go or they were all deaf to the chink, chink, chink as my relatives made their entrance. Toula's parents arranged overnight accommodation with friends for some of the Scottish contingent and when we all met the next day it transpired that there had been sing-songs all round the Ipswich area until the early hours. At more than one house the wedding guests came back and got stuck into what was left of their carry-outs, and when the 'landladies' got up and came downstairs they feared they were in for a ticking-off – until they asked if they could join them.

Toula and I were blessed with the safe arrival of Andrew and he is a credit to us both. He is in his mid-20s now and, thankfully, unaffected by his parents going their separate ways. As the person in the middle, he was only too well aware that we were having difficulties. I would have liked more children but Toula was happy to settle for just the one and although I respected her view I cannot deny that it caused some friction between us for a while. I like children and they seem to like me; when I am around them I'm like the Pied Piper the way they latch on to me. Because I was a well-paid, successful footballer we were able to have most, if not all, the things we wanted, but I am the first to admit that my lifestyle was not conducive to a successful marriage. I should think the divorce rate within the profession is fairly high, and whether it is simply a coincidence or not I cannot say, but half of the 12 players on duty for Ipswich when we beat Arsenal in the 1978 FA Cup Final were later divorced – Paul Cooper, Brian Talbot, Paul Mariner, Clive Woods, Mick Lambert and me. I don't mean to trivialise a very serious subject, but add other ex-colleagues at Portman Road, such as Eric Gates, Frans Thijssen, Jason Dozzell, Sergei Baltacha and Simon Milton, and it's not a bad side.

While a lot of former colleagues are still involved in professional football, as far as I am aware none of them carried on playing into their 50s. It is my intention to continue playing for as long as possible, which will be when my legs seize up and scream 'Enough, enough'. Since retiring in 1997 I have clocked up many a game, including around 200 during my eight seasons in the Licensed Trades League. In other words the local pub league, where we often have to remove dog mess from the pitch before the game can get under way. Friends, many of them ex-players who wouldn't dream of emulating me, think I am bonkers and, believe me, there have been times when I have questioned my own sanity. But the bottom line is that I enjoy playing, although I am seriously considering calling it a day and making the 2008-09 season my last at that level. SophtLogic have actually gone from the bottom division to the Premier, but once upon a time Phil dreamt of taking the club far higher. He actually wanted to start a team from scratch and take it up the football pyramid, all the way to the Football League if possible, but it soon became clear that even in Hollywood that couldn't happen. I'll tell you how keen I am to play – he bought England strips for us and I didn't refuse to wear it.

The pub league is another world from Wembley, the Nou Camp, or any of the other top grounds where I played as a pro. Some clubs don't even have changing facilities so it's a case of stripping off and putting your kit on in the car. One club we visited had borrowed a horsebox as a makeshift dressing room. You couldn't knock their enterprise but the smell was such that we quickly retreated to our individual cars, a far better option. Our home ground is Rushmere Sports Club in Ipswich, where the man in charge is my former Ipswich team-mate Roger

Osborne, who will always enjoy hero status in these parts for scoring the goal that brought the FA Cup to Ipswich for the one and only time in 1978. As manager I am responsible for just about everything you can think of. I take the training one night a week, I pick the team and I'm the guy who gets the text messages or phone calls telling me which players are unavailable, largely because of Saturday night excesses. There have been occasions when we have had to take the field with only eight players and not always 100 per cent fit. It happened when we were playing Man on the Moon – yes, there really is a pub of that name in Ipswich – and we were trailing 4-1 with just 20 minutes to go. Desperate measures were required so I moved up front and issued instructions to knock it long and hard, as we had the wind with us. The final score was 5-4 to us and I hit a hat-trick. Thankfully, there are very few opposition players who have thought it a good idea to kick the former World Cup player, although I did get a shock soon after I started playing at this level. I went up for a cross and headed the ball past the keeper, simple as you like. But just as the ball hit the back of the net an opponent clattered into the side of my head with his head, leaving me concussed. Welcome to the Ipswich & District Licensed Trades League!

We reached a semi-final not so long ago and I decided to give my team the big-time treatment. We booked into a hotel for a pre-match meal and I also arranged our own team bus as a one-off treat to transport us to the neutral venue, the home of Ridgeons League club Stowmarket. My nephew, Scott, who was with Ipswich as a kid and later played in the Football League for Rushden & Diamonds, was alongside me in defence. As we were warming up I could tell our opponents, Bardwell Wasps, were going to be difficult to overcome and so it proved. We did manage to take the lead but it was 1-1 at half-time and that was still the score with 15 minutes left. I told Scott I was going to move up front and see if I could help to swing the game our way. He floored me with his answer – "Don't do that, I'm knackered" – at which point I reminded him that while he was only 20 I was actually 50. We lost 3-1 in the end.

When I finish with Sunday morning football, however, I will certainly not be calling a halt to my involvement with the Liverpool Legends. We have been travelling the globe for a few years now and as long as the demand is there we will be happy to continue. We have been to Dubai, Hong Kong, Singapore, Malaysia, Canada, Scandinavia and Ireland in the time I have been involved, as well as at different locations all over the UK, and my team-mates include the likes of Bruce Grobbelaar, Bob Bolder, Phil Neal, Rob Jones, Alan Kennedy, Gary Gillespie, David Johnson, Mike Marsh, Mark Walters, John Aldridge, Ronnie Whelan, John Durnin, Jan Molby, Steve McMahon, Jimmy Case, Howard Gayle, Nigel Spackman, Michael Thomas, Jason McAteer and Paul Walsh. Ian Rush, John Barnes and Steve McManaman have also played a few games for us, but because of their other commitments they don't tend to be available as often as the others.

Football has brought us together, but I think each and every one of us would agree that we participate as much for the crack as anything else. It is always the dressing room banter that ex-pros miss and this is a way of replacing it, while helping numerous good causes at the same time. It never ceases to amaze me that a bunch of has-beens can still attract a crowd, but a good example of our pulling power came in Cork in March 2009 when a sell-out crowd of 12,000 paid good money to see us play the Celtic Legends. The matches are usually followed by a dinner and once a signed Liverpool shirt has been auctioned the charity receives another welcome boost. The Masters, an indoor six-a-side tournament, is another event I look forward to every year. I was in the Liverpool team that won the 2001 event and we won another in 2007 when we beat Manchester United in the Dubai Masters.

Football has opened my eyes through the travel opportunities it has provided. I didn't even own a passport when I joined Ipswich but even in my youth team days we went abroad and European football, which was virtually guaranteed every year, saw us visit Belgium, Holland, Sweden, the Canary Islands, Spain, Austria, Norway, Switzerland, Greece, Czechoslovakia, Poland, France, Germany and Italy, while we also played friendly games in Kuwait, Saudi Arabia, Israel, Canada, Dubai, USA and Malta, and went to the Caribbean on end-of-season trips. Add the places I visited as a Liverpool and Scotland player, and I haven't done too badly for a lad from Scotstoun in Glasgow. Without a doubt one of the funniest things that ever happened to me was during the away leg of a UEFA Cup-tie – I can't honestly remember the location – when I went down injured and our physio, Tommy Eggleston, came running on. I never went down unless I was in pain and on this particular occasion I had never been more pleased to see Eggo. But when he opened up his bag, instead of his various sprays and stuff, it was full of spare studs and pliers. An embarrassed Eggo said, "I've brought the wrong bag, let's just improvise". For the next minute or so, therefore, he pretended to be patching me up before leaving the field of play. I was still in pain but I was laughing so much I could hardly feel it and I managed to run it off. There was another occasion in Europe when Eggo ran on to treat an injured player but Paul Mariner had taken a knock at the same time and so we had two men down. Bobby Ferguson grabbed what he thought was the right bag and ran on to see what was wrong with PM. As he opened the bag it was full of wallets, watches and other valuables that the lads had collected because they didn't feel the dressing room was very secure. Again, laughter proved the best medicine.

There is no doubt that being a footballer, especially if you are fortunate enough to play at the top level, affords you certain privileges that would otherwise bypass you. That was how I regarded my involvement in *Escape to Victory* and I have been lucky enough to meet a number of top celebrities. I actually achieved an ambition when I met Billy Connolly backstage after his show in Ipswich just before Christmas in 1980. George Burley and I went into his dressing room and he was fantastic, just as I knew he would be. I have already related the story about how Rod Stewart led us in a sing-song in Puerto Banus following our exit from the World Cup in 1982, and I met up with him again more recently, in 2007, when he hosted a football day at his home near Epping. Former players from Ipswich, Norwich and Colchester got together to take on Rod's team. He wasn't able to play but he welcomed me with a big hug and a mug of tea. Rod has a full-size pitch in his garden and the playing surface was like a bowling green. The corner flags all feature the Celtic badge and his team wear the famous green and white hoops. The dressing rooms are alongside the stables and the set-up is a lot better than I am used to on a Sunday morning. Our team featured Geraint Williams, Simon Milton, Jason Dozzell, Mike Milligan and Dale Gordon, and I scored twice in our 3-3 draw, which was a great result considering Rod's team had an average age of about 25. I took Karen and Andrew along and after the game we adjourned to Rod's local, where Andrew couldn't stop ogling Rod's wife, Penny Lancaster. I was chatting to Rod and told him I had seen him in concert at Portman Road a few weeks earlier, when the heavens opened up and thousands were absolutely drenched. "Why didn't you let me know?" he said. "You could have come backstage." I'll remember the next time.

Just as some footballers have their favourite showbiz stars, the same applies in reverse and there are plenty of actors, singers etc who are into the game in a big way. I have turned out for Jess Conrad's Showbiz X1 in the past – Eddie 'The Eagle' Edwards was our goalkeeper – and that was a real hoot. Jess will always start the game, unless it's wet and windy, as these conditions can play havoc with his 'syrup'. I have also played for the Badgers, a side run by former *Soccer AM* host Tim Lovejoy and for whom I put in my one and only appearance at the Millennium Stadium, Cardiff. I also played for a team called the Carlsberg Veterans who took on their Real Madrid counterparts over in Spain. The game took place at Real's training ground and their big-name player was the Argentinean midfielder Fernando Redondo, 12 years my junior. We lost 5-1, but at least I had the consolation of scoring and we were taken to the Bernabeu Stadium to see Real play Athletic Bilbao. After Paul Mason and I quit playing for Ipswich we were asked to play for Woodbridge Town in an FA Vase quarter-final and I can't deny that the money on offer was attractive, although apart from a down-payment in advance we never received the rest as promised. Paul played in midfield and the ball just kept sailing over his head. Some people in the crowd, which was swelled by our presence, shouted "What a waste of money" in Paul's direction and they were clearly blind to the fact that he needed to be given the ball if he was going to make an impact. We lost the game, but had we won I think we would have been retained for the semi-final and after that I might have returned to Wembley.

But what about when I've kicked a ball for the last time, I hear you say. Well, I'll probably be a pensioner by then, so it won't matter too much. In all seriousness, I might join the after-dinner circuit. I've done it two or three times and it has gone well, so that's a possibility, or I could expand my personal trainer service and take on a second client. But I'm the type of person who has always been laid-back – 'Something will turn up' has long been my motto and generally it has. I'm glad I inherited that trait from my dad; my poor mum was undoubtedly the worrier in our family. I think the lyrics of my favourite Shirley Bassey song tend to sum me up pretty well:

I Am What I Am

I am what I am
I am my own special creation
So come take a look
give me the hook or the ovation
It's my world that I want to have a little pride in
My world and It's not a place I have to hide in
Life's not worth a damn till you can say
Hey world I am what I am

I am what I am
I don't want praise I don't want pity
I bang my own drum
Some think it's noise
I think it's pretty
And so what if I love each feather and each spangle
Why not try and see things from a different angle
Your life is a sham till you can say
Hey world I am what I am

I am what I am and what I am needs no excuses
I deal my own deck
Sometimes the ace
Sometimes the deuces
It's my life and there's no return and no deposit
One life, so it's time to open up your closet
Life's not worth a damn till you can say
Hey world I am what I am

Many a time I come back from the pub and play that song. My other favourites are *My Way* and, for obvious reasons, *You'll Never Walk Alone*. Mention of the Liverpool anthem reminds me of an incident that occurred a few years ago after my playing career had ended. I was in Glasgow and went out with several family members to a well known pub, the District Bar in Govan, which is frequented by Rangers fans. We were there from 12 noon onwards and that evening we went straight over to the Rangers Social club alongside Ibrox Stadium. When I went in the compére spotted me and said: "Maybe John will give us a song later." To be honest I was absolutely hammered, but when I was invited to take to the stage later on that night I immediately agreed. I grabbed the microphone and slowly started to sing "When you . . ." and at that point the place fell silent, apart from the sound of either a glass or a bottle smashing. I had completely forgotten that the Kop's favourite song is also sung by Celtic fans. Thankfully, before I got to the third word, walk, my cousin Findlay had leapt on to the stage, grabbed the microphone and told the audience: "Sorry about that. He's pissed and doesn't know what he's doing." He was right and I suppose I did well to get out of there alive.

Despite my success I have tried to be the same person throughout my life and hopefully those of you who know me best will agree. I owe a debt of gratitude to my family for making sure I kept my feet firmly on the ground. Any sign of arrogance and they'd have slapped me down – I hope. My older brother Alex was my guiding light. He pointed the way and for a while I followed his advice to a tee. I never smoked, I thought twice about having the Scotland the Brave tattoo that I had been eyeing up as a 14-year-old and as far as not drinking is concerned... well, two out of three isn't bad. I looked up to Alex to the extent that I even copied him in growing a moustache. I would have been about 17 at the time and at first it looked like I'd drawn it in, but I've had it for about 35 years and despite team-mates threatening to shave it off it is still very much a part of me. A lot of players grew them back then and in my case it is something of a trademark, even if people are always calling me Bruce (Grobbelaar) when I am on duty with the Liverpool Legends. My sister, Wilma, was like a second mother to me and although I had a five-year period where I didn't speak to my younger brother, Andy, I'm glad to say that our differences have long since been resolved and the family feud is no more. Karen played a huge part in making us see sense and I am glad she did. With Andy living in Ipswich, we see a lot of each other and he wasn't too far away from following in my footsteps at Portman Road. He also played for Drumchapel Amateurs and he was a high-scoring striker when he came south for a trial. Alas, it didn't work out for him and when I think back to when I was in a similar situation I realise how thin a dividing line often separates life's probables from the possibles.

When the curtain comes down for the very last time I would like my funeral to be more of a party, a celebration of my life. I don't want it to be a morbid occasion; instead I want the Morecambe and Wise theme tune *Bring Me Sunshine* to ring out loud and clear. And contrary to rumour I won't be leaving the 'tache in my will; I will definitely be taking it with me

MONEY MONEY MONEY

EVER WONDERED HOW MUCH a footballer was paid in the 80s and 90s? Nowhere near as much as they are paid today is the short answer, but when I came across my playing contracts from my time with Liverpool (1984-1988), Ipswich (1988-1990) and Middlesbrough (1990-1991) I thought I would tell you exactly how much I earned.

LIVERPOOL

I joined Liverpool on March 19 1984 and signed a four-year contract for a weekly wage of £851. I was guaranteed a rise every six months and on the last day of July and January in subsequent years I received an increase in line with the rise in the Retail Price Index. There were also a number of incentive clauses in my contract as follows:

LEAGUE CHAMPIONSHIP

Every time I played for the first team – or was a nominated substitute or 13th man – in the First Division I received an appearance fee of £25 and a bonus of £125 per point. If we won, therefore, it meant an extra £400 in my pay packet.

The bonus for winning the title was £5,000, for finishing runners-up £1,250 and for finishing third £425, paid on a proportionate basis dependent on appearances.

EUROPE

Every time I played for the first team – or was a nominated substitute or 13th man – in a European competition I received an appearance fee in the preliminary round or round one of £50, in round two £75, in round three £100, in round four £125, in the semi-final £150 and in the final £175.

The bonus for winning a game was £125 and for a draw £62.50.

The bonus for winning the European Cup was £6,250, for finishing runners-up £2,500 and for losing in the semi-final £1,250, paid on a proportionate basis dependent on appearances.

The bonus for winning the Cup Winners' Cup or the UEFA Cup was £5,000, for finishing runners-up £1,900 and for losing in the semi-final £950, paid on a proportionate basis dependent on appearances.

Prior to the semi-final stage, there was a crowd bonus of £6 for every 1,000 spectators over 28,000.

FA CUP

Every time I played for the first team – or was a nominated substitute or 13th man – in the FA Cup I received an appearance fee in round three of £25, in round four £50, in round five £75, in round six £100, in the semi-final £125 and in the final £150.

The bonus for a win in round three was £15 (draw £7.50), round four £20 (£10), round five £25 (£12.50), round six £30 (£15), semi-final £50 (£25) and final £60 (£30).

The bonus for winning the final was £5,000, for finishing runners-up £1,900 and for losing in the semi-final £950, paid on a proportionate basis dependent on appearances.

In the event of the final being drawn, an appearance in the replay was worth £625. Prior to the semi-final stage, there was a crowd bonus of £5 for every 1,000 spectators over 28,000.

LEAGUE CUP

Every time I played for the first team – or was a nominated substitute or 13th man – in the League Cup I received an appearance fee in round three of £25, in round four £50, in round five £75, in round six £100, in the semi-final £125 and in the final £150.

The bonus for a win in round three was £15 (draw £7.50), round four £20 (£10), round five £25 (£12.50), round six £30 (£15), semi-final £50 (£25) and final £60 (£30).

The bonus for winning the final was £5,000, for finishing runners-up £1,900 and for losing in the semi-final £950, paid on a proportionate basis dependent on appearances.

In addition to the above, the club paid £99 per week, rising every six months in line with the Retail Price Index, to a pension fund.

The club made a one-off payment of £185 on July 31 each year 'in respect of a fee for the player's services in connection with his promotional work for the club souvenir shop.'

I was reimbursed up to a maximum of £2,000 for relocation expenses – "curtains, carpets etc."

I was reimbursed with removal expenses – 'household effects, solicitors' fees including stamp duty and estate agents' fees, on both sale and purchase, actually incurred in his removal from Ipswich to Liverpool.'

The club agreed to pay 'return travel expenses from Ipswich and accommodation expenses on Merseyside for the player and his family, as considered necessary by the club, for a maximum period of six months.'

IPSWICH TOWN

I rejoined Ipswich Town on January 5 1988 and signed a two-year contract for a weekly wage of £600. The following incentive clauses also applied:

I received a signing-on fee of £45,000 to be paid in three equal instalments of £15,000 in January 1988, January 1989 and January 1990, and which were subject to income tax.

I received an appearance fee of £100 per game in Football League, FA Cup and League Cup games.

An extra payment was made according to the team's league position – £130 per game when top, £100 when second, £90 when third and £80 when fourth – after the first three games of the season.

A match bonus system paid £200 per win and £100 per draw in the League.

After an undefeated run of three consecutive Football League games, where at least five points were obtained out of a possible nine, an additional amount of £50 was paid for each win and £25 for each draw.

FA Cup appearance money was £100 for round three, £125 for round four, £175 for round five, £250 for round six, £500 for semi-final and £3,000 for final.

The bonus for winning the FA Cup was £3,000.

League Cup appearance money was £70 for round two, £80 for round three, £125 for round four, £175 for round five, £350 for semi-final and £2,500 for final.

The bonus for winning the League Cup was £2,500.

The club paid accommodation for the player for a period 'not exceeding 13 weeks' and also agreed 'to reimburse removal expenses between Ipswich and Liverpool, together with legal and estate agents' fees for the purchase of a house in the Ipswich area.'

MIDDLESBROUGH

I joined Middlesbrough on July 18 1990 and signed a two-year contract for a weekly wage of £800. The following incentive clauses also applied:

I agreed a signing-on fee of £80,000, but because I only remained for the first year of my contract I only received £40,000.

The bonus for winning the Second Division Championship was £200,000 to be distributed among the players on a pro rata appearance basis.

The bonus for gaining promotion to the First Division other than as champions was £100,000 to be distributed among the players on a pro rata appearance basis.

After the first three league games of the season positional bonus payments were paid – first to second £300 per win (£150 per draw), third to fifth £150 (£75), sixth to eighth £100 (£50), ninth to eleventh £75 (£25), below eleventh nil.

FA Cup and League Cup bonus payments were paid on a pro rata appearance basis – round three £5,000, round four £10,000, round five £15,000, round six £20,000, semi-final win £50,000, semi-final defeat £25,000, final win £150,000, final defeat £75,000.

Accommodation was provided by the club for the period July 19 1990 to October 19 inclusive.

The club agreed to provide me 'with a suitable motor car not less than 1600cc' and were responsible for the road tax and servicing. The insurance and petrol expenses were down to me.

CAREER STATISTICS

JOHN WARK
Born: Glasgow, 4 August 1957
Height: 5 ft 11 ins
Playing weight: 12 st 2 lbs

Honours
with Ipswich Town
FA Cup winners 1977/78, UEFA Cup winners 1980/81, Charity Shield runners-up 1978/79, League Division One runners-up 1980/81 & 1981/82, Second Division Champions 1991/92, PFA Player of the Year 1980/81,
European Young Player of the Year 1980/81,
Ipswich Town Player of the Year 1988/89, 1989/90, 1991/92, 1993/94

with Liverpool
Football League Division One champions 1983/84, 1985/86
Division One runners-up 1984/85 & 1986/87
European Cup runners-up 1984/85, League Cup runners-up 1986/87

with Scotland
1982 World Cup finals in Spain

Club football

IPSWICH TOWN
Debut: v Leeds United, 27 March 1975

Season	Club	League	FA Cup	Lge Cup	Other	Goals
74/75	Ipswich Town	3	2	0	0	0
75/76	Ipswich Town	3	1	0	0	0
76/77	Ipswich Town	33	3	2	0	10
77/78	Ipswich Town	18	7	0	1	7
78/79	Ipswich Town	42	5	1	7	9
79/80	Ipswich Town	41	4	2	3	15
80/81	Ipswich Town	40	7	5	12	36
81/82	Ipswich Town	42	3	8	2	23
82/83	Ipswich Town	42	3	2	2	23
83/84	Ipswich Town	32	2	4	0	11
Total	**Ipswich Town**	**266**	**37**	**24**	**27**	**134**

LIVERPOOL
Debut: v Watford, 31 March 1984

Season	Club	League	FA Cup	Lge Cup	Other	Goals
83/84	Liverpool	9	0	0	0	2
84/85	Liverpool	40	7	3	12	27
85/86	Liverpool	9	4	3	2	6
86/87	Liverpool	11	2	3	1	7
87/88	Liverpool	1	0	1	0	0
Total	**Liverpool**	**70**	**13**	**10**	**15**	**42**

IPSWICH TOWN
Debut: v Aston Villa, 16 January 1988

Season	Club	League	FA Cup	Lge Cup	Other	Goals
87/88	Ipswich Town	7	0	0	2	2
88/89	Ipswich Town	41	1	3	4	13
89/90	Ipswich Town	41	2	1	3	10
Total	**Ipswich Town**	**89**	**3**	**4**	**9**	**25**

MIDDLESBROUGH
Debut: v West Ham United, 25 August 1990

90/91	Middlesbrough	32	2	5	0	2
Total	**Middlesbrough**	**32**	**2**	**5**	**0**	**2**

IPSWICH TOWN
Debut: v Grimsby Town, 28 September 1991

91/92	Ipswich Town	37	5	1	3	3
92/93	Ipswich Town	37	4	7	0	7
93/94	Ipswich Town	38	5	3	0	4
94/95	Ipswich Town	26	2	0	0	4
95/96	Ipswich Town	14	2	1	2	2
96/97	Ipswich Town	2	0	1	0	0
Total	**Ipswich Town**	**154**	**18**	**13**	**5**	**20**

Ipswich Town	**679 appearances**	**179 goals**
Liverpool	**108 appearances**	**42 goals**
Middlesbrough	**39 appearances**	**2 goals**
Overall Totals	**826 appearances**	**223 goals**

International football

SCOTLAND
29 appearances, 7 goals

1. 19 May 1979, British Championship, Ninian Park, Cardiff
WALES 3 SCOTLAND 0 *Scorer: Toshack 29, 35, 75*
WALES: Davies, Stevenson, Jones, Phillips, Dwyer, Mahoney, Yorath (Nicholas), Flynn, James, Toshack, Curtis
SCOTLAND: Rough, Burley, F Gray, Wark, Hegarty, Hansen, Dalglish (c), Hartford, Wallace (Jordan 55), Souness and Graham.
Referee: Pat Partridge (England) Attendance: 20,371

2. 22 May 1979, British Championship, Hampden Park, Glasgow
SCOTLAND 1 NORTHERN IRELAND 0 *Scorer: Graham 76*
SCOTLAND: Wood, Burley, F Gray, Wark (Narey 46), McQueen, Souness, Dalglish (c), Hartford, Jordan, Hegarty and Graham (McGarvey 85).
NORTHERN IRELAND: Jennings, Rice, Nelson, Nicholl, Hunter, Moreland, Hamilton, McIlroy (Scott), Armstrong, Sloan and Spence.
Referee: Clive Thomas (Wales) Attendance: 28,254

3. 26 May 1979, British Championship, Wembley Stadium, London
ENGLAND 3 SCOTLAND 1 *Scorers: Barnes 45, Coppell 63, Keegan 70; Wark 21*
ENGLAND: Clemence, Neal, Mills, Thompson, Watson, Wilkins, Keegan, Coppell, Latchford, Brooking and Barnes.
SCOTLAND: Wood, Burley, F Gray, Wark, McQueen, Hegarty, Dalglish (c), Souness, Jordan, Hartford and Graham.
Referee: Antonio da Silva Garrido (Portugal) Attendance: 100,000

4. 2 June 1979, International Friendly, Hampden Park, Glasgow
SCOTLAND 1 ARGENTINA 3 *Scorer: Graham 85; Luque 33, 61, Maradona 70*
SCOTLAND: Rough (Wood 46), Burley, Munro, Narey, Hegarty, Hansen, McGarvey, Wark, Dalglish, Hartford (F Gray 70) and Graham.
ARGENTINA: Fillol, Olguin, Villaverde (Trossero), Passarella, Tarantini, Gallego, Barbas, Maradona, Houseman (Outes), Luque and Valencia.
Referee: Pat Partridge (England) Attendance: 61,918
5. 7 June 1979, European Championship Qualifying, Ulleval Stadium, Oslo

NORWAY 0 SCOTLAND 4 *Scorers: Jordan 32, Dalglish 39, Robertson 43, McQueen 55.*
NORWAY: Jacobsen, Karlsen, Kordahl, Grondalen, Pedersen (Hansen), Aas, Albertsen, Thunberg (Svendsen), Thoresen, Mathisen and Okland.
SCOTLAND: Rough, Burley (Hegarty 46) (Wark 64), Munro, Burns, McQueen, Gemmill (c), Graham, Dalglish, Jordan, Hartford and Robertson.
Referee: Ib Nielsen (Denmark) Attendance: 17,269

6. 12 September 1979, International Friendly, Hampden Park, Glasgow
SCOTLAND 1 PERU 1 *Scorers: Hartford 4; Leguia 85*
SCOTLAND: Rough, Jardine (c), Munro, Souness, McQueen, Burns, Cooper (Aitken 73), Wark (Graham 73), Dalglish, Hartford and Robertson.
PERU: Gastulo, Chumpitaz, Olaechea, Diaz, Velasquez, Leguia, Cueto, Mosquera, La Rosa and Labarthe (Ravello).
Referee: George Courtney (England) Attendance: 41,035

7. 17 October 1979, European Championship Qualifying, Hampden Park, Glasgow
SCOTLAND 1 AUSTRIA 1 *Scorers: Gemmill 75; Krankl 40*
SCOTLAND: Rough, Jardine, Munro, Souness, McQueen, Burns, Wark, Gemmill, Dalglish (c), Graham (Cooper 61) and Robertson.
AUSTRIA: Koncilia, Sara, Pezzey, Weber, Mirnegg, Kreuz, Hettenberger, Prohaska, Jara, Schachner (Steinkogler) and Krankl (Hintermaier).
Referee: Karoly Palotai (Hungary) Attendance: 72,700

8. 21 November 1979, European Championship Qualifying, Heysel Stadium, Brussels
BELGIUM 2 SCOTLAND 0 *Scorers: van der Elst 6, Voordeckers 47.*
BELGIUM: Custers, Meeuws, Gerets, Millecamps, Renguin, Cools, van Moer (Verheyen 66), Vandereycken, van der Elst, Ceulemans and Voordeckers.
SCOTLAND: Rough, Jardine (c), Munro (F Gray), Wark, Hansen, Miller, Dalglish, Souness, Jordan (Provan 61), Hartford and Robertson.
Referee: Eldar Azim-Zade (Soviet Union) Attendance: 14,289

9. 19 December 1979, European Championship Qualifying, Hampden Park, Glasgow
SCOTLAND 1 BELGIUM 3 *Scorers: Robertson 55; Vandenbergh 18, van der Elst 23, 30*
SCOTLAND: Rough, Jardine (c), McGrain, Wark, McQueen, Burns, Dalglish, Aitken, Johnstone, Bannon (Provan 46) and Robertson.
BELGIUM: Custers, Meeuws, Gerets, Millecamps, Martens, Cools, van Moer (Plessers 49), Vandereycken, van der Elst and Vandenbergh (Dardenne 73).
Referee: Heinz Aldinger (West Germany) Attendance: 25,389

10. 25 February 1981, World Cup Qualifying, Ramat Gan National Stadium, Tel Aviv
ISRAEL 0 SCOTLAND 1 *Scorer: Dalglish 54*
ISRAEL: Mizrahi, Mahnes, Bar, A Cohen, Y Cohen, N Cohen, Ekhoiz, Shum, Sinai, Damti and Tabak.
SCOTLAND: Rough, McGrain, F Gray, Souness, McLeish, Burns, Wark (Miller 46), Dalglish (A Gray 70), Archibald, Gemmill (c) and Robertson.
Referee: Otto Andreco (Romania) Attendance: 35,000

11. 25 March 1981, World Cup Qualifying, Hampden Park, Glasgow
SCOTLAND 1 NORTHERN IRELAND 1 *Scorer: Wark 76; Hamilton 70*
SCOTLAND: Rough (Thomson 84), McGrain, F Gray, Burns (Hartford 78), McLeish, Miller, Wark, Archibald, A Gray, Gemmill (c) and Robertson.
NORTHERN IRELAND: Jennings, J Nicholl, Nelson, McClelland, C Nicholl, O'Neill, Cochrane, McCreery, Hamilton (Spence 79), Armstrong and McIlroy.
Referee: Klaus Scheurell (East Germany) Attendance: 78,444

12. 9 September 1981, World Cup Qualifying, Hampden Park, Glasgow
SCOTLAND 2 SWEDEN 0 *Scorers: Jordan 21, Robertson 80 pen*
SCOTLAND: Rough, McGrain (c), F Gray, Wark, McLeish, Hansen, Provan, Dalglish (A Gray 70), Jordan, Hartford and Robertson.
SWEDEN: T Ravelli, Borjesson, Fredriksson, Hysen, Erlandsson, Bjorklund, A Ravelli, Borg, Svensson, Sjoberg and Larsson.
Referee: Andre Daina (Switzerland) Attendance: 81,511
13. 24 February 1982, International Friendly, Estadio Luis Casanova, Valencia

SPAIN 3 SCOTLAND 0 *Scorers: Victor 26, Quini 83 pen, Gallego 86*
SPAIN: Arconada, Camacho, Tendillo, Alesanco, Gordillo, Alonso, Saura, Sanchez Munoz (Gallego 55), Satrustegui (Quini 46) and Ufarte.
SCOTLAND: Rough, McGrain (c), F Gray, Strachan (Archibald 68), McLeish, Hansen, Brazil, Wark, Dalglish, Hartford and Souness.
Referee: Alfred Rudolph Thomas (Holland) Attendance: 30,000

14. 23 March 1982, International Friendly, Hampden Park, Glasgow
SCOTLAND 2 HOLLAND 1 *Scorers: Gray 13 pen, Dalglish 21; Kieft 31*
SCOTLAND: Rough, McGrain (c), F Gray, Narey, Evans, Miller, Dalglish (Brazil 46), Archibald (Burns 46), Jordan (Strachan 86), Bett and Wark.
HOLLAND: Van Breukelen, van der Korput, Krol, Spelbos, Hovencamp, Peters, Metgod, Rijkaard, Muhren, Kieft and Tahamata.
Referee: George Courtney (England) Attendance: 71,848

15. 28 April 1982, British Championship, Windsor Park, Belfast
NORTHERN IRELAND 1 SCOTLAND 1 *Scorers: McIlroy 52; Wark 32*
NORTHERN IRELAND: Platt, Donaghy, Nelson, J O'Neill, McClelland, Cleary, Brotherston, M O'Neill, Campbell, McIlroy and Healy.
SCOTLAND: Wood, McGrain (c), Albiston, Wark, McLeish (Hansen 75), Evans, Provan, Brazil, Dalglish, Hartford and Robertson (Sturrock 75).
Referee: John Hunting (England) Attendance: 20,000

16. 15 June 1982, World Cup Finals, Venue: Estadio la Rosaleda, Malaga
SCOTLAND 5 NEW ZEALAND 2 *Scorers: Dalglish 18, Wark 29, 32, Robertson 73, Archibald 80; Sumner 54, Wooddin 65*
SCOTLAND: Rough, McGrain (c), F Gray, Hansen, Evans, Souness, Strachan (Narey 84), Dalglish, Brazil (Archibald 53), Wark and Robertson.
NEW ZEALAND: Van Hattum, Hill, Almond (Herbert 65), Elrick, Malcolmson (Cole 77), McKay, Boath, Cresswell, Sumner, Rufer and Wooddin.
Referee: David Socha (USA) Attendance: 20,000

17. 18 June 1982, World Cup Finals, Estadio Benito Villamarin, Seville
BRAZIL 4 SCOTLAND 1 *Scorers: Zico 33, Oscar 49, Eder 65, Falcao 87; Narey 18*
SCOTLAND: Rough, Narey, F Gray, Souness (c), Hansen, Miller, Strachan (Dalglish 65), Hartford (McLeish 68), Archibald, Wark and Robertson.
BRAZIL: Valdir Peres, Leandro, Oscar, Luisinho, Junior, Falcao, Cerezo, Socrates, Serginho (Paulo Isidoro 80), Zico and Eder.
Referee: Luis Siles Calderon (Costa Rica) Attendance: 47,379

18. 22 June 1982, World Cup Finals, Estadio la Rosaleda, Malaga
SCOTLAND 2 USSR 2 *Scorers: Jordan 14, Souness 86; Chivadze 59, Shengelia 85*
SCOTLAND: Rough, Narey, F Gray, Souness (c), Hansen, Miller, Strachan (McGrain 70), Archibald, Jordan (Brazil 70), Wark and Robertson.
USSR: Dasaev, Sulakvelidze, Chivadze, Demianenko, Baltacha, Borovsky, Shengelia (Andreiev 88), Bessonov, Gavrilov, Bal and Blokhin.
Referee: Nicolae Rainea (Romania) Attendance: 45,000

19. 13 October 1982, European Championship Qualifying, Hampden Park, Glasgow
SCOTLAND 2 EAST GERMANY 0 *Scorers: Wark 54, Sturrock 74*
SCOTLAND: Leighton, Narey, F Gray, Souness (c), Hansen, Miller, Strachan, Wark, Archibald, Brazil (Sturrock 71) and Robertson.
EAST GERMANY: Rudwaleit, Trieloff, Kreer, Stahmann, Schnuphase, Hafner (Liebers 73), Dorner (Pommerenke 73), Baum, Pilz, Streich and Riediger.
Referee: Georges Konrath (France) Attendance: 40,355

20. 17 November 1982, European Championship Qualifying, Wankdorf Stadium, Berne
SWITZERLAND 2 SCOTLAND 0 *Scorers: Sulser 49, Egli 60*
SWITZERLAND: Burgener, Ludi, Egli, Geiger, Wehrli, Decastel (Barberis 61), Hermann, Favre, Ponte, Sulser and Elsener (Zwicker 85).
SCOTLAND: Leighton, Narey, Gray, Souness (c), Hansen, Miller, Wark, Strachan, Sturrock (Archibald 46), Brazil and Robertson.
Referee: Vojtech Christov (Czechoslovakia) Attendance: 26,000

21. 30 March 1983, European Championship Qualifying, Hampden Park, Glasgow
SCOTLAND 2 SWITZERLAND 2 *Scorers: Wark 70, Nicholas 76; Egli 15, Hermann 58*
SCOTLAND: Leighton, Gough, F Gray, Souness (c), Hansen (McLeish 46), Miller, Wark, Strachan, Dalglish, Nicholas and Weir.
SWITZERLAND: Burgener, Geiger, Wehrli, Egli, Ludi, Decastel, Favre, Hermann (Zwicker 69), Sulser (In-Albion 84), Ponte and Elsener.
Referee: Charles Corver (Holland) Attendance: 36,923

22. 24 May 1983, British Championship, Venue: Hampden Park, Glasgow
SCOTLAND 0 NORTHERN IRELAND 0
SCOTLAND: Thomson, Gough, Dawson, Simpson (Strachan 65), Hegarty (c), Narey, Wark, Bannon, A Gray, Burns and Nicholas.
NORTHERN IRELAND: Jennings, J Nicholl, Donaghy, J O'Neill (C Nicholl), McClelland, M O'Neill, Mullan, McIlroy, Armstrong, Hamilton (Brotherston) and Stewart.
Referee: Keith Hackett, England Attendance: 16,238

23. 1 June 1983, British Championship, Wembley Stadium, London
ENGLAND 2 SCOTLAND 0 *Scorers: Robson 13, Cowans 54*
ENGLAND: Shilton, Neal, Sansom, Lee, Roberts, Butcher, Robson (Mabbutt 23), Francis, Withe (Blissett 46), Hoddle and Cowans.
SCOTLAND: Leighton, Gough, F Gray, Narey, McLeish, Miller, Strachan, Souness (c), A Gray, Nicholas (Wark 67) and Bannon (Brazil 55).
Referee: Erik Fredriksson (Sweden) Attendance: 84,000

24. 21 September 1983, International Friendly, Hampden Park, Glasgow
SCOTLAND 2 URUGUAY 0 *Scorers: Robertson 24 pen, Dodds 55*
SCOTLAND: Leighton, Gough, Albiston, Souness (c), McLeish, Miller, Dalglish, McStay (Simpson 77), McGarvey (Dodds 17), Wark and Robertson.
URUGUAY: Rodriguez, Gutierrez, Acevedo, Diogo, Agresta, Gonzalez, Ramos (Montelongo), Barrios, Santelli (Aguilera), Saralegui and Acosta (De lo Santos).
Referee: David Richardson (England) Attendance: 20,545

25. October 12 1983, European Championship Qualifier, Hampden Park, Glasgow
SCOTLAND 1 BELGIUM 1 *Scorers: Nicholas 49; Vercauteren 30*
SCOTLAND: Leighton, Gough, Albiston, Wark (Aitken 80), McLeish, Miller (c), Dalglish, McStay, Nicholas (McGarvey 74), Bett and Robertson.
BELGIUM: Pfaff, Gerets, Millecamps, Meeuws (De Wolf 76), Wintacq, Vercauteren, Van der Elst, Claesen, Voordeckers, Coeck and Ceulemans.
Referee: Enzo Barbaresco (Italy) Attendance: 23,475

26. 16 November 1983, European Championship Qualifier, Kurt Wabbel Stadium, Halle
EAST GERMANY 2 SCOTLAND 1 *Scorers: Kreer 33, Streich 43; Bannon 77*
EAST GERMANY: Rudwaleit, Stahmann, Kreer, Troppa, Zotzsche, Pilz, Ernst (Raab 87), Backs, Steinbach, Streich and Richter.
SCOTLAND: Thomson, Gough, Albiston, Wark, McLeish, Miller (c), Strachan, McStay (McGarvey 61), Dalglish, Archibald and Bannon.
Referee: Franz Wohrer (Austria) Attendance: 18,000

27. 26 May 1984, British Championship, Hampden Park, Glasgow
SCOTLAND 1 ENGLAND 1 *Scorer: McGhee 12; Woodcock 36*
SCOTLAND: Leighton, Gough, Albiston, Wark, McLeish, Miller (c), Strachan (McStay 62), Archibald, McGhee (Johnston 62), Bett and Cooper.
ENGLAND: Shilton, Duxbury, Sansom, Wilkins, Roberts, Fenwick, Chamberlain (Hunt 75), Robson, Woodcock (Lineker 73), Blissett and Barnes.
Referee: Paolo Casarin (Italy) Attendance: 73,064

28. 1 June 1984, International Friendly, Stade Velodrome, Marseilles
FRANCE 2 SCOTLAND 0 *Scorers: Giresse 14, Lacombe 29*
FRANCE: Bats, Battiston, Le Roux, Bossis, Amoros, Giresse, Tigana, Platini, Fernandez (Genghini 67), Lacombe (Bravo 46) and Bellone (Six 67).
SCOTLAND: Leighton, Gough (Nicholas 67), Stewart, Miller (c), McLeish, Malpas, Strachan (Simpson 46), Wark, Archibald, Bett and Johnston.
Referee: Luigi Agnolin (Italy) Attendance: 21,641

29. 12 September 1984, International Friendly, Hampden Park, Glasgow
Scotland 6 Yugoslavia 1 Scorers: Cooper 12, Souness 18, Dalglish 31, Sturrock 64, Johnston 66, Nicholas 80; Vokrri 11
SCOTLAND: Leighton, Nicol, Albiston, Souness (c), McLeish, Miller, Dalglish (Sturrock 54), Wark (McStay 46), Johnston, Bett and Cooper (Nicholas 54).
YUGOSLAVIA: Pantelic (Stojic 46), Miljus, Baljic, Jesic, Matijevic (Jozic 65), Radanovic, Bahtic, Sliskovic, Vokrri (Pancev 46), Georgijevski (Gracan 65) and Batrovic.
Referee: Keith Hackett (England) Attendance: 18,512